THE VARIETY GUIDE
TO FILM FESTIVALS

THE VARIETY GUIDE TO FILM FESTIVALS:

The Ultimate Insider's Guide to Film Festivals Around the World

Steven Gaydos

Introduction by Peter Bart, Editor in Chief, *Variety*

A Perigee Book

A Perigee Book
Published by The Berkley Publishing Group
A member of Penguin Putnam Inc.
375 Hudson Street
New York, NY 10014

Consulting editors: Derek Elley, Patricia Saperstein

Editorial associates: Fiona Burt, Ronnie Gul

Listings editors: Steve Pemberton, Rio Hernandez

Special thanks to Peter Cowie, John Duff, Leonard Klady, Todd McCarthy, Andrew Paxman, Christopher Pickard and Joe Sutherland

First edition: October 1998

Published simultaneously in Canada.

The Penguin Putnam Inc. World Wide Web site address is
http://www.penguinputnam.com

Library of Congress Cataloging-in-Publication Data

The Variety guide to film festivals : an insider's guide to film
   festivals around the world / [edited by] Steven Gaydos ; with an
   introduction by Peter Bart. — 1st ed.
        p.   cm.
   Includes indexes.
   ISBN 0-399-52442-8
   1. Film festivals—Directories.   I. Gaydos, Steven.   II. Variety
(New York, N.Y.)
PN1993.4.V33   1998
791.43'079—dc21   98-24525
                                                    CIP

Printed in the United States of America

10 9 8 7 6 5 4 3 2 1

contents

contents

introduction

Over the years, I have traveled to many film festivals on many different missions. Sometimes my purpose was to buy pictures, other times to sell them, still others to judge them and, most often, to serve as a journalistic chronicler. I have been to festivals that were thriving to such an extent that they were all but overwhelmed by the attention (the Cannes 50th celebrations) and I've arrived at others when they were hanging the black curtains, having decided to go out of business (the late Prague Fest).

Whatever the conditions and circumstances, there are certain "givens" of the fest circuit—unavoidable facts of life one is sure to encounter. For one thing, the attendees will almost always be "up." There's an air of pervasive optimism, as though the festgoers fully believed that, sometime during the next hours or days, they would surely be both entertained and ennobled by witnessing a true work of art. People who attend festivals are ardent moviegoers and party-throwers—hedonists all. Which is doubtless the reason why, toward the end of every festival, almost everyone looks totally fried, as though they had seen too much, talked too much and drunk too much. Climb onto a plane with festgoers and you always hear the same exchanges: "I'm exhausted" . . . "I can't move" . . . "I had great fun, but I'm toast."

There's also a more serious subtext to all this. Film festivals have

introduction

created an international language of cinema. Even in the U.S., which in recent years has shown diminishing support for foreign-language films, the festivals nurture that subculture that still can't wait to see the latest entry from France, Italy or Japan. Even though the world of Fellini, Godard and Fassbinder may exist no longer, there is still a strong appetite to discover their successors.

And of course, there's no greater delight than a sense of discovery. At Cannes, no one in attendance will ever forget the astonishing premiere of *La Dolce Vita* or the thunderously boisterous reception given *MASH*. Not that every classic was accorded instant immortality: *L'avventura,* for one, was roundly booed at Cannes and around the fest circuit.

Not every festgoer's agenda focuses on the art of the cinema, to be sure. A key reason why fests keep proliferating is that they are good for the tourist business, whether it's winter in Palm Springs or summer in St. Petersburg (where the Pink Flamingo Gay and Lesbian Film Festival prevails). Tourists love to have a good excuse, even an arty excuse, to fly to some sybaritic destination, check out the sights, eat and drink in excess— oh, and also fit in a few movies. Without the tourist's dollar, all those cineastes out there would have a terrible time mounting their grand events.

In the forthcoming chapters, various *Variety* writers and critics, along with members of *Variety*'s extended family of contributors, will guide you through the bustling, occasionally overwrought but rarely boring world of film festivals. At times they will provide a virtual guerrilla guide to surviving these fests; at other times they will recommend things to keep you busy. But the writers of this book have one thing in common: They have traveled the circuit, they understand the curious global landscape of film fests and they're not holding back. Enjoy the ride.

—PETER BART

a short history of international film fests

Gerald Pratley and Leonard Klady

There's a fair degree of mythmaking in the history of film festivals, and ironically, given that journalists historically have been the mainstays of the fest circuit, few facts are recorded.

Monaco (the beginnings of Cannes, one could say) held a once-only festival of first films on New Year's Day in 1898; and the first-known prize-winning picture was Giovanni Vitotti's *Il Cane Riconoscente* shown in Rome (the beginnings of Venice, perhaps) in a 1907 movie contest. The awards were presented by the Lumière Brothers, who had by this time abandoned film production to manufacture photographic equipment.

The real beginning of modern film festivals was decades later, in 1932, as Italy was slowly pulling itself out of the Depression, when an organizer, whose name has been lost to time, struck upon the idea of an international exhibition of movies. With the personal endorsement of "Il Duce," and under the direction of his finance minister, Count Volpi de Misurata, the Venice Festival was launched. Production costs were a primary consideration even though this was a government event, money was tight and public funds scrutinized. Private sponsors were shunned (they would have tainted the art). Though no official awards were presented, according to the reports of the time, the audience proclaimed Rene Clair's *A nous la liberté* the most entertaining film of the event.

The French didn't present their first event in Cannes until 1939, under the patronage of Louis Lumière, then seventy-five years old. But World War II began in September, and the festival was interrupted by Hitler's invasion of Poland. The festival ran only for one night. Cannes had to wait for its first year of full-schedule glory until 1946 in a small theater in the original casino.

Berlin, the last of the big three European festivals, came later and unspooled in an environment drastically more dour than Venice and Cannes. In 1951, Berlin had nothing to offer but bombed-out buildings, with memories of the horrible conflagration, the death and destruction. This was a city without splendor where a film festival was expected to bring colorful spectacle and creative people into a divided world. And the festival worked: In the brighter years that followed, Berlin became the bridge between the filmmakers of Eastern Europe and the West.

The first decade of Berlin was a time of discovery. Satyajit Ray introduced the world to the cinema of India, courtesy of his *Apu* trilogy. Italy's Federico Fellini emerged as one of the visionary giants of auteur cinema, even as England's David Lean proved that epics could be constructed with intelligence. Sweden's Ingmar Bergman changed the vocabulary of cinema and explored the psychological dimensions of reality, while Italian Michelangelo Antonioni took and expressed postwar existential ennui via faces and terrains.

Finnish producer-writer-director statesman Jorn Donner, who produced Ingmar Bergman's *Fanny and Alexander*, and whose *A Sunday in September* shared the best first-film prize at Venice in 1963, recalls that the seriousness of the cinematic fare in decades past was counterbalanced by the casual ambiance of festgoing. In 1975, when Donner was on the jury of the Tehran Film Festival with actor Rex Harrison, he asked the organizers, in jest, whether it would be possible to serve his British co-member Harrison a Scotch and water during the morning screenings. "Thereafter," recollects Donner, "every day a young lady arrived at the cinema where we screened the films carrying two double Scotches for Rex and me. I could not stop it."

Later, new names emerged from the colorful festival scene, diverse in their approaches and talents but sharing a passion for filmmaking and the creative daring required to keep the art form bracingly alive. While individual mandates may have changed, festivals continue to play an important part in launching nonmainstream movies. In the '60s, it was the French *nouvelle vague*, along with Fellini, Bergman, Buñuel, Visconti and Ray among others. In the '70s, Herzog, Wenders and Fassbinder heralded a new era in German filmmaking.

Martin Scorsese's Palme d'Or–winning *Taxi Driver* helped explain America's fractious political and social situation to the world in 1976, just as British director Lindsay Anderson's *If* in 1969 and Robert Altman's 1970 black comedy *MASH* conveyed the tumultuous upheaval that characterized the era. An explosion of American independent film talent later received special festival treatment in the '80s and '90s, with Jim Jarmusch, Steven Soderberg, David Lynch, the Coen Brothers and Quentin Tarantino taking the global fest scene by storm.

The cinematic arts, however, haven't been the sole driving force behind the proliferation of international film festivals. These diverse and far-flung events are composed of a complicated mix of motives, politics and intentions, astonishing and bewildering financial whirlpools swirling around in culture, commerce and ideology. The hydra of art, commerce and tourism known as the film festival began to expand slowly across Europe before World War II, but it wasn't until 1956 that the first film fest arrived on American shores.

It's hard to imagine today, but there were *no* festivals in the U.S. until San Francisco struggled into being. One reason was the studio system and its collective loathing of all things festlike. That antifest bent first manifested itself in the studio's reluctance to cooperate with the overseas events.

When the studios were all-powerful, they provided very few films and then only to the big three—Venice, Cannes and Berlin—for diplomatic reasons. Films were entered by governments and not by producers. Not until the independents emerged and festival directors began to choose the entries did American films make a concerted appearance at festivals abroad. Now, every U.S. and foreign city, and hundreds of small hamlets, seem to have their own festivals.

Also, for decades, Hollywood was shunned by the festivals—big studio product was the enemy of the first film critics, especially the French who celebrated the mavericks and a few studio directors like Ford and Hawks while ignoring the likes of Zimmerman, Curtiz and Wyler. The perception of American film artistry changed with the emergence of the so-called "New Hollywood" of the late '60s and early '70s, which married distinctive, creative visions exemplified by directors such as Altman, Francis Ford Coppola, Scorsese and Jonathan Demme to the big studio production and marketing apparatus.

Tom Luddy, a founder of the Telluride Film Festival, remembers the commotion caused by the premiere of the unfinished *Apocalypse Now* in Cannes in 1979, when it shared the Palme d'Or with Volker Schlöndorff's *The Tin Drum*. Later, when the film's final version premiered at the Moscow Film Festival Luddy, a producer with Francis Ford Coppola's American Zoetrope Films, recalls that "many people thought the Russians wouldn't appreciate an American film about the Vietnam War, but the members of the North Vietnamese delegation were very appreciative to be able to see a film which presented the American participation in this way." It was a watershed event for American studio films, especially considering that the biggest studio picture about Vietnam before this was John Wayne's jingoist agit-prop actioner, *The Green Berets*. Clearly, the world was changing and American films were suddenly being seen as reflective of change, instead of resistant and reactionary.

What kept the mainstream U.S. product out of the festival mix here and abroad even *after* the cultural tide changed in its favor was the old studio prejudice against the "art" side of the "art and commerce" equation of moviemaking.

That prejudice is still grounded to this day in the fear that a high-profile festival launch makes a big-budget film a sitting duck and an easy, perhaps even inviting, target for the critics. The upside of critical praise versus the downside of public relations disaster hasn't been terribly persuasive in favor of festivals when it comes to the tough-minded calculus of the studio chiefs.

But despite the recalcitrance of the film businessmen, film festivals were an idea whose time was overdue in America. By the early 1960s, New York City had its own high-profile event, with Chicago, Dallas, Los

Angeles and other cities soon launching their own versions. Yugoslavian auteur Dusan Makavejev (*Montenegro, The Coca-Cola Kid*) remembers the early days of the New York Festival, citing the 1971 outing as "the most exciting" fest of his life. His landmark film *W.R.—Mysteries of the Organism* debuted at the New York fest on Makavejev's thirty-ninth birthday, and his distributor arranged for festivities that the director recalls included "a ten-foot-high birthday cake and sangria, which was followed by a stimulating discussion among film buffs of the themes of Wilhelm Reich's work, the source of *W.R.*

In about a dozen years, scores of specialized American festivals sprang up as the trickle burst into a torrent of film art spanning the country from Seattle to Sarasota. By 1985, the Foundation for Independent Film and Video guide to film festivals was listing nearly 150 events in the United States alone.

Today, in April and May, for instance, there's a six-week flow which begins with the Cleveland festival and segues into Orlando's event, the USA Festival in Dallas, San Francisco and Seattle. Almost a film distribution system unto themselves for "specialty product," or films that will roll out on fewer than six hundred screens nationally during their commercial run, fests are an essential means of creating word of mouth and visibility for the independent film firms. "By and large most American film festivals are local events," observes Orion Classics' Tom Bernard. "Because few of them get national coverage, the decision a distributor makes about showing one of his films is generally timed to when he plans a commercial run in that area. It can serve as a sneak preview, but you have to be very cautious that a film is seen in the best possible light."

From the European point of view, which has seen the foreign language films' market share in America drop from a high in the '60s of seven percent to the current level of seven-tenths of one percent, this "circuit" for foreign films isn't helping the bottom line. "For an auteur," says Donner, "it's a useful way to become known, but for producers, we just have the cost of bringing people to the festival. Mostly, it doesn't help in terms of getting distribution offers for European films."

What hasn't changed in forty years is the underlying devotion to films outside the mainstream. Still imbued in all festivals is this penchant for pushing the creative envelope, and many a director harkens back to the '60s as the era that shaped his filmgoing tastes. However, festival organizers and distributors of specialized product point to the irony that today's audience is both different and the same. The obvious difference is that the university student of today, unlike its '60s counterpart who rushed to Fellini, Truffaut and Bergman, is not the core audience anymore. Rather, the now-older, yuppified campus radical is still in the forefront of that audience.

While American festivals are thriving and using eclectic "best of fests" programming strategies that democratically cull from all parts of the globe, Europe's festival scene is not immune to the greater challenge facing their national cinemas. The European continent is tearing itself apart over the domination of its screens by American films which continue to attract huge audiences. Yet the large festivals are asking for more American films along with their celebrities. Such is the voracious appetite of the festival budgets that it demands the drawing power, and ticket sales, of these blockbuster movies.

In the beginning, Mussolini sought to propagate the image of fascist Italy and failed miserably. Today, the face of democratic America is familiar (with few exceptions) to moviegoers everywhere, and nowhere is it more in demand than at those film festivals that grew so big that their very existence depends on major work from Hollywood.

(Additional reporting by Todd McCarthy, Patricia Saperstein and Holly Willis.)

memories of late-but-not-always-lamented fests

P e t e r   C o w i e

Since the days of Mussolini and the Venice Mostra of the 1930s, film festivals have been used to achieve prestige through glamour. Millions of dollars are spent around the world each year by governments—and even dictators—seeking to buy acceptance in intellectual, glitzy and diplomatic circles.

In 1972, the Shah of Iran gave his blessing to a major new festival in Tehran. Spurred by the genuine movie buff personality of his wife, Farah Diba, this event spared no expense in summoning directors, stars, journalists and functionaries from some forty-seven countries. These distinguished visitors, cocooned in the luxury of first-class air travel and then in the lofty isolation of the Tehran Hilton, could drift from one extravagant party to another without even braving the screenings downtown. If you did venture into the teeming heart of the city, you ended up—as I did on one occasion—sharing a taxi with a goat and Rene Clair.

This assembly of stellar talent led to other amusing anomalies. The Shah's sister held a reception at their vulgar, dome-shaped abode one evening and for "security reasons" all guests were asked to travel in official buses. Gregory Peck, Stella Stevens, Frank Capra, Ann Miller, Leopoldo Torre Nilsson, Michael York, Hermes Pan—they all clambered aboard without protest. But Christopher Lee, a star of the second rank, demanded a limousine. "I've always had my own chariot," he said sniffily. And he got it.

The following week, a disgruntled Otto Preminger arrived at the Hilton after a long flight from New York. *"Vair's my sveet?!"* he barked in his distinctive accent. The receptionist explained that all the suites were occupied—except one, and that was reserved for Buster Keaton. "But Buster Keaton's been dead for years!" snapped a bewildered Preminger. Without missing a beat, the receptionist pointed at a poster announcing a Keaton retrospective. "He is arriving tomorrow, look at the dates," he declared with condescending gravity.

Preminger descended to the hotel restaurant and began devouring caviar (which in Tehran at that time could be had for about $5 a pop). Miraculously, his "sveet" was ready soon afterward. I asked how the problem had been solved. "I simply whispered to the concierge that if a suite were not free in ten minutes, he would be in chains," came the calm, chilling response.

Tehran as a festival lasted just a few years, until the shah's military regime was overthrown. The ever-present armored cars, the black market in foreign currency at every street corner, and the grotesque luxury of the regime should have persuaded us that the shah was doomed.

But film people tend to follow the money and the hospitality. The same happened in the Philippines, at the height of the Marcos dictatorship, when reputable critics from the West were offered villas and vacations on private islands in exchange for spreading the world about the Manila International Film Festival. Ferdinand's wife, Imelda Marcos, then governor of Metro Manila, mingled with her high-ranking visitors, distracting them from the mediocrity of the official selections. Manila had aspirations to be a major market, but although numerous companies trekked to the Philippines, it never quite jelled. At last the festival perished as the Marcoses' record on human rights became appallingly apparent.

Not all big, official national festivals need be so fascist in tone. When Marshal Tito still ruled Yugoslavia, binding those various republics together with his steely charisma, the national gathering in Pula was an exciting destination for any cinephile. Each evening, films would unfurl in the awesome surroundings of the Roman arena in Pula, on the Croatian coast. As many as six thousand people would sit on crude benches and cheer their favorites as they appeared onscreen, often in the presence of Tito himself. By day there was bathing in the Adriatic, excellent seafood and relaxed press conferences.

In the final analysis, small is indeed beautiful where festivals are concerned. Take for instance, the late-lamented Bergamo "Mostra," for experimental and new features, with a whopping five million lire (in the days when a lira was a lira) as a Grand Prize to the winning producer. This niche festival was the brainchild of Nino Zucchelli, a diminutive Italian whose effervescent personality persuaded Finns and French alike to submit their latest films before entering them anywhere else. The daily rhythm for a jury member could not have been more civilized: a leisurely breakfast, a screening at 11 A.M., followed by an even more leisurely lunch in one of the town's *osteria*. Then of course, a siesta, with a screening at 5. After that, well, it was time for an *aperitivo*, and a long, lingering dinner. A final screening at 11 P.M. meant you had seen your obligatory three films in the day and could go home to a well-earned rest in your hotel.

Ah, where indeed are the fests of yesteryear!

making and breaking films

Christopher Pickard

Like democracies, film festivals are far from perfect, but they are still the best system we have for giving movies an opportunity to be seen when commercial concerns are not the first priority. Film festivals can make or break movies and, given the odds, the risk of failure seems directly proportional to a movie's budget and the size of the festival. Perhaps that is why the major Hollywood studios and the larger independents have become so selective as to which movies will be unspooled when, and where.

The festival circuit is an alternative global distribution network. In fact, for many movies, a festival screening will be its one and only opportunity to be appreciated on a large screen. A festival screening is also the purest test screening a movie can have. For instance, the reception that Curtis Hanson's *L.A. Confidential* received at Cannes from the audience and the critics, although not the official jury, was the first clear indication to Warner Bros. that it had what was to become one of the most highly acclaimed films of 1997.

Festivals are also as much a part of the overall marketing plan for many films as a full-page ad in the *Los Angeles Times* or the *New York Times* or a television spot during the Super Bowl is to others. But for many filmmakers, the diversity of festivals today lets them take advantage of the circuit to "market" their own movies to potential distributors or sales agents. The distributors, in turn, will use bigger, higher-profile festivals to introduce the same films to the international buyers and, more important, to the general public and the media.

Good word of mouth draws the distributors and buyers to the screenings and helps a buzz build for future audiences. Thanks to the growing globalization of the media and the World Wide Web, that "buzz" (good or bad) can be circling the world in a matter of hours after a first festival or market showing.

Such was the case of a small indie film produced in Australia for just $4.5 million. The film, Scott Hicks's *Shine*, became an international hit, both commercially and critically, garnering seven Academy Award nominations, including best picture, and winning the best actor Oscar for Geoffrey Rush. Yet its success began not at the Academy Awards on March 24, 1997, but at the Sundance Film Festival a full fifteen months earlier.

Shine already had enjoyed a nice little buzz within industry circles going into the 1996 Sundance Film Festival. As a non-American film it wasn't going to screen in competition, but the word on the street was that it was one to check on. Before the official screening on the festival's first Sunday—the movie's world premiere—the top indie distributors started circling the film and making overtures to its producer. Miramax cochairman Harvey Weinstein, whose company had been tracking the film's progress, knew he could not make it to the official Sundance screening because of the Golden Globes, so he took the precaution of arranging a special showing of the film in Los Angeles early on the following Monday.

Shine received a rapturous ovation at its premiere in Park City, Utah, after which director Hicks told the audience: "It needs to get picked up." The ski gloves were off and the offers started to pour in to the movie's producer representative at Sundance, Jonathan Taplin. Bids came not only from Miramax but also October, Fox Searchlight, Sony Classics and Fine Line Pictures. As a result, the price for the North American rights climbed from $1.4 million at the start of the day following the screening to $2.5 million by close of business.

Yet, the figure was not staggering in itself. At the same festival Castle Rock bought the world rights to Lee David Zlotoff's *The Spitfire Grill* for $10 million. What made *Shine* stand apart was not only the reaction of the audience and the critics, or the number of interested buyers, but also the fact that those interested buyers were literally willing to fight one another to get hold of the film and this battle was reported in the popular press.

At first, Miramax's Weinstein thought he had won the bidding battle that tumultuous Monday, but Taplin had already signed with Fine Line president Ruth Vitale. A famous, some same infamous, scene ensued that evening in a popular Park City restaurant between Miramax's top man and the producer's rep: a scene that has since gone down in the annals of Sundance folklore. But the confrontation did not change the fact that Fine Line had the North American rights to *Shine* and Miramax did not.

Weinstein, a man never known to miss a marketing opportunity if he can possibly help it, was back at the very same restaurant the following morning to meet with the media. To the surprise of the assembled press not only did he wish Fine Line well with *Shine* in North America, but he also announced that Miramax and parent company Buena Vista had picked up the international rights to the movie in eight key foreign markets. The buzz had just gotten louder and it helped the Australian film outshine every other movie that went through Sundance that year, including the eventual competition winner *Welcome to the Dollhouse* and the high-priced *The Spitfire Grill*.

The story of *Shine* at the fests did not end with Sundance. Fine Line, recognizing that it had an exceptional property, also appreciated that the film needed to be handled sympathetically if it was to reach its target audience and beyond. The company chose to hold back the U.S. release of the movie until the end of 1996 as the film had clear Academy Award potential—arguably the ultimate marketing tool for any "specialty" or "art" picture—and would stand a better chance of being remembered by the Academy's members if it screened late in the year. A date of November 22 was finally set, and in September—to help remind audiences and critics alike about *Shine* and the reception it had received at Sundance—Fine Line took the picture to the Toronto Film Festival. It screened in competition and took home the top prize and the People's choice award. The snowball was gaining speed and size.

Two months after Toronto, *Shine* opened on seven U.S. screens and grossed $162,179 over its first weekend. By the end of the year the North

American gross stood at $4.2 million and by the night of the Academy Awards, *Shine* was playing on nearly one thousand screens in North America and had grossed $32.4 million. Not a bad result for a film made for $4.5 million and sold in the U.S. for $2.5 million. Yet it would never have happened if the film's producers had not had a plan as to how they would break out the film by using the festival circuit. They gambled, but they knew what they were doing and were well prepared.

There is no question that Sundance and Toronto are the two North American festivals that matter above all others. They matter not only for the interest they generate within the film industry, but also because what happens at the two festivals is also noted by a key faction of the theater-going public in the world's largest market and far beyond.

Toronto's late-September slot makes it a perfect platform for films awaiting their year-end opening in the U.S., in much the same way that the Berlin Film Festival is used in February for releasing films in Europe. Paramount used the Toronto festival in 1996 to position Albert Brooks's comedy *Mother*, while in 1997 New Line unveiled *Boogie Nights*, and Miramax *The Wings of the Dove*. But like Sundance, Toronto can also be used to place a film in front of the distributors. While *Shine* already had a name and a U.S. distribution deal when it screened in Toronto, that same festival helped the launch of *Kissed* and *Swingers*, which itself had been first noted a month earlier at Telluride alongside *Sling Blade*. That same year Toronto also introduced *Breaking the Waves*, which had made an impact at the Cannes Film Festival, to North American audiences.

In 1997 it was the turn of a small British film to demonstrate that good word of mouth is one of most potent and cost-effective marketing tools available to an industry that normally prides itself on its marketing savvy. The film was *The Full Monty*, which used the festival circuit to build up global word of mouth in advance of its commercial release in each territory. Even in the U.S. it premiered at the Sundance Film Festival a full seven months before its commercial bow. *The Full Monty* was no struggling independent production looking for representation, however, but nurtured globally by Fox Searchlight, a division of 20th Century Fox. The film ended 1997 as one of the most profitable ones released by the studio in recent times.

A similar strategy was employed in 1997 by Miramax for *Shall We Dance?* a Japanese movie premiered in the U.S. at Sundance after a very successful commercial run in its own country. It had been expected to open in the U.S. in May, immediately following a special benefit screening at the Cannes Film Festival, but Miramax chose to hold *Shall We Dance?* back until July as word of mouth continued to build following other festival screenings. The film has since gone on to become the most successful Japanese-language movie ever at the U.S. box office, grossing close to $10 million.

While festivals can and are used to place a film on the road to critical and commercial success, the competition is extremely fierce. Seven hundred and fifty new features from U.S. producers were submitted to the Sundance Film Festival for consideration in 1998, up from six hundred in 1997 and five hundred in 1996. For Sundance in '98, only thirty-two were chosen for competition and sixteen for the American Spectrum. More than seven hundred entries were sent off to look for another festival to call home.

When it comes to choosing which festival to attend or participate in, size can matter, yet bigger is never a guarantee that the experience is going to be any more satisfying or rewarding.

At the granddaddy of all the festivals, Cannes, an unknown filmmaker without connections is almost certainly wasting his time. Even directors and talent who have been pampered and fawned over at Sundance just four months earlier may find themselves back at the bottom of the food chain when they arrive on the French Riviera, unless their film is being handled by an established Cannes player who can protect them.

In 1987, Jean Gabriel Albicocco, the French director who is credited with being the father of Directors' Fortnight, a parallel and alternative festival to the main event at Cannes, was programming FestRio, Rio's short-lived and greatly missed international film festival, with Cosme Alves Netto, a key figure in Rio de Janeiro's main film library and archive, as his right-hand man. In August, Netto told Albicocco that he had just seen the film that he believed would win that year's festival. The film, *Baghdad Cafe*, by German director Percy Adlon, which had been submitted to Rio after it had been overlooked by every major European fest, did indeed go on to win the Golden Toucan and international success. FestRio put *Baghdad Cafe* and Adlon on the map. Despite its global reach, the international festival circuit is a relatively small, close-knit family that values the opinions of its fellow family members. And providentially for Adlon, among the jury in Rio was France's Daniel Toscan du Plantier, a close collaborator with the Cannes Film Festival. Adlon's next film, *Rosalie Goes Shopping*, would be chosen by Gilles Jacob to screen in competition in Cannes.

While film festivals can make a nobody a somebody overnight, they can also break the expectations of a larger film. Even the major Hollywood studios tiptoe gingerly around the fringes of Cannes unless they feel the film is right or has nowhere else to go.

For many major studios Cannes is an extended press junket for its upcoming slate of summer blockbusters. For Buena Vista, the parent company of Miramax, both *The Rock* and *Con Air* were unveiled for the first time to the international media and Buena Vista's global distribution partners during the festival. But the company, not the festival, controlled who got to see these films, where and how. The screenings and the access to the talent were never listed in any of the daily trades, and the vast majority of the media attending and covering the festival were strictly persona non grata.

Every couple of years a company like Buena Vista will throw a tasty bone to the festival to keep it happy. In 1990, it allowed the festival to have a special out-of-competition screening of Walt Disney's *The Little Mermaid* and in 1992, *Beauty and the Beast*. Miramax's movies and talent have brought Cannes many of its most memorable and uplifting moments during the '90s, and for that reason alone the festival will indulge Buena Vista when needed and give it the space to do its own business in and around the festival.

Even major-league players such as Clint Eastwood have been seduced by Cannes; he made his first appearance there in 1985 for the premiere of Warner Bros.' *Pale Rider*, of which he was director and star.

Eastwood's love affair with Cannes, and what it could do for his more personal films, especially those he had chosen to direct, had begun. He returned in 1988 with *Bird*, the biography of Charlie Parker, which won the best actor prize for Forest Whitaker. William Goldman, a juror that year, felt the film deserved more but warns that screening a film in Cannes means "no apologizing, no excuses; self-pity's been banished. Warts and all, it says, here I am, like me or not." Four months after Cannes, Eastwood chose the New York Film Festival for *Bird*'s U.S. premiere.

In 1990, Eastwood used a similar festival route for *White Hunter, Black Heart* and followed its Cannes premiere with screenings at the Telluride and Toronto film festivals before the U.S. opening in September. *Unforgiven* could have followed to Cannes but Warner Bros. chose an August (1992) window for the opening to position the film for the Academy Awards. Eastwood returned to the Riviera in 1994 when he presided over the festival jury, which discovered and had the courage of their convictions to give the Palme d'Or to Quentin Tarantino's *Pulp Fiction*.

Eastwood and Tarantino are not alone among Hollywood's biggest names to see the value of festivals. Tom Cruise is a big fan of Cannes, as are Paul Newman and Jack Nicholson. Steven Spielberg has gone against the trend of mainstream Hollywood directors, and, after winning best screenplay in 1974 for his first feature, *The Sugarland Express*, allowed Jacob to have *E.T. The Extra Terrestrial* as the closing-night film in 1982 and also screened *The Color Purple* out of competition in 1986.

Spike Lee is something of the odd man out, having carried on a love-hate relationship with the festival since his breakthrough film *She's Gotta Have It* screened in Directors' Fortnight in 1986. *Do the Right Thing* premiered in competition in 1989 but lost out to Steven Soderbergh's *sex, lies and videotape*. Lee's view of Cannes and the jury system was not made any better when two years later *Jungle Fever* lost out to Joel Coen's *Barton Fink*. Yet for all the downside, Lee has never missed the opportunity to use Cannes and other festivals to get his films maximum international exposure before their releases. Lee is the first to acknowledge that festivals can make and break films as well as talent.

For an independent movie to have a life longer than its first few festival screenings, it is going to have to be bought by a distributor or picked up for representation by a sales company. And where there are acquisition executives one also finds the more important film festival directors, or their scouts who are also there to acquire films, if only for their own festivals.

In the late '70s and early '80s, there was an influx of new talent on the selling and marketing side of the international independent film industry. For many of these young and unattached marketers film festivals seemed an easy way to have fun, see the world and visit some exciting global locations other than the inside of the Fiera Milano, home to Mifed, and the Beverly Hills Hilton, then home to the American Film Market.

Sales companies or distributors with international rights to sell were eager to service the growing number of international film festivals and attend, where possible, on the excuse that business might be done or the talent needed a chaperone. As the sales companies normally negotiated the movies directly with the festivals, it was quite simple: a ticket for the sales company executive and free accommodation or no film and no talent.

It did not take long for these road warriors to grow tired of living out of a suitcase and flying coach. The executives who grew older and matured along with their companies soon came to be more choosy which events they would attend and how. Some even started to charge festivals for prints and other ancillary costs associated with servicing festival requirements and would now have to be dragged screaming from their offices to actually attend another new event. Talent could still go if they wanted to, but they could go alone.

Today's marketing executive has the year's schedule pretty much mapped out, and because of the nature of the business, that schedule includes festivals and markets, and not just traditional film markets like the AFM, Mifed and Cannes, but also the key TV markets like Mip-TV, Mipcom and NATPE. It leaves very little time for the smaller, albeit often more colorful, festivals, which now are given as bonuses to junior staff in sales companies so long as it doesn't cost the company anything.

Festival slots, from the biggest to the smallest festivals, are often allocated on the basis of the relationships and friendships that good sales agents or distributors have developed. The facility to place their better films in the right festival program is one of the rewards of these hard-earned affiliations. Some agents are so well connected that they will even negotiate the slot in which they want their movie to play with promises of delivering talent on a specific day. Likewise, a festival may invite a sub-standard or inappropriate film just to get the talent attached to attend their festival and attract the media.

For the filmmaker looking to have a movie represented by a sales agent, it is vital to know and target the festivals that executives or their acquisition teams still attend on a regular basis. Besides the Triple Crown of international competitive festivals—Cannes (May), Berlin (February) and Venice (September)—they include, in North America, Sundance (January), South by Southwest in Austin, Texas (March), Seattle (May), Montreal (August), Toronto (September), Telluride (September) and, due to their proximity to Los Angeles, the American Film Institute's International Film Festival (October), the Los Angeles Independent Film Festival (LAIFF) (April), Santa Barbara (March) and Palm Springs (January).

The Independent Feature Film Market (September), while not a festival as such, is also seen as a key venue, as are the New York Film Festival (October) and the Hamptons (October), as both are in the backyard of many of the leading independent distributors including Miramax, October, Fine Line and Fox Lorber.

Events in London, such as the London Screenings (October) prior to Mifed, are similarly advantageous, due to their proximity to key acquisition personnel based in the city, although more business has resulted of late from Edinburgh (August).

On the European continent Rotterdam (February), Locarno (August) and, to a lesser extent, San Sebastian (September), are seen as the leading independent venues after the big three of Cannes, Berlin and Venice and the Mifed market.

To get a film into a festival is only the beginning of the work. The real objective is to put bums on seats and to have the *right* bums on those seats. It's about courting the media, the buyers, the distributors and, then, the public.

Jean Gabriel Albicocco had a good understanding of what attracts the media: When he was with FestRio he would advise the filmmakers to bring the actresses in their films with them to Rio, and leave the actors at home. While not necessarily politically correct, Albicocco knew the value of a photo of a pretty actress on a Rio beach in promoting both the festival and the film in the international marketplace. He was rarely wrong.

Even in Cannes a good screening in the Directors' Fortnight can be more important to the success of a film than being an also-ran in competition. The list of directors who have had their films screened and discovered in Directors' Fortnight is a who's who of top talent: Theo Angelopoulos, Bruce Beresford, Bernardo Bertolucci, Atom Egoyan, Stephen Frears, Werner Herzog, James Ivory, Jim Jarmusch, Spike Lee, Ken Loach, George Lucas, Manoel de Oliveira, Nagisa Oshima, Michael Radford, Tim Robbins, Glauber Rocha, Fred Schepisi, Martin Scorsese and Fernando Solanas, to name just a few.

"We also had what we called 'white sessions,' " Albicocco explained of the early days of Directors' Fortnight. "That is screening times that were left open for directors who arrived at the last minute with a print under their arm and nowhere else to show it." He continued the policy in Rio, where one year Jonathan Demme turned up with David Byrne for a screening of *Stop Making Sense* but brought under his arm a print of *Something Wild*, which he had just completed.

But times have changed since the early carefree days of Directors' Fortnight and FestRio. Space to screen at any festival is at as much of a premium today as finding screen space at the local U.S. multiplexes during the heavy summer release schedule. In a ten-day period in January, for example, Sundance screens more than one hundred features.

Although breaking a film at a market often comes as a surprise to those involved, it is, in fact, the aim of the exercise. But with these surprises also comes the more crushing reality that filmmaking is as much a business as an art. Being unprepared for the fallout can have disastrous results, as Jonathan Nossiter learned the hard way. His film, *Sunday* had the rare distinction of winning two of the major prizes at Sundance in 1997, including best film, but the deals for U.S. distribution and sales representation got bogged down, so international buyers had to wait until Cannes to buy the film. This pushed *Sunday* back on release schedules so that the success of Park City was all but forgotten, including in the U.S., where it struggled to find an audience.

Kevin Smith, the director of *Clerks*, noted when the film he had reportedly made for $27,000 was discovered at Sundance: "I came to the festival a wage slave. Twenty-four hours later I had a filmmaking career."

indie influence

The discussion of the relationship between independent filmmakers and festivals often begins with Steven Soderbergh's *sex, lies, and videotape* and the Sundance Film Festival in 1989. As the histories go, the film inaugurated a new kind of filmmaking and sparked a heightened interest in the offbeat films frequently featured at the festival. However, as many fest-savvy pundits eagerly point out, *sex, lies, and videotape* was not recognized by the festival's grand jury; instead, like many of the best films every year, it was endorsed by audiences who gave it their own prize. Further, rather than inspiring filmmakers, the popularity of *sex, lies, and videotape* and its subsequent box office success alerted distributors to an untapped market, and this was the film's real accomplishment. Suddenly, acquisitions executives realized that the festival might harbor other gems and that these might, like *sex, lies and videotape*, draw audiences. The festival in some ways shifted as a result; rather than being a cozy, receptive site for film lovers, Sundance, along with a series of other top-notch international festivals, became a place for doing business. Subsequently, festivals now are divided between those that offer a filmmaker access to potential business relationships and those that are more concerned with particular films and their effect on an audience.

Since 1989, Sundance has grown increasingly powerful as the primary domestic showcase for buyers and critics interested in independent films. Key films—*Reservoir Dogs* in 1992, *Clerks* and *Go Fish* in 1994, and *Star Maps* in 1997, among others—all in some way offered a forecast for what would be hot throughout the rest of the year, which has in turn contributed to Sundance's growing power in defining the trends and aesthetic issues of the independent scene. Some of these trends include the excitement around queer cinema in the early '90s, the flurry of extremely violent films like *Man Bites Dog*, as well as an interest in the lazy aesthetic sparked by *Slacker*.

Other festivals used to boast this power of setting trends. "In Los Angeles, Filmex was for many years incredibly important," notes Emily Gerstman, co-president of Zeitgeist, a New York–based distributor. "There's been a sea change in the circuit so that some of the festivals that were so important ten years ago are now less so. And then festivals like Sundance that weren't so significant have grown to be extremely important, and this is due mainly to the increased interest in independent films."

There are also many more festivals now than ever before; many have sprung up to complement Sundance—the Los Angeles Independent Film Festival and South by Southwest are two new fests to watch—while international programmers have become more and more enamored of American independent films, finding them both entertaining and lucrative. Overall, in the last decade, Sundance, as well as a long list of other American and international festivals, has become an essential part of a film's life, not only offering a venue for attracting buyers but also establishing a space for filmmakers to show off their talents for future projects. However, it's important to note that there have been dramatic changes over the last ten years.

The first change is simple: thanks to both the continued excitement around the do-it-yourself ethic and the increasingly more expensive and professional second and third efforts of many previously successful indie directors, the annual output of American filmmakers has increased steadily over the years. "A thousand independent films are made in the United States every year now," says Peter Broderick, president of Next Wave Films, a company funded by the Independent Film Channel to supply finishing funds to ultra-low-budget independent films. "With all of these films chasing a finite number of festival slots, competition increases."

Broderick hastens to add, however, an often overlooked fact: "Not every independent film is a festival film, and it's very important for filmmakers to evaluate their films to see if they really should launch at a festival or if they might do better to host their own screening for acquisitions executives." Broderick continues: "More conventional genre films may not work at festivals, but they might thrive in theaters; it's important for people not to confuse the festival life of a film with mainstream theatrical distribution. They are very different."

The kind of films both being made and labeled "independent" has also shifted. "When Toronto started to establish itself as a major festival, the American component tended to be very low budget films, and the reason for including them was to hear voices that hadn't been heard," explains Noah Cowan, associate director of programming at Toronto's Festival of Festivals. "Films like *Killer of Sheep* and *Daughters of the Dust* were radically different films, very scrappy, very guerrilla." Cowan goes on to point out, however, that now the range of American independent films has expanded beyond these rough, low-budget efforts. "Now $8 million films are considered independent," he says, adding, "It's healthy. For Toronto, it's very easy now to show that we're covering the range, and in general, festivals are showing more of a blend, from the very-low-budget films to the higher-budgeted independents."

If festival programmers are suddenly inundated with more submissions, including films that have relatively large budgets, how do filmmakers stand out? Broderick notes that now more than ever the first ten minutes of a film need to be compelling. "Will the opening spark interest?" he asks, adding, "The title is also important." Filmmakers like Joe Carnahan, who was the first filmmaker to receive finishing funds from Next Wave Films and premiered his film in Sundance's Midnight section in 1998, have taken this advice to heart. Carnahan's title? *Blood, Guts, Bullets & Octane*. And the first ten minutes? An explosive flurry of murder and mayhem that will not get untangled until the film's final fifteen minutes.

Filmmakers will also often try to generate interest by getting one of the growing number of festival scouts or a producers' reps interested. People like Mary Glucksman, Bob Hawk and Berenice Reynaud routinely advise festivals on brand-new films that they find exciting, and by wooing the scout or rep, a filmmaker can establish a champion for the film who will help marshal it through the selection process.

For filmmakers who lack either a festival scout or producer's rep pushing for the film, all is not lost. According to Cowan, unknown films do still have a chance. "Obviously we'll watch a film with greater scrutiny when it comes from someone we trust," he says. "But then there are those unknown tapes that come through, and we'll put one of them up and find ourselves enraptured. I hope and believe that a film that is doing something new and interesting, whether or not it has its champions, will find a place in the festival."

As the competition grows increasingly fierce for the limited number of festival slots, filmmakers are now encouraged to plan their strategy carefully. "The question of which festival to play first is crucial," claims Broderick. "The second, third, and fourth festivals don't matter as much. With the first festival, however, you want to be at one where there is serious coverage by distributors. If you get an enthusiastic response at that first festival, the rest can be easier. After a film's festival premiere, you've lost that moment of high anticipation. If it doesn't click at the first festival, it can be all uphill from there."

Given the complexity of the rules for premieres and the hesitation to exhaust a film's theatrical audience in a particular city with a festival screening, many filmmakers often feel nervous about putting together an appropriate festival strategy. For Kirby Dick, who finished his documentary film, *Sick: The Life and Death of Bob Flanagan, Supermasochist*, just in time for the 1997 Sundance deadline, the whole festival scenario seemed daunting. "I didn't know anything about festivals when I started," he says. "I called Darryl Macdonald, the director of the Seattle International Film Festival, as well as several directors who had just spent the previous year at festivals, to get some advice." With these various contacts, Dick cobbled together an education in festival strategy and etiquette. "You have to do your homework," he says.

Dick adds that people tend to respond well to filmmaker inquiries. "Generally people involved with festivals love films and filmmakers, so they're open to helping. I've also found that they realize that this information is incredibly arcane and that their knowledge can be extremely beneficial for filmmakers." Broderick echoes Dick, noting that research is necessary for assessing which festivals might be right for a certain film. "This shifts from year to year depending on the director of the festival and the various programmers. And this is where you really have to do your homework by calling people and getting advice. This information is not in a book. It's not on-line. It's not in any single source. And you have to do this work again with every subsequent film."

Once Dick's film was accepted into Sundance, he got the assistance of Mark Urman, who was then a publicist for Dennis Davidson and Associates. Urman would prove to be invaluable at the festival, and indeed, another shift in the festival scene is the importance of handling a film's festival premiere correctly. Playing that first festival is no longer merely a matter of showing up and hanging out; filmmakers now have to learn how to work the parties and the press with well-rehearsed lines and an intriguing public persona. "Having someone who knows the festival circuit can really make a difference," Broderick notes. "It's really a person-to-person business. And this isn't good or bad . . . it's just the way it works."

Filmmakers quickly learn how small the "person-to-person" festival network is. "The scene is surprisingly tight," comments Dick. "There is a network of people who go from festival to festival all over the world, and gossip is in large part the glue of the circuit." Dick's advice? Be professional and polite. "The last thing you want to do is alienate people or try to muscle programmers," he says. "They'll be around for a long, long time."

Indeed, many veteran producers recommend that filmmakers remember to think long-term about their festivals. "If the filmmaker made the film and his or her goal was to be able to make more movies, and the film goes to festivals and audiences see it and an agent or producer spots the filmmaker's talent and wants to provide support for his or her next film, then the filmmaker has succeeded even if the film isn't picked up by a large distributor," says Broderick. "Having made one movie, it's easier to make a second."

Festivals thus offer filmmakers access to audiences, acquisitions executives and other filmmakers. They also may be the first place in which a film is critically assessed. "At Toronto, there is a huge collection of critics and buyers, and this becomes very important for filmmakers," says Cowan. "We see it as our duty to provide an environment that is conducive to filmmakers, and one of the ways that we try to do that is in being careful to create positive critical essays in our catalogs. This is the first piece of writing an audience will see about a film, and it should be a list of the film's qualities or offer a sense of a film's value."

Festivals also offer a crucial venue for some films. For documentaries, for example, many of which are shot on 16mm, which lessens their chances for theatrical release, the festival circuit may be the only way of showing the film to the public. Festivals also tend to be adventurous in their programming and will thus cheerfully screen films that may have trouble in more mainstream venues. "Festivals like to explore certain boundaries that the theaters in a particular city might be hesitant to explore," explains Dick, and indeed, films like Bruce LaBruce's *Super 8 1/2*, Chris Smith's *American Job* or Beth B's *Two Small Bodies*, while certainly deserving a theatrical release, may find that their most discerning audiences are the ones attending festivals.

International festivals have also grown increasingly more interested in American indies. "For a lot of people, American independent films are where it's at," explains Gerstman. "It's also hard to ignore them. Now Cannes, Berlin, and Rotterdam all have important indie sections." Gerstman also notes that the international interest in American indies may have been sparked by the fact that in the late '80s, foreign television entities began funding American independent filmmakers; having these films screen for foreign audiences was a natural extension of that involvement.

Gerstman also notes that several European festivals have done their share to foster American independent production. "Rotterdam was always important," she explains, "but now it's incredibly significant, and this is because they work hard getting the films that you don't see at other festivals, and they've also groomed certain filmmakers. They're extremely loyal, and the larger festivals just don't have the time to do that."

Another key attribute at foreign festivals is the way European interest can carry over to American audiences. Gerstman recalls as an example the reception of Bruce Weber's *Let's Get Lost* at the Berlin Film Festival in 1989. "It was terribly exciting to see the audience so enthusiastic about this independent American documentary," she says, adding that the reception of *Poison* a few years later was equally thrilling. "I would say that gay and lesbian work really came to light at festivals in general, and at foreign festivals in particular. The screening of *Poison* at Berlin was wild. And then the interest in gay and lesbian work dovetailed with what was going on in the U.S."

Overall, then, both international and domestic film festivals have worked hand in hand with independent filmmakers to generate increased interest in and support for a wide range of provocative films; distributors have also helped, picking up and then marketing many of these often challenging films to audiences unaccustomed to the low-budget films that frequently flourish at festivals. While the increased emphasis on festivals as marketplaces and launching grounds may be troubling relative to the festival scene of the past, the burgeoning of festivals in cities all over the world seems to bode well for promoting film culture and diverse filmmaking talents.

the tech new world of international film fests

S t e v e n   G a y d o s

Today, virtually every festival can be reached via e-mail, and the number of fests with Web sites increases daily. But stepping outside this guide and onto the streets of a film festival at the dawn of the millennium is a more bracing, dazzling display of how far fests have technologically traveled in the past decade.

The ubiquitous cell phones that have cropped up on every corner at fests from Cannes to Sundance have linked filmmakers and deal-makers so that commerce occurs speedily, from planning lunch dates to sealing foreign sales contracts. Computerized ticketing systems (when they work) have alleviated one of the fest manager's greatest nightmares.

"The first time my wife, Anne, and I came to Cannes more than thirty years ago," recalls producer Arnold Kopelson (*Platoon*, *The Fugitive*, *Seven*), the phones were these antiquated black boxes with long cords and every call had to go through an operator. You literally couldn't call next door in your own hotel. So the next year we came in, I brought walkie-talkies and it was a huge improvement. And it caught on for several years."

Though the business side of fests and markets has improved immeasurably, perhaps the greatest beneficiaries of the dramatic technological advances in fest- and market-going are also one of the key components of the international festival scene: journalists. For those filing stories, reviewing pictures and interviewing filmmakers and stars, the tech revolution has transformed the very nature of the task. Laptop computers, Internet research, Web sites, e-mail, digital photography, CD-ROM press kits, mini-disc audio recorders, satellite linkups to lightweight minicams and rolling video edit bays, all add up to a revolution in festival reporting.

In his lively remembrance of Cannes, "Two Weeks in the Midday Sun," *Chicago Sun Times* film critic Roger Ebert recalls the cumbersome copy flow he faced in the '60s and '70s, when he "typed the stories on a manual typewriter, and took them to the telex booth of the festival where foreign-speaking typists copied an approximation into their telegraph machines." In one story he was reporting the release of "900 balloons" at a party for Farrah Fawcett, which metamorphosed via the telex transcribers into a report on the release of "900 falcons," which led to virulent protests from animal-rights activists. At least this mistake was absurd enough to earn Ebert $12 when he sold the text of the *Sun Times*'s correction of the incident to *The New Yorker*.

Slamdance, the fest initiated in 1995 as a companion/competitor to the famed January Sundance fest, was one of the first film fests to tap into the power of the Internet.

"The festival goes on one week a year, and we're trying to help new filmmakers, so it seems absurd to stop there," Slamdance director Peter Baxter says. The rest of the year the Web site is an interactive global film community hall, where filmmakers can compare notes on past fest experiences, share information and advice on filmmaking and swap resources. One part of the Web site is called War Stories, while another, dubbed the Digital Marketplace, links filmmakers, scripts and financing sources, offering film clips on-line.

Sweden's Gothenburg Film Festival in '97 rolled out an innovative way to expand the reach of its seminars and workshops. A perennial problem of film fests is the jammed screening and panel schedules that force festgoers into making impossible choices between watching must-see films or attending can't-miss discussions.

Bengt Toll, organizer of the Gothenburg fest's "My American Friend" panel, snagged a cross-section of international film figures including Jorn Donner, Agnieszka Holland, Nik Powell and Angus Finney. The discussion ranged from European quotas designed to block Hollywood product to the travails of specialty film financing. Out of the tens of thousands of festgoers, only a couple of hundred were able to catch the lively repartee. But Toll and fest director Gunnar Bergdahl solved the problem by downloading the highlights of the panel onto an audio CD, which was then sent out to industryites and international press, and distributed at the Swedish film booth at the Cannes fest several months later.

At the Karlovy Vary (KV) International Film Festival in 1997, there was a quiet cyber breakthrough that the festival's board of directors was at first reluctant to endorse. If they had polled film critics and reporters, they would have quickly discovered that plugging the festival into the Internet is rapidly shifting from an option to a necessity.

Brad Kirkpatrick is one of the tens of thousands of young American expatriates living in Prague. Undaunted by the KV's lack of enthusiasm, he found allies in the younger rank and file of KV fest workers and volunteers and solicited aid from Datron Tech, a Prague-based PC computer distributor.

Having just wired up the Council of Europe conference held in Prague, Kirkpatrick knew the potential of applying digital technology to live cultural events. "We went in with digital cameras and filmed things as they were happening. Reporters recorded interviews on minidiscs. Then they took all the material to the technical team at workstations, who scanned and coded and organized everything on a work management system put together by Oracle, another of our sponsors. All of this was then sent to a server and was distributed to the world via Web pages."

This brave new tech world of cultural event coverage means the dramatic reduction in reporting time from days via traditional means to minutes via e-mail. In addition, the digital world offers bonuses for researchers.

Festival web sites themselves not only become vehicles for reporting and disseminating information but also are an essential and reliable resource for attendees and reporters alike. And there are festivals popping up that are not only aided by digital technology; they're *about* digital tech, such as San Francisco's pioneering ResFest, which is entirely dedicated to exploring the world of live-action narrative and animation digital shorts, many of which were created completely on desktop computers. Traditional fests such as the AFI Los Angeles film festival also plan to have films showing on their Web sites as soon as streaming video technology is improved.

how to launch a community fest

Darryl Macdonald

So you want to start a film festival, and you don't know where to begin? It's actually pretty simple: Just take a look around your community. That will dictate a good deal of what you will need for your start. Different strategies apply, depending on the kind of community the event is to be launched in; the things that work in one setting are not necessarily applicable to another. And while there are many kinds of film festivals held currently in every corner of the country, two main models provide the prime examples for successful local film festivals: the urban film festival, such as those held annually in New York, Toronto and Seattle; and the resort community film festival, exemplified by those in Sundance, Telluride and Palm Springs.

In general, the big-city film festival relies on a large, somewhat sophisticated and diverse local populace to provide the audience for an eclectic mix of contemporary "independent" film programming from around the world, while the resort community festival must rely largely on an audience drawn both from its own smaller local filmgoing community as well as from cineastes and tourists in the nearby metropolitan market who are attracted both by the films at the festival and the ambience of the resort or small town.

The least complicated model by far is the urban film festival. Many of the elements needed to mount a festival already exist in abundance in the city, from potential audiences, sponsors and staff to the theaters, hotels and other infrastructural requirements needed to host a viable film event. It's also a lot easier to attract films in an urban setting. Film distributors and suppliers are more likely to give serious consideration to an event that can attract a sizable audience and provide the kind of press coverage and word of mouth that will increase their chances for a successful run of their films after the festival has come and gone. The main thing that attracts filmmakers and film suppliers to a festival is the promise of increasing their chances for success in the theatrical marketplace, and cities have a natural advantage in this equation.

That said, heightening a film's profile is certainly not the sole province of big city festivals. Sundance provides the most obvious example of a resort-based festival that can do wonders for filmmakers and film suppliers alike.

But starting a film festival in a remote rural community presents problems one would rarely encounter in the city. I remember the resistance I ran into when I first started programming the Hamptons Film Festival. Distributors I had been dealing with successfully for years in Seattle were at first very skeptical about providing films to yet another upstart U.S. festival, let alone one that they saw little need for, situated two hours away from New York City by car. More than one distribution executive said to me: "Why would I want to put my films in a festival for rich people? Those people don't even go to the movies!" I countered with the two strengths I knew the Hamptons could provide: The huge New York City media base was naturally drawn to the Hamptons, because of all the entertainment industry players and business mavens who had getaway homes there; and these "celebrities" were the hook to get the entertainment press out to the Hamptons to cover the festival, which in turn provided ample opportunity to get lots of coverage for films and filmmakers who participated in the event.

The other intangible I pushed was the presence of the many New York–based opinion makers with weekend homes in the Hamptons, who would presumably return to New York after a weekend watching films at the festival raving about the new film they'd caught from France or England or wherever. This wasn't a glib fabrication on my part. That is exactly what happened at the Hamptons Film Festival, and it provides a valuable lesson: Know your marketplace and promise only what you can genuinely deliver. The incentive I offered distributors wouldn't have worked a second time if no press or opinion makers had come that first year, but resort areas like the Hamptons have a special appeal to press, industry and filmgoers from out of town: they figure that even if the films aren't that great, they can still make the most of a minivacation in a beautiful area.

The Palm Springs Film Festival required a similar strategy to get film suppliers to pony up. While the town was no longer a hot vacation destination for the industry, its location in the desert made it an easy sell to members of the press and film industry from Europe and other parts of America who were only too eager to take a free trip to a sun-baked resort town in the middle of winter. In addition, Palm Springs was still perceived by filmmakers and industry in other parts of the world as the glamorous movie star getaway it once had been. This made it an especially enticing place in which to host a festival. The key ingredient the festival needed to succeed—apart from the films—was enough of a budget for hotel rooms and airfares to be able to invite key filmmakers, buyers and sellers and press to attend the festival as our guests. That's where Sonny Bono came in.

Sonny Bono had recently become the mayor of Palm Springs and was looking for a way to put the fading resort town back on the map as a tourist destination. His background in the entertainment industry led him to the conclusion that pushing Palm Springs's fabled reputation was the key to bringing back an aura of glamour to the city, and a film festival seemed the obvious means to do that. Using his clout with both the city council and the businesses based in Palm Springs, Sonny put together an incredible support network for the event, rustling up a healthy amount of cash funding from the council through their tourism promotion budget and hitting up local businesses, hotels and a major airline to provide the remaining means to launch a major film festival with a great chance to succeed.

With abundant means at our disposal to invite the filmmakers, industry and press to take a busman's holiday in the desert in the middle of winter, getting the hot, new films that provided the main justification for them to come was made much easier. The L.A.- based press and industry, who in this case may have been skeptical about a festival in tired old Palm Springs, were drawn by the enticing menu of international films that the festival lined up; and the end result was a thriving new festival that served everybody's purposes: it put filmmakers and suppliers in direct contact with the distributors and national press based in L.A. and brought a financial boon and press attention to a fading resort area in an otherwise fallow season.

The Hamptons provided altogether different problems as the host of an international film festival, and it represents another set of concerns that must be addressed in starting up a resort fesitval. While the struggle to get films from suppliers was a relatively straightforward problem to deal with, getting the mayor and the town itself to embrace the idea of a festival was the hardest part of the endeavor. The Hamptons are an enchanting, pastoral chain of villages set at the eastern tip of Long Island, populated by a strange mix of farmers, fishermen and a rarified blend of the rich and famous.

While the village of East Hampton retains the charm and old-money mansions of the Gatsby era, a more recent, eclectic mix of *nouveau riche* entrepreneurs, artists, writers and show business types has moved into the town, summering there and spending getaway weekends during the rest of the year. In this bucolic setting, both the longtime locals and the recent *arrivistes* resent the intrusion of outsiders and press, fearing that the beauty of the Hamptons will somehow be sullied by the presence of outsiders—particularly the "wrong element" (i.e., celebrity gawkers and paparazzi). In this setting, it was neccessary to get the cooperation of the mayor, the police department and several other local powers-that-be in order to move forward with planning the festival. The local chamber of commerce proved to be a major ally, as did several board members who had strong relationships with the town leadership and other merchants.

Even then, the one ingredient that all resort-style festivals must include to really provide a festive ambience for guests and filmgoers is some large and stellar parties. While Palm Springs had more than adequate facilities in which to hold those events indoors, in the Hamptons we were forced to hold the parties in a tent large enough to accommodate hundreds of revelers. The various logistics and permissions needed to pull off these parties—such as the opening- and closing-night galas—were a case study in the difficulties of staging a world-class film festival in a community that may welcome the infusion of cash that an off-season event can provide, but loathes the disruption to their normal routine that an event like this can bring.

Seattle is probably more typical in the type of financial support most large- or medium-sized cities will devote to this type of endeavor. The city, county and state arts commissions, as well as a number of high-profile foundations, took some convincing but eventually kicked in four-figure grants in support of the festival. What Seattle already had that made the going easier was a large, sophisticated filmgoing public (Seattle has the highest per capita filmgoing audience in the country) who supported the festival in large numbers from day one. They, in turn, attracted the kind of corporate support that made our job of fund-raising a lot easier.

In general, three things are essential to the success of the urban-based film festival: solid sponsorship support, strong programming and aggressive promotion and marketing. While each of these is also neccessary for the resort festival to succeed, it must rely much more heavily on two local non-filmgoer elements if it is to thrive. A supportive local government and business community must buy into the event, which is not always as easy as it may sound.

MONEY, MOVIES AND MARKETING

While many organizers start out naively thinking that all you have to do is announce the intention of starting a film festival and the world will beat a path to your door, the truth is that there is a saturated marketplace where film suppliers feel there are already way too many festivals. So before you begin the battle for films, you need money to attract the elements that will achieve the best programming you can present.

Unless you can find one or two angels who are prepared to underwrite your initial costs, you'd better be able to raise funds and support from sponsors yourself or hire a good fund-raiser who can do it.

Festivals are an expensive animal, so whether you do it yourself or use start-up funds from board contibutors to hire a fund-raiser, the first step is to pursue corporate or government funds to underwrite the costs of hiring a staff and finding offices from which to mount the festival. Look for sponsoring companies that will benefit from aligning themselves with your event. Research which companies sponsor similar arts events in your community. Attend chamber of commerce meetings, approach consulates or cultural orgainzations, and always keep in mind that your corporate partners will want to connect with your audience demographics or the prestige of being associated with an artistic endeavor that aims at a broad public spectrum.

As for government funding, don't count on a lot of support. I've run big-city festivals and resort-community festivals, and apart from the festival I programmed in Vancouver, there are precious few U.S. festivals that receive much of anything from any level of government. (The chief exception to this was the Palm Springs Festival, which attracted major underwriting from the city council, given the mayor, Sonny Bono's, participation.)

Identifying your audience is crucial both to getting sponsors to support the event and to the basic financial well-being of the fesitval through ticket sales. Is there a large student population or university campus nearby? Do you live in a community with a large and diverse ethnic population? Is there a distinct and underserved special-interest group or groups you can cater to like seniors or gays and lesbians or religious or other communities who form a base of consumers for the event? Each of these elements will dictate, to a certain extent, both the viability of starting up a film festival in your community and what you can expect in the way of potential audience size, sponsorship, availability and even the costs involved in mounting an event.

You need to realize before you even begin to map out a game plan that *nothing is more important than the films.* While that may seem evident to anyone, I'm always amazed when I get a call from someone wanting to start a film festival who thinks that some kind of blueprint exists that will make everything simple; there is nothing simple about mounting a film festival—film festivals are three-ring circuses that require a lot of juggling to keep everyone happy and all constituents served. In order to mount a festival, you need to have access to films, and that is not nearly as simple as it may seem.

Most of the people who provide films for festivals want something out of the event. U.S. distributors want to increase the market for their films, so if you can promise them lots of free publicity for the films you're requesting, they'll be much more disposed to play ball, particularly if your festival is based in a city where they already book films to theatrical exhibitors. If you're in a smaller resort community, you may be able to offer them two things: building the audience for their films by increasing the local audience's appetite for movies; or, if it's a resort community like Sundance, Palm Springs or the Hamptons, you can offer them national publicity for their films, provided that you are committed to spending the money to bring in press from major media markets such as New York or Los Angeles. Promising press coverage also means a large hospitality budget to offer free travel and lodging to both press and filmmaking guests. These perks won't be as neccessary once the festival has developed its reputation and draw. Filmmakers and media will spend their own company's money to travel to your festival once you've established a "must go" reputation for the event.

In the meantime, while a lot of press people from these major media centers are delighted to accept free trips to glamourous resort destinations, they can't neccesarily give you any coverage unless they find something to write home about, such as some name stars or directors. At the very least, they require the film lineup to be top-notch, including at least a few premieres, or their editors, who are responsible for what gets column inches or airtime, will ignore any coverage they proffer.

Other, smaller distributors may be happy to settle for film rental instead of press coverage of the films you request from them, but this is a costly way of booking films (particularly if they insist upon a percentage of the admissions) and negates the possibility of having money in the budget to bring in filmmakers or press. There are, of course, other sources of films for your lineup, including international sales agents (most of whom will want film-rental and shipping charges covered, if they bother to respond to you at all), film producers (a discerning and picky lot) or film directors—many of whom are begging for the exposure a film festival can offer because their films have already been rejected by distributors or sales agents. Their big hope is that your festival can provide the kind of audience response, awards or press coverage that will ignite interest from film buyers.

Let's assume that you are able to put a lineup of films together for a festival because you can offer film suppliers what they are looking for. The eternal question that comes next: If you build it, will filmgoers come? The answers rely to a great extent upon who your audience is and how good your promotional and marketing abilities are. Never assume that just because there's a large college audience nearby, they will beat a path to your door. In truth, most of them will run in the opposite direction, probably to the nearest multiplex playing *Scream 7* or *Batman 5*. The demographics of film festivals have changed drastically over the last ten to fifteen years, and it's a safe bet that the largest share of your audience lies in the thirty to fifty age group, so target them in all of your marketing plans, unless you plan on playing films that are very mainstream. The largest audience for foreign and independent films in this country lies in this mature sector who were brought up on a film diet of Fellini and Buñuel, Sayles and the Coen Brothers.

This rule of thumb applies even if you are hosting a festival aimed squarely at an ethnic or special-interest-group audience. The main point of a festival is to serve an audience that is starved for alternatives to Hollywood films. By and large, the mainstream audience won't cross the street to see a film with subtitles or without a major star or director attached to it.

What elements are needed to reach the audience? Advertising helps, though the costs are sometimes prohibitive. Concentrate instead on putting out flyers listing your lineup and make sure you get them into bookstores, video shops, libraries, campuses, community centers and other theaters, as well as the myriad other places where your demographic targets pursue their recreational pleasures. A good publicist or promotions staff is invaluable to get free publicity by pursuing newspaper, television and radio coverage and promotion, often by offering the media outlet a promotional tie-in as the "official" radio station or newspaper sponsor of the event. The media are very promo-savvy—after all, it's their business to be—and they are often looking for special events such as festivals to build their audience and demographic reach. What they offer in return is free promotional and advertising time or space for your event.

While the prudent decision is not to try pulling off this Herculean task, for those of you who will push forward despite the odds, the following list of definite "do's" may help to get you rolling in the right direction. Whether you live in a large or small city or a remote resort community, there are certain things you need to put in place before you get into the details of programming and promoting the festival. Chief among them are:

1. A board of directors or trustees—Look for key members of your community who have a keen inerest in the arts, preferably a love of film, and who are either connected to sources of sponsorship, political support and funding or are motivated "worker bees" who will lighten the organizational workload. If your board choices do not include a lawyer and an accountant, solicit board members who have connections to individuals who will provide these services, and others, *pro bono*. This will save you major bucks and grief down the road.

2. Nonprofit status—Hire a lawyer, or go to your nearest library for a Volunteer Lawyers for the Arts chapter, or get a board member who's a lawyer or an accountant to handle the paperwork involved. You will need to file articles of incorporation, a certificate of incorporation and, if at all possible, a coherent mission statement that identifies your purpose and corporate goals.

3. A realistic budget—This should cover the first eighteen months of operation, including the actual staging of the first festival. While this may seem obvious, too many inexperienced festival directors really don't have any idea of all the items to include in the budget for a festival operation. Among the neccessities:

Income Categories: Admissions income, development income (fundraising and grants), special events, membership, submission fees, program advertising sales, merchandise sales, in-kind sponsorships (including free advertising, hotel rooms, airline tickets, etc.). Although this latter category does not represent cash, it can offset major costs on the expense side of the books.

Expense Categories: Personnel costs, contract labor (including legal and accounting services and advertising/marketing firm, etc.), rent and utilities (offices as well as theatrical venues), office operations (including stationery, office supplies, postage, phone and fax, auto, travel and entertainment, equipment rentals, etc.), delegate expense (for filmmaking guests and national press), advertising and promotions, program catalog costs, film rental (unless you have the connections to get all the films for free— and don't count on that if you're pursuing films from sales agents or archival sources), ticket printing costs or fees, taxes and license fees (particularly at the state and local level), print shipping, insurance and merchandise expense. And whether you think you need it or not, throw in a contingency expense line item (ideally 5 percent of the overall budget), because no matter how well prepared you think you are, you aren't prepared for everything that can and will crop up.

4. The best staff you can get your hands on—Energy and motivation are the strongest attributes your staff can have, but experience is essential in such categories as programming, publicity and promotion, shipping and guest/delegate travel. You can still put on a film festival with an inexperienced staff, but chances are you'll never get to present a second festival because the word will be out after the first year's effort that the event is disorganized and the people running it don't know what they're doing. This type of reputation doesn't sit well with film suppliers, sponsors or audiences. It's worth noting that the opposite also applies: if you get things right the first time out, film suppliers, sponsors and audiences will eagerly await your second edition, and building your festival into a force to be reckoned with will be immeasurably easier.

the festivals

The following is a chronological list of film and television festivals and markets around the world, as well as selected trade conferences, conventions and other industry events.

Although it includes most major events and is as up-to-date as possible, some events may be omitted because of lack of information, and some that are included may change their plans.

Figure in parentheses after the fest's name indicates the edition of the event as of 1998.

Dates listed are for 1997–98 festival editions. All information is supplied by fests and subject to change. We recommend contacting festivals for confirmation of current status of scheduling, personnel, fest programming, etc. Figures in parentheses before telephone or fax numbers are area codes within the country. TBD is noted when dates are not available for determination as of press time.

Note: FIAPF recognition refers to fests that are officially sanctioned by Fédération Internationale des Associations de Producteurs de Films. Many American festivals have no affiliation with this body, and the FIAPF designation is primarily utilized by fests with international competitive sections.

JANUARY

KidFilm Festival (14th)

2917 Swiss Ave.
Dallas, TX 75204
Phone: (214) 821-6300
Fax: (214) 821-6364
Contact: Alonso Duralde
Web site: www.usafilmfestival.com
Dates: Jan. 5–18
Deadline: Oct. 19

America's longest and oldest children's festival. Noncompetitive. FIAPF recognized.

Nortel Palm Springs International Film Festival (9th)

1700 E. Tahquitz Canyon Way, #3
Palm Springs, CA 92262
Phone: (619) 322-2930
Fax: (619) 322-4087
Contact: Craig Prater
Web site: www.psfilmfest.org
Dates: Jan. 8–19
Deadline: Nov. 1

Emphasis on international films, seminars and awards gala honoring industry greats. Noncompetitive. FIAPF recognized.

At the tenth-anniversary point in 1999, the Nortel Palm Springs International Film Festival is poised either to emerge as an important outlet for specialty films or to retrench into simply being a nice diversion for a resort community.

The 1998 edition yielded several discoveries from overseas, including Polish helmer Juliusz Machulski's *Killer*, which made the front page of *Variety* during the fest when it was grabbed for remake rights by *Men in Black* director Barry Sonnenfeld. The deal drew attention to Palm Springs's exciting *Wild Wild East* sidebar on contemporary Central and Eastern European cinema and reminded Hollywood filmmakers that the remake business was yet another lucrative usage of festgoing.

Though discoveries such as this are good for boosting the Palm Springs fest's claim to international status, the fest remains in a somewhat ambiguous state, with ambitious programming accompanied by a lack of financial resolve to mount a truly first-rate fest. Events such as a black-tie gala honoring Sylvester Stallone with a lifetime achievement award may help pay for the fest, but Stallone's decidedly mixed body of work created a critical backlash both in and out of the fest infrastructure that threatened to diminish the fest's very substantial progress over the past decade in planning and programming.

Founded by the late Sonny Bono, who at the time was serving as mayor of the desert community two hours east of Los Angeles, the Palm Springs Fest was first programmed by Seattle Fest director Darryl Macdonald, who left in the fourth year after a rancorous split with the board over the direction in which the fest would be headed. Palm Springs took several years to recover from Macdonald's defection, but by 1997 it was again being talked about in Hollywood and international filmmaking circles as a fest with promise. Much of the credit for that turnaround goes to former artistic director Paola Freccero, who arrived in '97 and left in early '98, and program director Paul Gachot.

The fest has traditionally slotted in large numbers of films that are in the heat of the mid-January quest for the best foreign language film Oscar, a strategy that has led to high-profile bows of award-winning films such as *Burnt by the Sun*, *Belle Epoque*, *Cinema Paradiso* and *Mediterraneo*. In 1998, thirteen films in the fest were official Oscar submissions from countries around the globe. The '98 fest rolled out 106 films, of which 42 were U.S. premieres and 12 were world premieres.

The main section of the fest is traditionally a survey of current world cinema, and the only awards granted at the fest are audience prizes, voted on by moviegoers and presented to the top-five vote getters. Winners in '98 were: two Czech films, *A Forgotten Light* and *Mandragora*; *Character* from the Netherlands; a U.S. documentary, *The Long Way Home*; and *Elles* from Luxembourg. The fest also provides a bounty of lively panels on subjects from indie filmmaking and financing to the role of the film critic. The '98 fest also included a film sidebar focused on film preservation as well as several gala film premieres to entertain the bejeweled locals.

—*Steven Gaydos*

International Film Festival of India (29th)

Directorate of Film Festivals
Ministry of Information &
Broadcasting
Government of India
4th Floor, Lok Nayak Bhavan
Khan Market, New Delhi 110003,
India
Phone: (91-11) 461-5953, 469-7167
Fax: (91-11) 462-3430
Contact: Malti Sahai
Dates: Jan. 10–20
Deadline: Nov. 30

The best of international cinema, with a competition for Asian filmmakers. FIAPF recognized.

You would expect that a government-sponsored film festival in the biggest film-producing country in the world (eight hundred features a year) should be grandiose, and in its majestically elephantine way, the Indian festival is unforgettable.

Until 1998, the International Film Festival of India (IFFI) was the only major festival in the world that changed its location every year. Even-numbered years saw its gaudy banners unfurl at the three-screen Siri Fort complex in New Delhi, home base of the Directorate of Film Festivals. Visitors during odd-numbered years were directed to Trivandrum, Calcutta, Madras, Bombay or whichever city copped the hotly contested sweepstakes to host the event. Now the government has changed all that: the festival has been fixed permanently in Delhi. In reaction to the location freeze, three new independent festivals have sprung up in Trivandrum (April), Calcutta (November) and Mumbai/Bombay (November).

IFFI is an exotic festival in any case, mingling joys with frustrations. The latter stem from the festival's close ties to the Indian government and its ministers, whose behind-the-scenes politicking and onstage preening are an endemic part of IFFI. Bureaucracy vies with colorful local chaos to make life difficult for guests, but in the end, the determined ones somehow manage to see most of the films they're interested in. Several years ago, tight security measures were instituted to ensure that film prints coming from abroad remained in safe hands throughout the festival.

The wonder is how this cumbersome machinery unspools some two hundred feature films each year in mid-January. Over the past three decades, IFFI has undergone a gradual shift away from being a meeting point for Soviet-bloc and Western films (a parallel to India's role as a nonaligned country during the Cold War) to focusing increasingly on Asian cinema. Fest chief Malti Sahai has given space to imaginative programming by Cinemaya editor Aruna Vasudev and others, hatching the laudable idea of a competition section dedicated to Asian women directors.

A large Cinema of the World section contains a few world premieres from countries off the beaten track like Syria and Sri Lanka. The U.S. section has become substantial, thanks to the cooperation of the American majors, and includes an occasional indie. The film market is a tank heavily fished by local distributors, who buy thirty to fifty fest titles for India. Any Western picture in the fest lacking Indian distribution is virtually guaranteed to make a deal. The reason is an arcane law that gives films screened at the festival automatic censorship approval, making them instantly buyable.

Minutely covered by the local press, which delights in ferreting out "scandals" and whose film reviews provide amusing morning reading, the event has only scatter-shot coverage abroad. This is a pity, since the Indian Panorama section represents a fine opportunity to view the best of the year's local production as well as a chance to meet the leading filmmakers. This sidebar, a mixed bag of some twenty features, contains all the country's new art film production, meaning those pictures that are potentially exportable to the West. (India's commercial song-and-dance films are not part of the festival.)

Though the atmosphere varied with the location (Bombay furnished the most stars and glamour, Delhi, a constant stream of embassy parties), India has a great deal to offer the rough-and-ready traveler. Accommodations for some one hundred guests are top quality, and the festival has bus outings to nearby tourist spots like the Taj Mahal. It is wise to count on one day in bed with Delhi belly. Bring a huge stock of business cards, as the locals like their Japanese counterparts, cherish the card exchange tradition.

—*Deborah Young*

FIPA—International Festival of Audiovisual Programs (11th)

14 rue Alexandre Parodi
75010 Paris, France
Phone: (33-1) 4561-0166
Fax: (33-1) 4074-0796
Contact: Marie France Pisier
Dates: Jan. 13–18
Deadline: Nov. 14

Fiction, series, documentary, news, music and short TV productions. Competitive.

Sundance Film Festival (14th)

P.O. Box 16450
Salt Lake City, UT 84116
Phone: (801) 328-3456
Fax: (801) 575-5175
Contact: Geoff Gilmore
E-mail: sundance@xmission.com
Web site: www.sundance.org
Dates: Jan. 15–25
Deadline: Oct. 3 (shorts), Oct. 10 (features)

Showcase for the best American independent films in dramatic and documentary categories, with emphasis on the discovery of new talent. Competitive.

Nestled in the Wasatch Mountains of Utah, this premiere event for U.S. independent films has truly humble origins. The forerunner to what's become eleven days in January of snow, cell phones and mega deals for the latest discovery didn't occur in Park City, Utah, and wasn't even called Sundance.

In 1978, the United States Film Festival was established in Salt Lake City by a group of businessmen and cinephiles. Like so many other similar unspoolings, it was a selection of the new and the old; mainstream, foreign and oddball pics for people who hungered for something they couldn't find in their local movie houses.

The legend is that Robert Redford, whose Sundance Institute established in 1981 was an hour away, was invited to attend and support the struggling local festival. It wasn't a particularly distinctive program, but he recalled that there was an excitement about the screenings of Stateside independents.

"There were two factors that led me to get involved," he says. "I thought I could increase the opportunity for the filmmakers themselves and, for more selfish reasons, I was having trouble getting attention for the institute. I thought if we could create a symbiosis between exhibition and distribution, maybe all this would help draw attention to the filmmakers' lab."

The seeds of what was to become Sundance were planted, and in 1985, the financially troubled film festival was absorbed into Redford's orbit. While screenings continued in Salt Lake City, the main event moved to Park City. Six years later, it would officially be renamed the Sundance Film Festival.

The turning point came in 1989 when *True Love* by Nancy Savoca was crowned best of fest. However, it was the Audience prize winner, *sex, lies and videotape*, that made the industry stand up and notice. Produced for slightly more than $1 million, it was acquired by upstart distributor Miramax and went on to win at Cannes and gross more than $70 million at the global box office.

First the indies and then Hollywood descended upon the ski resort to ferret out the next hot film property or talent. That feeding frenzy has escalated to the present, creating an unusual climate of industry nabobs and those who aspire to the throne. Movie stars and wannabes huddle under layers of clothing for warmth and to share the excitement.

"This could be the greatest festival in the world if Redford loved to surf," observed *Vogue* film critic John Powers.

For all that it is, Sundance can also be a logistical nightmare and arguably has the worst screening facilities of any major international film event. For fifty weeks of the year, Park City caters to skiers and tourists. It has one aging triplex that shows mainstream fare, so hotel facilities and school auditoriums have been converted into screening facilities to accommodate the demands of ever-increasing crowds. It can all grind to a halt when flurries blow to blizzard force and shuttles to the far-flung locations get mired in snow and ice.

One also has to wade through the arcane and the questionable to find the gems, as one might logically expect from any festival that's devoted to work by first- and second-time filmmakers. In addition to the Premieres selections and the main competition—in which prize winners seldom seem to go on to commercial success, despite being hotly courted by acquisitions executives—the fest offers the somewhat edgier American Spectrum selection and the World Cinema section, which has premiered hits such as *The Full Monty*. These sections also program an unparalleled selection of important documentaries, some of which draw nearly as much attention from distributors as the fictional fare.

What's surprising, considering its myriad problems, is that Sundance has retained an almost unique niche on the circuit. Program director Geoff Gilmore has confessed that a fall festival with a similar agenda could take some pressure and expectation off of Sundance's shoulders. To date, only the Los Angeles Independent Film Festival in March has come along as a viable alternative.

Back in Park City, there's competition from Slamdance, organized in 1995 by filmmakers who'd been passed over by Sundance's selection committee. It's the equivalent of the Cannes Directors' Fortnight, playing more raw and off-beat fare. In 1997, Slamdance presented an even more downscale alternative, and in 1998 Slamdunk took a stab at grabbing press attention. But at least for the moment, it's every American indie's dream to trek up the mountain and become the rage of Sundance.

—*Leonard Klady*

Slamdance Film Festival

6381 Hollywood Blvd #520, Los Angeles, CA 90028, USA
Tel: (1-213) 466-1786
Fax: (1-213) 466-1784
Contact: Peter Baxter
Web site: www.slamdance.com
Dates: Jan 16–23
Deadline: Nov. 12

Takes place in Park City, Utah, during Sundance Festival. Competitive.

Angers Film Festival (Premiers Plans d'Angers) (10th)

54 rue Beaubourg
75003 Paris, France
Phone: (33-1) 4271-5370
Fax: (33-1) 4271-0111
Contact: Claude-Eric Poiroux
Web site: www.anjou.com/
premiersplans/
Dates: Jan. 16–25
Deadline: Nov. 10

Showcase for new European films directed by first-time directors. Competitive.

New York Festivals

(Nonbroadcast Media & TV
Programming & Promotions)
780 King Street
Chappaqua, NY 10514
Phone: (914) 238-4481
Fax: (914) 238-5040
Contact: Bilha Goldberg
Dates: Jan. 16–25
Deadline: Sept. 30

Cinelatino (5th)

Osterbergstr. 9
D-72074 Tubingen, Germany
Phone: (49-7071) 56960
Fax: (49-7071) 569696
Contact: Paulo Roberto de Carvalho
E-mail: filmtage.tubingen@t-online.de
Web site: www.cityinfonetz.de/
filmtage/oo.html
Dates: Jan. 16–Feb. 7
Deadline: Nov. 30

Features and shorts from Latin America. Noncompetitive.

Midem (32nd)

Reed Midem Organization, BP 572
11 rue du Colonel Pierre Avia
75726 Paris Cedex 15, France
Phone: (33-1) 4190-4400
Fax: (33-1) 4190-4409
Contact: Jane Gardson
Dates: Jan. 18–22

Music industry market.

National Association of TV Program Executives (NATPE)

2425 Olympic Blvd., Suite 550E
Santa Monica, CA 90404
Phone: (310) 453-4440
Fax: (310) 453-5258
Contact: Kate Chester
Dates: Jan. 19–22

Market for international and domestic TV program buyers and sellers. Moves annually.

Meetings With the Central and Eastern European Cinema (9th)

Alpe Adria Cinema, Via San
Rocco 1
34121 Trieste, Italy
Phone: (39-40) 311-153
Fax: (39-40) 311-993
Contact: Tiziana Finzi
E-mail: aac@intertrade.it
Web site: www.intertrade.it/aac
Dates: Jan. 19–25
Deadline: Nov. 30

Young and independent features and shorts emerging from Central and Eastern Europe. Competitive.

Solothurner Filmtage (33rd)

P.O. Box 140
CH-4504 Solothurn, Switzerland
Phone: (32) 625-8080
Fax: (32) 623-6410
Contact: Ivo Kummer
E-mail: filmtage@cuenet.ch
Web site: www.cuenet.ch/filmtage
Dates: Jan. 20–25
Deadline: Oct. 31

National festival with special screening of European films. Noncompetitive.

Tromso International Film Festival (8th)

Georgernes Verft 3
5011 Bergen, Norway

Phone: (47-55) 322-590
Fax: (47-55) 323-740
Contact: Hans Henrik Berg
E-mail: tiff@bgnett.no
Web site: www.bgnett/tiff
Dates: Jan. 21-25
Deadline: Nov. 1

Focuses on contemporary art films and documentaries from all continents. Noncompetitive.

Brussels International Film Festival (25th)

50 Chaussee de Louvain
B-1210 Brussels, Belgium
Phone: (32-2) 227-3980
Fax: (32-2) 218-1860
Contact: Christian Thomas
E-mail: infoffb@netcity.be
Web site: ffb.cinebel.com
Dates: Jan. 21–31
Deadline: Oct. 31

European features and shorts. Main award comes with support for distribution in Europe. Competitive. FIAPF recognized.

Floating Film Festival (5th)

15366 17th Ave.; Suite 441
White Rock, BC, Canada V₄A IT9
Phone: (604) 531-7462
Fax: (604) 530-3558
Dates: Jan. 22– 31
Deadline: Dec. 1

Programs include international and American studio premieres plus tributes to classics, screened aboard a ship. Noncompetitive.

Women In Cinema Film Festival & Market

Seattle International Film Festival
801 E. Pine St.
Seattle, WA 98122 USA
Phone: (1-206) 324-9996
Fax: (1-206) 324-9998
e-mail: mail@seattlefilm.com

Contact: Kathleen McInnis
Dates: Jan. 23–29
Deadline: Nov. 15

Competitive.

Clermont-Ferrand International Short Film Festival (20th)

26 rue des Jacobins
63000 Clermont-Ferrand, France
Phone: (33-4) 7391-6573
Fax: (33-4) 7392-1193
Contact: Roger Gonin, Christian Guinot
E-mail: festival@gdebussac.fr
Web site: shortfilm.gdebussac.fr
Dates: Jan. 23–31
Deadline: Oct. 15

International and national competitions for shorts plus additional programs and market. Competitive.

Capacity, overflow and *sold out* are the watchwords at the Clermont-Ferrand International Short Film Festival—aka the "Cannes of Short Films." Be they animated or live action, short films have always been taken seriously in France; after all, the very first films were French and, by default, *very* short: fifty-two hand-cranked seconds. From ultra-modest beginnings two decades ago, fest attendance has risen a hundredfold to 120,000; and Clermont-Ferrand, which hands out a generous array of prizes in separate national and international competitions, has grown to resemble Mecca for filmmakers whose movies run less than an hour.

The setting for Marcel Ophuls's classic documentary *The Sorrow and the Pity* as well as headquarters for the Michelin Tire company, Clermont-Ferrand is a three-and-a half-hour train ride south of Paris. The part-industrial, part–quaint town sports a population of 136,000, of which some 30,000 are students. Given the dense crowds pressing to get into fest screenings, one might conclude that everyone is playing hooky to attend.

Demand to see the winning entries (there are roughly twenty prizes, some with cash awards worth as much as $30,000) is so strong that the fest schedules three consecutive identical programs on closing night to handle more than 4,500 ticketholders.

Many of the original organizers, who were college students in 1979, still run the nonprofit association that manages the overwhelming logistics of programming more than 250 short films from 45 different countries (including 76 in the international competition and 68 in the national competition in 1998) that unspool on nine screens in seven different locations during eight days. Lines form as much as an hour before screenings and would-be viewers are routinely turned away for lack of space. French filmmakers tend to take such rabid interest in stride, but visiting directors can't get over Clermont-Ferrand's unflagging devotion to short films.

Countless French names who went on to feature success unveiled attention-getting shorts in Clermont-Ferrand. These include Jean-Jacques Beneix (1979) of *Diva* fame; Jean-Pierre Jeunet and Marc Caro (1982), later to make *Delicatessen* and *City of Lost Children*; Leos Carax (1982), future director of *Lovers on the Bridge*; Pascale Ferran (1984), who won the Camera d'Or at Cannes with *Coming to Terms with the Dead*; and Cyril Collard (a prize winner in 1986), whose *Savage Nights* swept the Césars. Hot talents Arnaud Desplechin, Mathieu Kassovitz, Manuel Poirier and Cedric Klapisch made Clermont-Ferrand debuts; and Alain Berliner, whose first feature was *Ma Vie en Rose*, showed his short *Rose* there in 1994.

The Short Film Market—in its thirteenth edition in 1998—began as a handful of tables and has grown to occupy spacious quarters where business is brisk. Unlike the majority of film markets, a market badge in Clermont-Ferrand costs nothing.

Fest screenings are casual and egalitarian to a fault: tickets are a mere 15 francs (less than $3) in a country where viewing commercial releases costs roughly $8 and admission is first come, first served. Encounters and panel discussions with filmmakers are lively. Although filmmakers and buyers who travel the circuit also give high marks to the short film lineups in Brest (European shorts), Annecy (international animation), Angers and Poitiers (student shorts) in France and Tampere in Finland (28th edition in 1998), Clermont-Ferrand rules the roost for sheer size.

The Short Film Fest is such an ingrained fixture in the city's life that municipal authorities are building new headquarters to house the nonprofit association that runs the event.

—*Lisa Nesselson*

Filmfestival Max Ophuls Prize (19th)

Mainzerstr. 8
66111 Saarbrücken, Germany
Phone: (49-681) 39452
Fax: (49-681) 905-1943
Contact: Christel Drawer
E-mail: filmhaus@aol.com
Dates: Jan. 27–Feb. 1
Deadline: Nov. 15

Presents young directors from German-speaking countries. Competitive.

Gerardmer Fantastic Arts

36 rue Pierret
92200 Neuilly, France
Phone: (33-1) 4640-5500
Fax: (33-1) 4640-5539
Contact: Lionel Chouchan
E-mail: publics@imaginet.fr
Dates: Jan. 28–Feb. 1
Deadline: Jan. 11

International fantasy and sci-fi festival with films, videos, comics and other art forms. Competitive.

Rotterdam International Film Festival (27th)

P.O. Box 21696
3001 AR Rotterdam, The Netherlands
Phone: (31-10) 411-8080
Fax: (31-10) 413-5132
Contact: Simon Field
E-mail: iffr@luna.nl
Web site: www.iffrotterdam.nl
Dates: Jan. 28–Feb. 8

Major international showcase of independent film, incorporating Cine-Mart, an international co-production market for indie films. Competitive.

To celebrate its twenty-fifth anniversary in 1996, the Rotterdam International Film Festival replayed the entire program of thirty-six titles—plus several that were invited but unavailable at the time—from its inaugural edition in 1972. More than just a nostalgia trip, the exercise served to show how, a quarter of a century on, the greatly expanded Dutch event has remained true to the aims of its founder, Hubert Bals.

A passionate supporter of Third World, political, underground and independent cinema—as well as documentary, experimentalism and avant-garde filmmaking—Bals saw the need for an international film showcase in the Netherlands, where theatrical distribution at that time was anchored firmly in the commercial mainstream and showed scant regard for the new trends emerging from Europe, Asia and the U.S.

His 1972 lineup included work by maverick filmmakers such as Peter Bogdanovich, Rainer Werner Fassbinder, Philippe Garrel, Paul Morrissey, Wim Wenders, Marcel Ophuls and Frederick Wiseman. Also included were several African, Latin American, Middle Eastern and Asian films, with a particularly strong showing from Japan. The legacy of that first selection is clearly visible in the program of more than two hundred features plus one hundred short films, videos and CD-ROMs that constitutes the fest today.

The world's largest seaport, Rotterdam's downtown area was largely reconstructed after World War II and lacks the physical beauty of many other festival destinations. But despite its sterile setting, the fest has blossomed into a major international event. Its relaxed atmosphere and friendly social scene, its tight physical focus within a few city blocks, its richly eclectic lineup and the continuity of its initiatives to extend support beyond the confines of the ten-day event have made Rotterdam a regular industry stopover between Sundance and Berlin.

A nurturing force behind independent film, the fest's activities range from investment coordination and partial funding through screening the finished product and, recently, providing postfest distribution via a small theatrical-releasing arm. The fest's latest development is a sponsorship program for young film critics.

The five-day finance workshop, Cinemart, which takes place during the fest, selects just fewer than fifty feature projects each year, throwing the filmmakers together with financial backers and distributors from various territories. The Hubert Bals Fund administers more than $600,000 per year in seed money to be awarded to productions from developing countries. Films that obtained initial financing from HBF include Chen Kaige's *Life on a String*, Moufida Tlatli's *The Silence of the Palais* and Zhang Yuan's *East Palace, West Palace.*

Alongside lesser-known names, Rotterdam's main program regularly features directors such as Atom Egoyan, Hal Hartley, Takeshi Kitano, John Sayles, Tsai Ming-Liang, Wong Kar-wai and Abbas Kiarostami, as well as profiling idiosyncratic filmmakers like Alain Cavalier, Tatsumi Kumashiro, Karel Kachyna and Alexandr Sokurov. In 1995, the fifteen-title Tiger Awards competition for first and second features was introduced, offering three prizes of $10,000 each. Discoveries have included Ryosuke Hashiguchi's *Like Grains of Sand* and Naomi Kawase's *Suzaku*, which went on to win the Camera d'Or at Cannes.

The fest's innovative sidebars have included Fake Films, focusing on mockumentaries and other fact-and-fiction fusions; Pink Pictures, taking in erotica from Japan; 1998s the Cruel Machine, which looked at radical approaches to violence on-screen; and the first fest spotlight on films from the Mekong region.

In 1997, Simon Field, formerly the director of cinema of the distribution arm of London's Institute of Contemporary Arts, took over as director of the fest at the end of Emile Fallaux's five-year tenure. The new chief has established his intention not to stray too far from the model developed by his predecessor, the success of which has begun to pose a threat to the more established Berlin fest. Wrestling with its neighboring event over premieres looks to be an ongoing problem for Rotterdam, but the Dutch fest's active involvement in projects from script and preproduction stage ensures a strong prior claim to no small number of features.

—*David Rooney*

Cinequest (The San Jose Film Festival) (8th)

P.O. Box 720040
San Jose, CA 95172-0040
Phone: (408) 995-6305
Fax: (408) 995-5713
Contact: Mike Rabehl
E-mail: sjfilmfest@aol.com
Web site: www.webcom.com/sjfilm
Dates: Jan. 29–Feb. 4
Deadline: Oct. 15

Maverick cinema with features, shorts, documentaries and After Hours films. Competitive.

Gothenburg Film Festival (22nd)

Box 7079
S-40232 Göteborg, Sweden
Phone: (46-31) 410-546
Fax: (46-31) 410-063
Contact: Gunnar Bergdahl
E-mail: goteborg.filmfestival@
mailbox.swipnet.se
Web site: www.goteborg.se/kultur/
filmfestival/
Dates: Jan. 30–Feb. 8
Deadline: Dec. 1

National film festival of Sweden with an international and Swedish program. Noncompetitive.

Since 1997, the twentieth anniversary of the Gothenburg Film Festival, the fest's late January–early February unspooling has carried the added cachet of its designation as the official film festival of Sweden, granted by the Swedish Film Institute. The west coast seaport town may be a frigid spot in winter; however, that doesn't stop the long-established fest from drawing more than one hundred thousand moviegoers and many of the top filmmakers from all over the world.

The second-decade mark was celebrated with a number of festivities and special events, including the launching of Cine Bosnia, an ambitious fund-raising project for rebuilding a film theater in war-ravaged Bosnia. The project raised $25,000 from moviegoers in its first go-round. The fest also benefited from the presence of the European Film Academy meeting set in Gothenburg during the 1997 unspooling, a gathering that attracted filmmakers such as Istvan Szabo, Agnieszka Holland, Jorn Donner, Nik Powell, Daniel Bergman, Reinhard Hauff and Mika Kaurismaki. These noted Euro film figures were joined by more than one hundred film directors invited to celebrate the anniversary.

Scandinavian cinema since the retirement of Ingmar Bergman in the '80s has generally not quickened the hearts of foreign film fans, outside the occasional success of a Lasse Hallström or Bille August. Luckily for Gothenburg, the fest's recent outings have coincided with the emergence of a new generation of Scandinavian filmmakers who are more market driven and audience friendly. The result is a heightened international awareness of an emerging Scandinavian film scene in the '90s and popular local successes such as Kjell Sundvall's *The Hunters* in Sweden and the stylish Danish crime drama *Pusher*. Interestingly enough, both of these films have been picked up for Hollywood for remake rights, an enterprise that is quickly becoming a mainstay of the international fest circuit. The fest also is benefiting from high-profile Scandinavian film critical successes such as Norwegian films *Junk Mail* and *Insomnia*, both of which were picked up for U.S. distribution in 1998.

Gothenburg hosts several engaging film panels each year, including "My American Friend," a wide-ranging seminar bringing together Euro and American filmmakers to dialogue on key issues of film art and commerce. Fest organizers cleverly repurposed these discussions into a CD publication, which was later distributed at other fests such as Cannes.

Sections at the fest include "Distant and Far," which is the contemporary world cinema frame; a "Close Up" section focused on one of the Scandinavian nations as well as a spotlight on the latest Swedish cinema offerings. Fest director Gunnar Bergdahl describes the fest as bifurcated between "home (Scandinavia) and the world." The key prizes at Gothenburg include a Nordic Film Prize, which includes a $7,000 cash award as well as an audience award, a Swedish critics award and a City of Gothenburg award for best Swedish film. The '98 lineup included 430 films from forty-four countries, with sidebars on China, Japan and Iran, as well as a tribute to the late Bo Widerberg and a day of screenings and other projects focused on the work of Bertolt Brecht.

—*Steven Gaydos*

Miami Film Festival (15th)

Film Society of Miami
444 Brickell Ave., #229
Miami, FL 33131
Phone: (305) 377-3456
Fax: (305) 577-9768
Contact: Nat Chediak
Web site: www.filmsocietyofmiami.com
Dates: Jan. 30–Feb. 8
Deadline: Nov. 1

Shows the best of international feature films and shorts. Noncompetitive.

Florida's leading film event, the Miami Film Festival, has introduced U.S. audiences to the likes of Regis Wargnier, Lasse Hallström, Atom Egoyan and Fernando Trueba. Miami works on the principle of quality rather than quantity, typically screening around thirty films, once each, at a single, large venue. Given those limitations, it draws a solid attendance of as many as forty thousand.

Miami owes its prestige largely to co-founder and president Nat Chediak, who has demonstrated a keen eye for unknown talent. For the inaugural Miami fest in 1984, he programmed *Dark Habits* by a debuting Spanish cineast, Pedro Almodovar. The following year he selected the Spaniard's second picture, *What Have I Done to Deserve This?* which drew the attention of programmers for the New Directors, New Films series at New York's Museum of Modern Art. And so Almodovar's reputation in the U.S. began to take off—as did that of his leading man, Antonio Banderas. Meanwhile, Chediak's fest has continued to spotlight bright novices; in fact, almost one-third of the films in the 1998 Miami festival were made by debut filmmakers.

The fest is best known as a forum for Spanish-language directors, who often contribute a third of its slate. The 1998 edition hosted stateside premieres of five films, which included Catalan director Bigas Luna's *The Chambermaid and the Titanic*, *In Praise of Older Women* from Spaniard Manuel Lombardero and *Little Miracles* by Argentine auteur Eliseo Subiela. But Chediak also unearths non-Hispanic jewels. Among past U.S. premieres at Miami are Stephen Frears's *My Beautiful Launderette* and Hallström's *My Life as a Dog*.

Miami has a tradition of strong supplementary events. In 1985, Georges de la Rue conducted the University of Miami Symphony Orchestra in a series of pieces he had composed for the films of Truffaut—the first time he had ever done so in the U.S., and without charging a cent. In the 1990s, the fest has staged several cinema and literature symposia, featuring big names who have worked both in film and in print. The rosters have boasted John Sayles, Guillermo Cabrera Infante, Bertrand Blier, Susan Sontag, Alain Robbe-Grillet and Sam Fuller. Seminars accompanying the festival also focus on filming in South Florida, a popular location for Hollywood and home to a small but vibrant and multicultural indigenous industry.

Miami tends to be director studded rather than star studded, but A-list talent is no stranger to the city. Fest or no fest, Hollywood actors often are drawn to the lively club circuit of Miami Beach. Moreover, Sylvester Stallone has served three times as the fest's "honorary international chairman." A local resident, Sly has lent more than his name to the event: in 1997 he donated $75,000, and an equal sum to the Gusman Center, a magnificently restored 1926 movie palace with a fifty-foot-tall screen that is the festival's only venue and seats 1,700. Chediak has resisted the temptation to turn the festival competitive, but in 1998 he did introduce an Audience Choice Award.

—*Andrew Paxman*

International Film Fest Belgrade

Sava Centar, Milentija Popovica 9
11000 Belgrade, Serbia-Montenegro

Phone: (381-11) 311-4961
Contact: Nevena Djonlic
Dates: Jan–Feb
Deadline: TBD

FEBRUARY

Hungarian Film Week (29th)

Magyar Filmunio
Varosligeti Fasor 38
1068 Budapest, Hungary
Phone: (36-1) 351-7760
Fax: (36-1) 351-7766
Contact: Katalin Vajda
Dates: Feb. 6–10

Showcase for Hungarian productions from the past year. Competitive.

Santa Clarita International Film Festival (4th)

P.O. Box 801507
Santa Clarita, CA 91380-1507
Phone: (805) 257-3131
Fax: (805) 257-8989
Contact: Chris Shoemaker
Dates: Feb. 6–13
Deadline: Jan. 5
Web site: www.sciff.org

Family-themed festival for films and screenplays. Competitive. FIAPF recognized.

Pan African Film Festival (6th)

P.O. Box 2418
Beverly Hills, CA 90302
Phone: (213) 295-1706
Fax: (213) 295-1952
Contact: Ayuko Babu
Dates: Feb. 6–16
Deadline: Oct. 15

More than fifty new films and videos from the U.S., Africa, the Caribbean, South America, Europe, the South Pacific and Canada, made by or about people of African descent. Noncompetitive.

Milia (5th)

Reed Midem Organization
BP 532
11 rue du Colonel Pierre Avia
75726 Paris, Cedex 15, France
Phone: (33-1) 4190-4460
Fax: (33-1) 4190-4470
Contact: Laurine Garaude
E-mail: 100321,1310@compuserve.com
Dates: Feb. 8–11
Deadline: Nov. 14 (CD-ROMs and Web)

International digital media exhibition and conference.

European Film Market

Budapester Strasse 50, D-10787
Berlin, Germany
Phone: (49-30) 25 48 92 25
Fax: (49-30) 25 48 92 49
Contact: Beki Probst
Dates: Feb 12–22
Deadline: TBD

Berlin International Film Festival (48th)

Budapester Strasse 50
10787 Berlin, Germany
Phone: (49-30) 254-890
Fax: (49-30) 254-89-249
Contact: Moritz de Hadeln
Dates: Feb. 12–23
Deadline: Nov. 25

Competition (headed by Moritz de Hadeln), Panorama of World Cinema (Wieland Speck), New German Cinema (Heinz Badewitz) and the International Forum of Young Cinema (Ulrich Gregor). Competitive. FIAPF recognized. European Film Market (headed by Beki Probst) attached.

The Rorschach test question for any festivalgoer—on a par with whether you like your martinis shaken or stirred—is: "Berlin or Venice?"

Very few are equally passionate about both, and most are frequently violently partisan: It's a simple matter of North vs. South, snow vs. swelter, logical German efficiency vs. charming Italian chaos, and tough, sassy envelope pushers vs. safer, more traditional, art house–cultural fare.

It has not always been so, though the Berlinale's feisty character was shaped by the unique postwar history of the metropolis— a tiny stronghold of Western Bloc capitalism in a sea of Eastern Bloc communism. Like Cannes in its early years, it started partly as an industry showcase, though with a more political edge, founded by Alfred Bauer in 1950 as a showpiece by the Western powers. Only in 1967 was a company separate from the Berlinale set up to give it some kind of cultural independence.

As at Cannes in the 1960s, pressure started to grow for the event to reflect the new forces in filmmaking. Mirroring the introduction of the Directors' Fortnight at Cannes in 1969, the Berlinale gained a provocative parallel showcase, the International Forum of New Cinema, in 1971; its founders, Ulrich and Erika Gregor, still run it to this day with a personal passion.

Soviet Bloc countries finally started attending Berlin in the mid-'70s, and when film critic Wolf Donner took over in 1977 the fest entered a new era, taking on its present character. Donner took advantage of new cultural subsidies being poured into Berlin by the federal government, moved the fest from balmy June to freezing February, and raised its profile as a direct challenge to Cannes.

Donner's brief reign was tumultuous, antagonizing the Soviets (who pulled out in 1979 in protest against *The Deer Hunter*), the forum and Hollywood. His successor, former Locarno fest boss Moritz de Hadeln—who heads the Official Selection and shares co-directorship of the whole event with Ulrich Gregor— has brought to the job a showman's appetite for controversial choices and a combative approach to the press and rival fests, tempered by canny diplomatic skills.

With the fall of the Berlin Wall in 1989 and opening up of Central Europe, the city lost some of its edgy character and the fest struggled for some years to build a new profile. But De Hadeln has played a patient game that has started to pay off in recent years: ever aware of the mighty Cannes lurking three months hence, he has courted the Hollywood majors, laid out a welcoming carpet for East Asia (especially Chinese-language) cinema, and battled annually with the forum for the best of (among others) Central and Eastern European filmmaking.

Berlin still is the unrivaled, first litmus test of the year among truly international fests, with an attached European Film Market—run by veteran Swiss exhibitor Beki Probst—that works in close synergy with the main event and is a particularly useful entree to Europe for U.S. indie filmers. First-timers to the Berlinale often need a computer to negotiate the packed schedule but, unlike some other fests (and definitely unlike Cannes), it's totally logical and surprisingly friendly and democratic, once you know your way around.

Currently located in the heart of the hard-partying, hard-eating city, in the flavorsome Zoo district—though soon set to move to the characterless, newly developed Potsdamer Platz—the main fest is eleven days and about 160 films: the bad and the beautiful, straight and gay, glitzy and grungy. Just like Berlin itself, in fact.

—*Derek Elley*

Mardi Gras Film Festival (20th)

P.O. Box 1081, Darlinghurst
NSW 2010, Australia
Phone: (61-2) 9332-4938
Fax: (61-2) 9331-2988
Contact: Tony Grierson
E-mail: info@queerscreen.com.au
Web site: www.queerscreen.com.au
Noncompetitive.
Dates: Feb. 12–26
Deadline: Nov. 30

Features and shorts about, made by or of interest to gays and lesbians.

Portland International Film Festival (21st)

Northwest Film Centre
1219 S.W. Park Ave.
Portland, OR 97205
Phone: (503) 221-1156
Fax: (503) 226-4842
Contact: Bill Foster
Web site: nwfilm.org
Dates: Feb. 12–March 1
Deadline: Nov. 15

Showcasing more than 100 features from around 30 countries. Competitive.

Yubari Fantastic Adventure Film Festival

Hokkaido
Hakuba Building, 4th Floor
Kanda Jumbocho 1-24
Chiyoda-ku, Tokyo 101
Phone: (+813) 3219-3231
Fax: (+813) 3219-3235
Dates: Feb. 13– 17
Deadline: TBD

Certainly not one of the biggest events on the international film circuit, Yubari is probably one of the coldest. The festival, held in this northern Japanese mining town, takes place in midwinter in one of the country's frostiest locations. Despite the harsh conditions, the festival has a hearty following, and it is known for the first screenings of some of the coolest films to hit Japan.

Yubari was a boomtown more than a century ago when coal was discovered there. In the 1950s, the town had as many as 120,000 inhabitants, and eighty pits were in operation. But as the nation found other energy sources, Yubari's population dwindled while the economy went sour. But under the guidance of charismatic Mayor Tetsuyi Nakata, the town started to bill itself as a tourist attraction after the 1972 Winter Olympics were held in nearby Sapporo.

The mines were turned into museums, other attractions were added and hotel rooms increased while Nakata used his charm to sell a town that offers skiing six months of the year and some of the best sashimi in Japan.

Yubari was conceived as being a twin to the Festival International du Film Fantastique at Avoriaz, held at the French ski resort. Founder Yoichi Komatsuzawa was a regular participant in the French festival, and he wanted to bring a similar event to Yubari as a way to revitalize the mining town.

About forty films are screened at the event, and there are prizes in the Young Fantastic Competition as well as an award given out for best video production. The Grand Prix comes with a prize of about $7,500.

The festival is striving to cast the spotlight on young directors who are just emerging as skilled helmsmen.

The big event in 1997 was the Japan premiere of Wes Craven's *Scream*, where the director was also the major guest at the fest. Some of the other notable films on recent screening roles included Tim Burton's *Mars Attacks!* and *Microcosmos* from Claude Nuridsany and Marie Perennou.

The Japanese government picks up the entire tab for the frigid film fest.

—*Jon Herskovitz*

Transmedia Video Fest

Klosterstrasse 68-70, Berlin, Germany 10179
Phone: (49-30) 2472 1907
Fax: (49-30) 2472-1909
Contact: Mickey Kuella
E-mail: videofest@mediopolis.de
Dates: Feb. 13–22
Deadline: Nov. 14

Competitive

International Forum of New Cinema

Budapester Strasse 50 D-10787
Berlin, Germany

Phone: (49-30) 2548 9229/9246
Fax: (40-30) 2548 9249/2615025
Contact: Karen Moeller
Dates: Feb 13–23
Deadline: Nov. 30

*Competitive.An important part of the
Berlin International Film Festival, its
function is to inform its patrons
about new formal and thematic developments in film in all countries.*

World Animation Celebration

30101 Agoura Court, Ste. 110
Agoura Hills, CA 91301 USA
Phone: (1-818) 991-2884
Fax: (1-818) 991-3773
Contact: Lesley Sullivan
Dates: Feb. 17–22
Deadline: Nov. 1

Competitive.

Brussels Cartoon & Animated Film Festival (17th)

Rue de la Rhetorique 19
1060 Brussels, Belgium
Phone: (32-2) 534-4125
Fax: (32-2) 534-2279
Contact: Philippe Moins
E-mail: folioscope@skynet.be
Web site: www.awn.com/folioscope/
festival
Dates: Feb. 17–Mar. 1
Deadline: Nov. 1

*A showcase for the newest and most
innovative work in animation. Noncompetitive.*

Locations '98

835 N. Stanley Ave.
Los Angeles, CA 90046
Phone: (213) 852-4747
Fax: (213) 852-4904
Contact: Maggie Christie
E-mail: maggiec@ix.netcom.com
Dates: Feb. 20–22

*The only trade show for worldwide
location and production services.*

Monte-Carlo Television Festival & Market (38th)

4, Blvd. du Jardin Exotique
MC98000 Monaco
Phone: (377) 9310-4060
Fax: (377) 9350-7014
Contact: Wilfred Groote (festival),
David Thomatis (market)
Web site: www.tvfestival.monaco.mc/
Dates: Feb.20–26; Market, Feb. 23–
26
Deadline: Dec. 4 (news); Nov. 20
(fiction)

*Competition of fiction and news pro-
grams with attached market. Awards
Gold and Silver Nymphs. Competitive.*

Fantasporto-Oporto International Film Festival

Rua da Constituicao 311
4200 Porto, Portugal
Phone: (351-2) 550-8990/1/2
Fax: (351-2) 550-8210
Contact: Mario Dorminsky
E-mail: fantas@caleida.pt
Web site: www.caleida.pt/
fantasporto
Dates: Feb. 20–28
Deadline: Dec. 15

*Specializes in fantasy and sci-fi films,
with a New Directors' Week and a
retrospective dedicated to Spanish
cinema. Competitive.*

American Film Market (18th)

10850 Wilshire Blvd., 9th floor
Los Angeles, CA 90024
Phone: (310) 446-1000
Fax: (310) 446-1600
Contact: Brady Craine
E-mail: info@afma.com
Web site: www.afma.com
Dates: Feb. 26–Mar. 6
Deadline: Jan. 9

Film market.

66

the variety guide to film festivals

Sedona International Film Festival (4th)

P.O. Box 2515
Sedona, AZ 86339
Phone: (520) 282-0747
Fax: (520) 282-5358
Contact: Daniel Schay
E-mail: scp@sedona.net
Web site: www.sedona.net/scp
Dates: Feb. 27–Mar. 1
Deadline: Jan. 1

Celebration of cinema dedicated to "intimacy and excellence." Competitive.

NatFilm Festival (9th)

St. Kannikestr. 6
1169 Copenhagen K, Denmark
Phone: (45) 3312-0005
Fax: (45) 3312-7505
Contact: Kim Foss & Andreas Steinmann
E-mail: natfilm@centrum.dk
Web site: www.filmfest.dk
Dates: Feb. 27–Mar. 8
Deadline: Dec. 10

Screens 150 feature films and special programs including documentaries, shorts and video art. Noncompetitive.

Green Screen (5th)

114 St. Martins Lane
London, WC2N 4AZ, U.K.
Phone: (44-171) 379-7390
Fax: (44-171) 379-7197
Contact: Victoria Cliff Hodges
Dates: end of Feb.
Deadline: Nov. 30

Showcase for entertaining and lively films with environmental issues including debates and discussions. Competitive.

Fajr International Film Festival (16th)

Farhang Cinema
Dr. Shariati Ave.
Gholhak, Tehran 19139, Iran

Phone: (98-20020) 888-990
Fax: (98-20020) 267-082
Contact: Ezzatollah Zarghami
Dates: Feb. (Exact dates TBD)

Provides a focal point for Eastern and Western cinemas. Competitive. FIAPF recognized.

MARCH

Dublin Film Festival (13th)

1 Suffolk St.
Dublin 2, Ireland
Phone: (353-1) 679-2937
Fax: (353-1) 679-2939
Contact: Aine O'Halloran
E-mail: dff@iol.ie
Web site: www.iol.ie/dff/
Dates: early Mar.
Deadline: Nov. 24

Annual showcase of the best in Irish and international features, shorts and documentaries. Noncompetitive. FIAPF recognized.

Fribourg Film Festival (12th)

Rue de Locarno 8
1700 Fribourg, Switzerland
Phone: (41-37) 222-232
Fax: (41-37) 227-950
Contact: Martial Knabel
Dates: Mar. 1–8
Deadline: Dec. 1

International film festival focusing on Asia, Africa and Latin America. Competitive and noncompetitive.

International Film Festival for Children

17 Kasr El Nil St.
Cairo, Egypt
Phone: (202-392) 3562
Fax: (202-393) 8979
Contact: Saad Eldin Wahbah
Dates: Mar. 1–8
Deadline: TBD

Competitive. Focuses on films for children.

U.S. Comedy Arts Festival

c/o Home Box Office
2049 Century Park East, 42nd floor
Los Angeles, CA 90067
Phone: (310) 201-9200
Fax: (310)201-9445
Contact: Stu Smiley
Dates: Mar. 4–7
Deadline: Dec.15

Showcase of new and innovative comic artists performing in the various disciplines of the comic arts: film, television, animation, theater, live performances. Noncompetitive.

Tampere International Short Film Festival (28th)

P.O. Box 305
FIN-33101 Tampere, Finland
Phone: (358-3) 213-0034
Fax: (358-3) 223-0121
Contact: Kirsi Kinnunen
E-mail: film.festival@tt.tampere.fi
Web site: www.tampere.fi/festival/film
Dates: Mar. 4–8
Deadline: Jan. 5

One of the biggest international showcases for shorts, incorporating a market with 1,500 entries and the Multimedia Parlour. Competitive. FIAPF recognized.

Viewpoint (4th)

Sint-Annaplein 63
9000 Ghent, Belgium
Phone: (32-9) 225-0845
Fax: (32-9) 233-7522
Contact: Cis Bierinckx
E-mail: Studio.Skoop@net7.be
Web site: www.cinebel.com/studioskoop
Dates: Mar. 4–11
Deadline: Dec. 14

International festival with a section of rarities and classics, New(s) from Flanders and Human Rights Watch. Noncompetitive.

San Francisco International Asian American Film Festival (16th)

346 Ninth Street, 2nd Floor
San Francisco, CA 94103
Phone: (415) 863-0814
Fax: (415) 863-7428
Contact: Corey Tong and Paul Yi
E-mail: naata@sirius.com
Web site: www.naatanet.org
Dates: Mar. 5–12
Deadline: mid-October

Presenting more than 100 titles from around 20 countries, festival is premier showcase in North America for Asian and Asian-American cinema, with films from the greater Asian-Pacific diaspora. Noncompetitive.

Santa Barbara International Film Festival (13th)

1216 State Street, #710
Santa Barbara, CA 93101
Phone: (805) 963-0023
Fax: (805) 962-2524
Contact: Diane M. Durst
E-mail: sbiff@west.net
Web site: www.west.net/-sbiff
Dates: Mar. 5–15
Deadline: Dec. 1

Showcase of international independents, retrospectives, salutes, workshops, seminars and galas. Competitive.

For its first dozen years, the Santa Barbara International Film Festival ambled along amiably as a virtual definition of a regional festival, a welcoming, audience-friendly event held in a relaxed, picturesque setting that brought in enough exotic titles and name personalities to excite the locals but never developed

the variety guide to film festivals

sufficient heat to make it a must for out-of-towners.

Santa Barbara has always been a most agreeable festival, to be sure, a pleasant getaway destination in March, an off time of year on the fest circuit. But the programming has always tended toward the "nice," and away from the sort of rough, cutting-edge films that one sensed might offend the presumably delicate sensibilities of the festival's generally genteel, well-heeled sponsors.

In its thirteenth year, however, directorship of the festival was taken over by veteran Hollywood producer and local resident Renee Missel, and the lineup of films and participating talent gave every indication that Santa Barbara is intent on seriously raising its profile, if not on the international fest circuit, at least in terms of the American industry. Involvement on the part of the major studios increased markedly, as did the number of significant world premieres and major names brought in for tributes and seminars. In terms of physical location and reputation, Santa Barbara's position has always been roughly analogous to that of the Palm Springs Film Festival; both are easy two-hour drives from Los Angeles and would represent attractive destinations for industryites if they offered something essential from a business point of view.

For all their popularity with their local constituencies, however, neither Santa Barbara nor Palm Springs has managed to become a real magnet for distributors, the press, talent or those looking for same. On the basis of the 1998 event, Santa Barbara looks as though it might be getting ready to take its shot.

—*Todd McCarthy*

Guadalajara Film Festival

Griegos 120, Col. Altimira
Zapopan, Jalisco 45160, Mexico
Phone: (52-3) 6332-670 and 560-927
Fax: (52-3) 6332-492
Contact: Maria Ines Contreras
Dates: Mar. 6–13
Deadline: Dec. 15

Devoted to the promotion of new Mexican films, as well as screening Spanish and South American product. Noncompetitive.

The "Muestra," or showcase, held each year in Mexico's second city is one of Latin America's most reputable film events. Other festivals in Mexico have come and gone, and events elsewhere in Latin America tend to be big and shambolic. But Guadalajara soldiers on with quiet efficiency, enticing not only directors from around Latin America but also a number of film buyers from the U.S. who hope to discover the next *Like Water for Chocolate*.

Quality has suffered, however, due to a dearth of local pics. Mexico's film output has been so minuscule in recent years—averaging fifteen films a year, including co-productions—that organizers have stooped even to accepting dross that has lain in cans for several years to make up a Mexican section of eight or nine new pics within the overall slate of thirty-five to forty. Attempts to bolster the event with South American and Spanish films have had mixed results: since the event is noncompetitive—but for an audience award and two critics' prizes—it tends to draw films that are fine but a little old, or new but second-rate. As Mexico's film industry continues to limp along in moribund fashion, the reputation of Guadalajara is at risk—which is a shame, not least because the city is a good venue for a festival, being a populous, friendly and architecturally pleasing locale. Still, the state increased subsidy coin in late 1997, and with Mexico's economy now humming along nicely and moviegoing up sharply over the last two

years, production should soon start to revive.

Begun in 1985, the Muestra was conceived by filmmaker Jaime Humberto Hermosillo as a forum for student pics from the University of Guadalajara. The institution's rector, Raul Padilla, lent financial and administrative support and assumed the role of fest president. In the late 1980s, when the film industry was still producing about one hundred films per year (most of them admittedly exploitation films), the fest became a platform for the best of local cinema. In the early 1990s, Padilla ceased to be rector and so created a festival board, which today includes actor Pedro Armendariz, Jr., producer Bertha Navarro and the historian Emilio Garcia Riera. The university—joined by the film institute Imcine—continues to provide most of the $400,000 budget. Lately, there have been three changes of fest director in as many years, but the 1998 topper, film critic/lecturer Susana Lopez Aranda, hopes to lead the event for some time.

Mexican films preeming at the Muestra in the '90s have included Alfonso Arau's *Like Water* . . . , Alfonso Cuaron's *Solo con tu Pareja* (Love in the Time of Hysteria) and

Guillermo del Toro's *Cronos*—and all three of these directors are now working in Hollywood. Last year's *Cilantro y Perejil* (Recipes for Staying Together) by Rafael Montero went on to become the top domestic pic of 1997.

Guadalajara is also a popular meeting place for producers and distributors from around Latin America. In 1997, the fest saw the launch of La Red, an alliance of distributors from twelve Latino territories—among them Brazil's Rio-Filme and Mexico's Jorge Sanchez—who agreed to form a pool of films for all-rights distribution in each other's countries. La Red members hope that a steady stream of product will enable them to secure a continuous relationship with exhibitors, the increased theatrical exposure in turn stimulating downstream sales in each arena.

—Andrew Paxman

Bradford Film Festival (4th)

National Museum of Photography, Film and TV
Pictureville, Bradford, BD1 1NQ, U.K.
Phone: (44-1274) 773-399, ext. 241
Fax: (44-1274) 770-217
Contact: Chris Fell
Web site: www.nmsi.ac.uk/nmpft
Dates: Mar. 6–22
Deadline: Jan. 15

Shows new and classic international features as well as a wide-screen festival. Noncompetitive.

International Istanbul Film Festival (17th)

Istanbul Foundation for Culture and Arts
Istiklal Caddesi, No.146 Luvr Apt.
Beyoglu 80070, Istanbul, Turkey
Phone: (90-212) 293-3133
Fax: (90-212) 249-5575
Contact: Hulya Ucansu
E-mail: film.fest@istfest_tr.org
Web site: www.istfest.org
Dates: Mar. 7–22

Focusing on films dealing with the arts. Also a panorama of international and Turkish cinema. Competitive. FIAPF recognized.

Gaining in importance year by year, the International Istanbul Film Festival held its sixteenth round last April, during the twenty-fifth anniversary of its parent organization, the Istanbul Foundation for Culture and Arts. "Films about the arts" (literature, music, cinema, dance, etc.) is the theme of the international competition and an apt description of the overall atmosphere—intelligent and well-heeled—a model for festival-of-festival programming.

Though the whole festival unspools over the first two weeks of April, a hundred foreign guests, including filmmakers and press, turn up only for the last seven days, when most of the 160 feature films are repeated. Fest venues are full to crowded. As Turkey sails a stormy course between Europe and the Islamic East, the festival has become a beacon of liberalism for local film-lovers.

While government support for the event has virtually been cut off, the festival has managed to keep afloat by increasing private sponsorship and using ticket sales to pay for many of its expenses. The city of Istanbul, straddling Europe and Asia, remains cosmopolitan and exotic. The five screens scattered along the popular shopping street, Istiklal, in the picturesque Beyoglu area are packed with ticket holders eager to see new work from world cinema. Sponsored TV and radio commercials plugging the films undoubtedly account for the large admissions, which last year tallied 85,000.

The festival has had a decisive impact on art house distribution in Turkey. Commercial theaters, which once shunned art films and any foreign film unless it was American, now feature titles like *Kolya*, *Shine* and *Breaking the Waves* on their marquees. Istanbul has also launched niche directors like Ken Loach, Arturo Ripstein and Theo Angelopoulos into commercial release. "The festival has fulfilled its mission of helping

quality films find regular distribution," says longtime director Hulya Ucansu. A staunch opponent of censorship, she has screened *Crash*, *Kama Sutra* and *Empire of the Senses*, despite criticism from the conservative press. To her relief, the screenings went off without a hitch and *Crash* headed for commercial release virtually uncut.

All this means the festival is a favorite with art house sellers, even those with difficult Euro titles on their hands. Organizers claim that most fest films get sold to Turkey after the festival for theatrical release or TV, especially French titles. In general, glamour takes a backseat to the movies, themselves, although lifetime achievement awards (most recently received by Peter Greenaway and Claude Sautet) assure some star names. Superb hospitality and excellent Turkish organization have also developed a loyal following of foreign press.

American movies have been increasingly prominent in the fest. A new sidebar dedicated to American indie production, opening with *Welcome to the Dollhouse*, was an instant hit.

The festival has been actively courting Hollywood's Foreign Press

Association, which sent a delegation recently, promising that Turkish films would be carefully considered for Golden Globe noms. Most of the diminishing Turkish film industry is collected in a ten- to twelve-title Turkish section tailored to the needs of critics and programmers from abroad.

—*Deborah Young*

Local Heroes International Screen Festival (14th)

3rd floor, 10022—103St
Edmonton, Alberta, T5J 0X2, Canada
Phone: (403) 421-4084
Fax: (403) 425-8098
Contact: Debbie Yee
E-mail:filmhero@nsi-canada.ca.
Web site: www.nsi-canada.ca
Dates: Mar. 8–14
Deadline: Dec. 5

Canadian and international independents, with daily seminars and Canadian shorts. Noncompetitive.

International Festival of Films on Art (16th)

640 St. Paul Street West, #406
Montreal, Quebec, H3C 1L9, Canada
Phone: (514) 874-1637
Fax: (514) 874-9929
Contact: Rene Rozon
E-mail: fifa@maniacom.com
Web site: www.maniacom.com/fifa.html
Dates: Mar. 10–15
Deadline: Oct. 10

Films and videos on all art forms: printing, drawing, sculpture, dance, music, architecture, cinema, design, fashion, etc. Competitive.

Newport Beach International Film Festival (3rd)

4400 MacArthur Blvd., 5th Floor
Newport Beach, CA 92660
Phone: (714) 851-6555
Fax: (714) 851-6556
Contact: Jeffrey S. Connor
Web site: www.nbiff.org
Dates: Mar. 12–22
Deadline: Jan. 1

A showcase of 100 films from around the world, including features, documentaries, animation and shorts, with seminars and a screenwriting. Competitive.

London Lesbian and Gay Film Festival (12th)

National Film Theatre
South Bank, London, SE1 8XT, U.K.
Phone: (44-171) 815-1323/4
Fax: (44-171) 633-0786
Contact: Adrian Wooton
Dates: Mar. 12–26
Deadline: Dec. 15
E-mail: jane.ivey@bfi.org.co
Web site: www.bfi.org.uk

Showcase for films and videos dealing with lesbian and gay identity and experience. Noncompetitive. FIAPF recognized.

South by Southwest (SXSW) Film Festival (5th)

P.O. Box 4999
Austin, Texas 78765
Phone: (512) 467-7979
Fax: (512) 451-0754
Contact: Nancy Schafer
E-mail: sxsw@sxsw.com
Web site: www.sxsw.com
Dates: Mar. 13–21
Deadline: mid-Dec.

New American independentss, both competitive and noncompetitive.

Established in 1994 as an offshoot of the long-running South by Southwest Music and Media Conference, the South by Southwest (SXSW) Film Festival still is very much a work in progress. Even so, the Austin, Texas–based event is well on its way to gaining recognition as one of the country's more important film forums.

Right from the start, says SXSW film coordinator Nancy Schafer, the festival was able to attract an audience from far beyond the active Austin film community. "People came here at first," she admits, "because they knew they'd have a good time partying in Austin. But they've come back because we have a good festival, and we show good movies."

The festival also presents, along with nine days of regional and world premieres, a five-day SXSW Film Conference that has featured such panelists as Quentin Tarantino, John Sayles, Richard Linklater (an Austin resident) and Kevin Smith. The conference also offers one-on-one mentor programs and demonstrations of new filmmaking technology.

As might be expected, the Austin festival showcases independent productions by Texas filmmakers, along with premieres of other movies filmed in the state. The sneak-

preview world premiere of John Sayles's *Lone Star* was a highlight of SXSW '96. In 1997, the festival premiered *Still Breathing* (partially filmed in San Antonio and subsequently picked up by October Films), *Traveller* and *Full Tilt Boogie*. Even so, Schafer emphasizes that "the percentage of films from Texas is no greater than the percentage from other places." Indeed, past festival programs have included everything from Japanimation (*Ghost in the Shell*) and Italian farce (Roberto Benigni's *The Monster*) to music documentaries (*Hype!*) and Luis Buñuel classics.

A major part of the SXSW Film Festival's appeal is its low-stress, audience-friendly atmosphere. Many of the dramatic and documentary features are shown at the intimate Dobie Theatre, a multiplex located near the University of Texas campus. Other films are shown at the beautifully restored Paramount Theatre, just a few blocks away from the dusk-to-dawn club scene of the city's celebrated Sixth Street.

—*Joe Leydon*

Kino Festival of New Irish Cinema (2nd)

48 Princess St.
Manchester, M1 6HR, U.K.
Phone: (44-161) 288-2494

Fax: (44-161) 237-3423
Contact: John Wijowski
Dates: Mar. 13–21
Deadline: Jan. 14

Shorts, low-budget features and a sidebar for expatriate Irish filmmakers. Competitive.

Ankara International Film Festival (10th)

Bulten Sok. No. 64/2
06700 Kavakladere
Ankara, Turkey
Phone: (90-312) 468-7745
Fax: (90-312) 467-7630
Contact: Mahmut T. Ongoren
E-mail: servis2.net.tr
Dates: Mar. 13–22
Deadline: Feb. 10

National competitions for Turkish features, shorts and documentaries, and an international competition for short animated films. Also noncompetitive sections.

Cinema du Reel (20th)

BPI—CNAC Georges Pompidou
19 rue Beauborg
75197 Paris Cedex 04, France
Phone: (33-1) 4478-4521/4516
Fax: (33-1) 4478-1224
Contact: Suzette Glenadel
Dates: Mar. 13–22
Deadline: Nov. 1

Documentaries with an ethnological or sociological interest, plus focus on a country. Competitive.

Brussels International Festival of Fantasy, Thriller and Science Fiction Films (16th)

144 Avenue de la Reine
B-1030 Brussels, Belgium
Phone: (32-2) 201-1713
Fax: (32-2) 201-1469
Contact: Bozzo Freddy
Web site: www.concentra.be/fantasy
Dates: Mar. 13–28
Deadline: Dec. 31

Showing international fantasy and sci-fi films as well as thrillers, long features and shorts. Competitive. FIAPF recognized.

Bergamo Film Meeting (16th)

Via G. Reich 49
24020 Torre Boldone, Italy
Phone: (39-35) 363-087
Fax: (39-35) 341-255
Contact: Fiammetta Girola
E-mail: bfm@alasca.it
Web site: www.alasca.it/bfm
Dates: Mar. 14–22
Deadline: Jan. 20

Italian premieres of international films, tributes and retrospectives. Competitive.

Sportelamerica (2nd)

6040 Blvd. East, #27c
West New York, NJ 07093
Phone: (201) 869-4022
Fax: (201) 869-4335
Contact: Liliane and William Vitale
Dates: Mar. 16–18
Deadline: Nov. 30

International TV program market devoted exclusively to sports. Noncompetitive.

Ann Arbor Film Festival (36th)

P.O. Box 8232
Ann Arbor, MI 48107
Phone: (313) 995-5356
Fax: (313) 995-5396
Contact: Vicki Honeyman
E-mail: vicki@honeyman.org
Web site: www.citi.umich.edu/u/honey/aaff
Dates: Mar. 17–22
Deadline: Feb. 15

Showcasing 16mm independent and experimental films, with more than 300 entries from around the world.

New York Underground Film Festival

225 Lafayette St. Ste. 401
New York, NY 10012 USA
Phone: (1-212) 925-3440
Fax: (1-212) 925-3430
e-mail: festival@nyuff.com
Contact: Ed Halter
Dates: Mar. 18–22
Deadline: Jan. 7

Competitive

Nordic Film Festival

22 rue de la Champmesle
Rouen 76000, France
Phone: (33-2) 3598-2846
Fax: (33-2) 3570-9208
Contact: Jean Michel Mongradien
Dates: Mar. 18–29
Deadline: Jan. 31

Presenting films from Scandinavia and the Baltic countries. Noncompetitive.

Cleveland International Film Festival (22nd)

1621 Euclid Ave., #428
Cleveland, OH 44115
Phone: (216) 623-0400
Fax: (216) 623-0103
Contact: David W. Wittkowsky
Web site: www.ciff.org
Dates: Mar. 19–29
Deadline: Nov. 30

Full survey of contemporary international filmmaking, including U.S. independents, student and short films and documentaries. Competitive for shorts.

New Directors/New Films

Film Society of Lincoln Center
70 Lincoln Center Plaza, 4th Floor
New York, NY 10023
Phone: (212) 875-5610
Fax: (212) 875-5636

Contact: Richard Pena
Web site: www.filmlinc.com
Dates: Mar. 20–Apr. 7
Deadline: Jan. 17

International films from first-time or overlooked directors. Noncompetitive.

Independent Film Days Augsburg (13th)

Filmburo Augsburg
Schroeckstr. 8
86152 Augsburg, Germany
Phone: (49-821) 153-077
Fax: (49-821) 349-5218
Contact: Franz Fischer
Dates: Mar. 22–29
Deadline: early Feb.

Documentary and independent features of all formats and lengths, with retrospectives, regional or national focuses and an International Documentary Film Symposium. Competitive for documentaries.

Diagonale — Festival of the Austrian Film (4th)

Obereaugartenstr. 1
A-1020 Vienna, Austria
Phone: (43-1) 216-1303
Fax: (43-1) 216-1303-200
Contact: Christine Dollhofer
E-mail: wien@diagonale.at
Web site: www.diagonale.at
Dates: Mar. 24–29
Deadline: Dec. 31

Panorama of Austrian film and video production. Noncompetitive.

Cartagena International Film Festival (38th)

Baluarte de San Francisco
Calle San Juan de Dios
A.A. 1834, Cartagena, Colombia
Phone: (57-5) 664-2345 or 660-0966
Fax: (57-5) 660-0970 or 660-1037
Contact: Victor Nieto

Dates: Mar. 26-Apr. 2
Deadline: Jan. 10

*Ibero-Latin American film festival in-
cluding shorts, documentaries, international film show and TV and video
market. Competitive. FIAPF recognized.*

Festival of Yugoslav Documentary &
Short Film

Jugoslavia Film, Makedonska
22/VI
11000 Belgrade, Yugoslavia
Phone: (381-11) 324-8554
Fax: (381-11) 324-8659
Contact: Vojislav Vucinic
Dates: Mar. (Exact dates TBD)
Deadline: Feb. 15

Competitive.

International Women's Film Festival
(20th)

Maison des Arts
Place Salvador Allende
94000 Creteil, France
Phone: (33-1) 4980-3898
Fax: (33-1) 4399-0410
Contact: Jackie Buet
Dates: Mar. 27–Apr. 5
Deadline: Dec. 31

*Focuses on recent feature films, doc-
umentaries and shorts directed by
women. Competitive.*

Festival Internationale de Cinema
Jeune Public de Laon (16th)

8 rue Serurier, BP 526
02001 Laon Cedex, France
Phone: (33-4) 2320-3861
Fax: (33-4) 2320-2899
Contact: Marie-Therese Chambon
Dates: Mar. 30-Apr. 9
Deadline Dec. 10

*Shows a selection of international fea-
ture films for children and young
adults. Competitive.*

Moving Pictures (The Traveling
Canadian Film Festival) (5th)

1008 Homer Street, #410
Vancouver, B.C., V6B 2X1, Canada
Phone: (604) 685-8952
Fax: (604) 688-8221
Contact: John Dippong
E-mail: john@viff.org
Web site: www.netshop.net/~jfulton

*Brings a weekend-long festival of
strictly Canadian films to small cities
in Western Canada. Noncompetitive.*

It's All True—International
Documentary Film Festival (3rd)

Rua Cristiano Viana 907
05411-001 Sao Paulo, BP Brazil
Phone: (55-11) 852-9601
Fax: (55-11) 852-9601
Contact: Amir Labaki
E-mail: itstrue@ibm.net
Dates: Mar. 30-Apr. 9
Deadline: Jan. 15

*Presents fresh and original documen-
tary films and aims to promote international discussion on the subject.
Competitive.*

New England Film & Video Festival
(23rd)

1126 Boylston St., #201
Boston, MA 02215
Phone: (617) 536-1540
Fax: (617) 536-3576
Contact: Cherie Martin
E-mail: nefvfest@aol.com
Web site: www.actwin.com/BFVF/
Dates: late Mar.-early Apr.
Deadline: mid-Nov.

*Showcases narrative, documentary,
experimental and animated films and
videos by independents and students
from the six New England states.
Competitive.*

Jewish and Israeli Films Festival (15th)

500 Boulevard d'Antigone
34000 Montpelier, France
Phone: (33-67) 4150-876
Fax: (33-67) 4150-872
Contact: Jean-Paul Benkamoun
Dates: Mar. (Exact dates TBD)
Deadline: early Dec.

Showcase for Jewish and Israeli films. Competitive.

Femme Totale Film Festival

Klepping Strasse
21-23 D-44122
Dortmund, Germany
Phone: (49-231) 50 25 162
Fax: (49-231) 50 22 497
E-mail: 106212.3237@
compuserv.com
Contact: Silke Johanna Rabiger
Dates: Mar.
Deadline: Dec.

APRIL

Cognac International Thriller Film Festival (16th)

36 Rue Pierret
92200 Neuilly, France
Phone: (33-1) 4640-5500
Fax: (33-1) 4640-5539
Contact: Lionel Chouchan
E-mail: publics@imaginet.fr
Dates: early Apr.
Deadline: Mar. 14

International thrillers and film noir, with competitions for features and French shorts.Competitive.

Singapore International Film Festival (11th)

29A Keong Salk Road
Singapore 089136
Phone: (65) 738-7567
Fax: (65) 738-7578

Contact: Philip Cheah
E-mail: filmfest@pacific.net.sg
Web site: www.filmfest.org.sg
Dates: early April
Deadline: December

Screens 150 features and shorts. Competitive for Asian films. FIAPF recognized.

The annual Singapore International Film Festival (SIFF) is a two-week event and the only one in the world that highlights Southeast Asian films. Its director, Philip Cheah says it functions like an outpost for European festival directors to keep tabs on what's happening in the Asian film industry. It was in 1991 that Cheah determined that the fest should focus on Asian films to establish its identity in the field, and in 1997, half of the 160 films screened were products from Asia.

SIFF's Silver Screen Awards recognized achievements in Asian films. The cash prizes—ranging from S$5,000 to S$15,000—are important to the young filmmakers. SIFF's annual showcasing of Asian film was responsible for local TV station TV12's weekly showing of such product. For all its effort, however, SIFF lacks glamour. This is hardly surprising, as it has not attracted any major Hollywood name to grace the annual event and its Silver Screen Awards fare poorly before audiences who have grown accustomed to live telecasts of Hollywood's Academy, Emmy and Golden Globe Awards.

SIFF's competition of short films is a major event. Eric Khoo, thirty-two, the director of the award-winning *12 Storeys,* a film that shows the underbelly of Singapore, attributes his interest in film to SIFF. He first entered the shorts competition in 1990—and won. In 1997, *12 Storeys* won two Silver Screen awards. A year before, Khoo's first feature film, *Mee Pok Man,* also won an award.

But SIFF fans—including its regular Western guests—love it, proclaiming it to be a two-week, noncommercial window to the world. Indeed, as a result of SIFF, the world, too, has come to Singapore: Japanese, French, German, Canadian and British film weeks are becoming regular annual events in the film calendar. Fortunately for SIFF, the more liberal film-rating standards in recent years have meant that films are no longer cut to suit the official measure of morality, but are allowed artistic rein.

—*Mary Lee*

Carolina Film and Video Fest

100 Carmichael Bldg.
Greensboro, NC 27412 USA

Phone: (1-910) 334-5360
Fax: (1-910) 334-5039
Contact: Kate Malec
E-mail: akheilsb@
hamlet.uncg.edu
Dates: Apr. 1-4
Deadline: March 10

Aspen Shortsfest (7th)

110 East Hallam, #102
Aspen, CO 81611
Phone: (970) 925-6882
Fax: (970) 925-1967
Contact: Laura Thielen
E-mail: geldred@aspenfilm.org
Web site: www.aspen.com/filmfest
Dates: Apr. 1-5
Deadline: Jan. 15

Showcase for short dramas, comedies, documentaries and animation. Competitive.

Canyonlands Film and Video Festival

435 River Sands Rd., Moab, UT 84532 USA
Phone: (1-801) 259-9135
Contact: Nicholas Brown
E-mail: cfvf@moab-utah.com
Dates: Apr. 2-4
Deadline: Mar. 1

Competitive. Emphasis on Southwestern regional works.

New Haven Film Fest

111 Clinton Ave.
NH, CT. 06513 USA
Phone: (1-203) 865-2773
Fax: (1-203) 865-2773
Contact: Wayne Buck
E-mail:film Fest New Haven
@compuserv.com
Web site: ourworld.compuserv.com/
hompages/Film_Fest New Haven

Dates: Apr. 3-5
Deadline: Feb. 1

Competitive.

**Mip TV International Television
Program Market (35th)**

Reed Midem Organization
P.O. Box 572, 11 rue du Colonel
Pierre Avia
75726 Paris Cedex 15, France
Phone: (33-1) 4190-4580
Fax: (33-1) 4190-4570
Contact: Andre Vaillant
Dates: Apr. 3–8
Web site: www.miptv.com

*Professional TV market for the buy-
ing and selling of international TV
programming.*

**Hong Kong International Film
Festival (22nd)**

Level 7, Administration Bldg.
Hong Kong Cultural Centre
10 Salisbury Road, Tsimshatsui
Kowloon, Hong Kong
Phone: (852-27) 342-903
Fax: (852-23) 665-206
Contact: Lo Tak-sing
Dates: Apr. 3–18
Deadline: Dec. 30

*Feature films, documentaries, anima-
tion and shorts. Showcase for Asian
cinema and Hong Kong retrospective.
Noncompetitive. FIAPF recognized.*

During the early to mid-'80s, when
East Asian filmmaking was firing on
all cylinders, there was only one
place for aficionados to be every
Easter—the Hong Kong International Film Festival. Those days are
long gone, and since the major Eu-
rofests started platforming and gar-
landing Far East cinema from the
late '80s, Hong Kong has lost its
pulling power for major premieres.

But while other countries in the
region (China, Taiwan, South Korea, Japan) have sputtered in their
attempts to start up or maintain international festivals with serious
profiles, Hong Kong has, with the
support of the Urban Council, become the de facto veteran of the region, benefiting from the territory's
East-West outlook, nonparochial
mindset and English-language fa-
miliarity.

Apart from being the only festival in the world held on the mainland (Kowloon) and a neighboring
island (Hong Kong), it's also based
in one of the world's great cities,
with more wealth, color, energy,
people and eateries crammed into
its area than anywhere else on the
planet. Though it's a long haul for
most Westerners to get there,
there's plenty else going on in the
town—around the clock—if the
movie's a stinker.

Launched in 1977, and initially
held in June/July, the H.K. fest was
a logical step waiting to happen.
Though the territory was (and remains) one of the world's largest
movie producers numerically, the
appetites of its educated local youth
and Western ex-pats for quality in-

ternational cinema were mostly ca-
tered to by a film society (Studio
One) and occasional national showcases. "Culture" meant concerts
and plays, not films or film appreciation, especially not in a town
where the moviemaking ethos was
"get it out, mop up and move on."

Programmed by cine-literate
buffs, and supported by excellent,
bilingual dossiers from the get-go,
the fest was well positioned to benefit from the explosion of the Hong
Kong New Wave in 1979–80 and
the arrival of the so-called Fifth
Generation of filmers in China some
four or five years later. (No one who
was present at the first, historic
screening outside China of Chen
Kaige's *Yellow Earth* in 1985 will
ever forget the experience.) The
only blot on the fest's copybook was
its slowness to screen movies from
the emergent Taiwan New Wave,
owing to pressure from Beijing.

Of equal, and continuing, importance has been the festival's
genre retrospectives, of everything
from kung-fu and costume martial
arts movies to comedies and melo-
dramas. These effectively helped to
encourage a film appreciation culture that led to the Urban Council's
setting up the badly needed Hong
Kong Film Archive in 1993.

The fest has remained noncompetitive and without any aspirations
toward setting up a market. It's also
extremely well organized, despite
its minimal budget. In the run-up to
the handover to China in July 1997,
fears were expressed often about its
future independence; but in the
short term, at least, no other festival
in the region has the international
smarts or experience to stage a similar event. (Shanghai's attempts
have been chaotic; Taipei is still too
parochial and isolated.)

Though Hong Kong, under-
standably, has been unable to
screen any cutting-edge Mainland
pics or thumb its nose—as some
Western fests do—at Beijing, it
could conceivably benefit from now
being a part of Greater China by becoming an international showcase
for its big brother's industry. The
major East Asian titles still look to
be going to fests in Europe and the
U.S., but Hong Kong, with its scholarship, organization and infrastructure, still has a place on the festival
map.

—Derek Elley

**Montevideo International Film Festival
(16th)**

Lorenzo Carnelli 1311
11200 Montevideo, Uruguay
Phone: (598) 482-460

Fax: (598) 494-572
Contact: Manuel Martinez Carril
E-mail: cinemuy@chasque.apc.org
Dates: Apr. 4–19
Deadline: Jan. 12

Promoting high-quality shorts and full-length features, as well as documentaries, experimental, Latin American and international films. Competitive. FIAPF recognized.

Intercom '98 Film and Video Festival (34th)

32 W. Randolph St., Ste. 600
Chicago, IL 60601
Phone: (312) 425-9400
Fax: (312) 425-0966
Contact: Jim Healey
E-mail: filmfest@wwa.com
Web site: www.chicago.ddbn.com/filmfest/
Dates: Apr. 10–12
Deadline: Mar. 1

Sponsored film and video industrial, corporate image and independent video production as well as interactive media. Competitive.

International Grenzland-Filmtage Selb (21st)

P.O. Box 307
95622 Wunsiedel, Germany
Phone: (49-9232) 4770
Fax: (49-9232) 4710
Contact: Adele Troger
E-mail: grenzland-filmtage@t-online.de
Web site: www.t-online.de/home/grenzland-filmtage
Dates: Apr. 16–19
Deadline: Jan. 31

Presenting films of all genres with a special focus on Eastern Europe. Noncompetitive.

Taos Talking Picture Festival (4th)

216M North Pueblo Road, #216
Taos, NM 87571
Phone: (505) 751-0637

Fax: (505) 751-7385
Contact: Kelly Clement
E-mail: ttpix@taosnet.com
Web site: www.taosnet.com/ttpix/
Dates: Apr. 16–19
Deadline: Feb. 1

Multicultural celebration of cinema artists, their art and its audience. Noncompetitive.

Los Angeles Independent Film Festival (4th)

5455 Wilshire Blvd., #1500
Beverly Hills, CA 90036
Phone: (213) 937-9155
Fax: (213) 937-7770
Contact: Robert Faust
Web site: laiff.com
Dates: Apr. 16–20
Deadline: Jan. 14

Showcase for independent cinema. Noncompetitive.

St. Barts Caribbean Film Festival (3rd)

410 W. 24th St., 16K
New York, NY 10011 USA
Phone: (1-212) 989-8004
Fax: (1-212) 727-1774
Contact: Joshua Harrison
e-mail: jpharris@interactive.net
Dates: Apr.16–20
Deadline: Mar. 5

Concentrates on Caribbean cinema with films by Caribbean filmmakers or with Caribbean themes.

Turin International Gay and Lesbian Film Festival (13th)

Via Tasso 11
10122 Torino, Italy
Phone: (39-11) 534-888 or 535-046
Fax: (39-11) 535-796
Contact: Giovanni Minerba
E-mail: glfilmfest@assiomia.com

Web site: www.assiomia.com/
glfilmfest
Dates: Apr. 16–22
Deadline: Feb. 15

*Showcase for gay filmmaking includ-
ing a panorama of new productions,
retrospectives, tributes and special
events. Competitive.*

USA Film Festival (28th)

2917 Swiss Ave.
Dallas, TX 75204
Phone: (214) 821-6300
Fax: (214) 821-6364
Contact: Alonso Duralde
Web site: www.usafilmfestival.com
Dates: Apr. 16–23
Deadline: Mar. 2

*The best new American and foreign
films, National Short Film & Video
competition, tributes and retrospectives. Competitive.*

**Arizona International Film Festival
(7th)**

Arizona Media Arts Center
P.O. Box 431
Tucson, AZ 85702
Phone: (520) 628-1737
Fax: (520) 628-1737
Contact: Giulio Scalinger
Web site: www.azstarnet.com/
~azmac
Dates: Apr. 16–26
Deadline: Feb. 27

*Southwestern showcase for American
and international independent film
and video. Competitive.*

Italian Film Festival (5th)

Italian Institute
82 Nicholson St.
Edinburgh, EH8 9EW, Scotland
Phone: (44-131) 557-0560
Fax: (44-131) 557-0560
Contact: Allan Hunter
Dates: Apr. 17–26
Deadline: Feb. 28

*Sponsored by the Italian Cultural In-
stitute, this is a showcase for new Italian cinema and retrospectives. Noncompetitive.*

**Palm Beach International Film
Festival (3rd)**

7108 Fairway Drive, #235
Palm Beach Gardens, FL 33418
Phone: (561) 626-0026
Fax: (561) 626-9119
Contact: Mark Diamond
Web site: www.pbfilmfest.org
Dates: Apr. 17–26
Deadline: Mar. 1

*Films from around the world. Non-
competitive.*

**WorldFest Houston (Houston
International Film Festival) (31st)**

P.O. Box 56566
Houston, TX 77256
Phone: (713) 965-9955
Fax: (713) 965-9960
Contact: J. Hunter Todd
E-mail: worldfest@aol.com
Web site: www.zannezar.com/
worldfest
Dates: Apr. 17–26
Deadline: end of Feb.

*Focuses on independent films. Com-
petitive.*

If any film festival can be described
as embodying the vision and spirit
of a single individual, it's World-
Fest/Houston. After more than three
decades, chairman and founding director J. Hunter Todd remains the
guiding force behind an annual ex-
travaganza that has somehow managed to survive relocations, identity
crises and economic downturns.
Despite drastic expansions and

contractions of its size and scope, not to mention its relative lack of national recognition, the festival continues to be supported by a small but loyal audience. Indeed, it has been successful enough to encourage Todd to establish a "sister festival," the WorldFest/Charleston in South Carolina.

The thirty-first annual World-Fest/Houston in 1998 was actually the twentieth Houston edition of a festival Todd previously operated in Atlanta, Miami and the Virgin Islands. Until 1995, the Houston event claimed a local art house, the Greenway 3 Theatre, as its primary base of operations for its annual ten-day run. During this period, the festival's major claim to fame was its successful relaunching of Ivan Passer's *Cutter's Way* (1981) after that film's less-than-successful debut in New York.

Despite the infamous "oil bust" that ravaged the Texas economy during the mid-1980s, the Houston International Film Festival (as it was originally known) maintained a slow but steady growth. Kirk Douglas and Alan Alda were among the notables who appeared to present new films or collect lifetime achievement awards.

In 1992, however, the renamed WorldFest/Houston got too big for its own good, and Todd's policy of inviting film submissions without the normal "weeding out" process led critics of the WorldFest to question its standards for entry. By his own admission, Todd seriously miscalculated the appeal of his festival when he ambitiously expanded his program to cram some 140 features into three venues over ten days. At the end of WorldFest '92, a disappointed Todd promised to reinvent his showcase as "a lean, mean movie machine." The following year, WorldFest/Houston presented 70 features. In 1995, the year WorldFest shifted over to two screens of General Cinema's Meyerland Plaza multiplex, the downsizing continued with a slate of 48 features.

Todd makes no apologies for what some wags have described as the "Incredible Shrinking Festival." In his view, less is more, and fewer films means a greater number of repeat screenings. Just as important, cutting back on slots to fill has allowed him to reduce the number of low-budget exploitation pictures and made-for-cable features that frequently appeared on WorldFest programs and to emphasize "truly independent" productions in a schedule of thirty to thirty-five films.

The festival awards gold, silver, and bronze prizes in several juried competitions, with categories ranging from "New Media/Interactive" and "Best Music Video" to radio advertisements and student films.

Throughout the thirty-one-year history of his festival, major jury prizes have gone to such up-and-coming filmmakers as Oliver Stone, Robert Rodriguez and John Sayles. In 1996, the best feature film prize was bestowed on *Once Upon a Time . . . When We Were Colored* and the top prize in 1997 went to *For Roseanna*.

—Joe Leydon

Chicago Latino Film Festival (14th)

600 S. Michigan Ave.
Chicago, IL 60605
Phone: (312) 431-1330
Fax: (312) 360-0629
Contact: Pepe Vargas
Dates: Apr. 17-27
Deadline: Feb. 2

Presents some 100 films and videos of all genres from Spain, Portugal, Latin America and the U.S. Noncompetitive.

Minneapolis/St. Paul International Film Festival (16th)

2331 University Ave. S.E., Ste. 130B
Minneapolis, MN 55414-3067
Phone: (612) 627-4431
Fax: (612) 627-4111
Contact: Al Milgrom
E-mail: filmsoc@tc.umn.edu

Web site: www.umn.edu/nlhome/9023/filmsoc/
Dates: Apr. 17-30
Deadline: Jan. 15

Over 100 films from 38 countries, including an Emerging Filmmakers competition. FIAPF recognized.

Nyon International Documentary Film Festival (29th)

18 rue Juste-Olivier, CP 593
1260 Nyon 2, Switzerland
Phone: (41-22) 361-6060
Fax: (41-22) 361-7071
Contact: Jean Perret
E-mail: docnyon@iprolink.ch
Web site: www.webdo.ch/visions_97.html
Dates: Apr. 20-26
Deadline: end of Jan.

Showcase for international documentaries. Competitive.

Oslo Animation Festival (5th)

PB 867 Sentrum OR Skippergt. 17
0104 Oslo, Norway
Phone: (47-22) 478-050
Fax: (47-22) 478-060
Contact: Kristine Kjolleberg
E-mail: oaf@manelyst-filmenshus.no
Web site: web.sol.no/anima/
Dates: Apr. 23-26
Deadline: Jan. 25

Only animation festival in the Nordic and Baltic countries. Noncompetitive.

Golden Rose of Montreux (38th)

Television Suisse Romande
Quaie E. Ansermet 20/ CP 234
1211 Geneva 8, Switzerland
Phone: (41-22) 708-8599
Fax: (41-22) 781-5249
Contact: Pierre Grandjean
E-mail: gabrielle.bucher@tsr.srg-ssr.ch
Dates: Apr. 23-28
Deadline: Jan.

Presents light entertainment TV pro-grams. Competitive.

Oberhausen International Short Film Festival (44th)

Grillostr. 34
46045 Oberhausen, Germany
Phone: (49-208) 825-2652
Fax: (49-208) 825-5413
Contact: Angela Haardt
E-mail: Kurzfilmtage_oberhausen@uni-duisburg.de
Web site: www.uni-duisburg.de/HRZ/OKF/home.html
Dates: Apr. 23–28
Deadline: Feb. 1

International short film festival, open to all genres and formats, including video. Competitive for children's shorts. FIAPF recognized.

The oldest festival of its kind, the Oberhausen International Short Film Festival was founded in 1954 and continues to offer a forum for avant garde and up-and-coming filmmakers from Germany, Europe and around the world.

Amongst highlights of the fest's history are counted the 1962 "coup" by a group of disgruntled young German filmmakers who came together to sign the Oberhausen Manifest in which "Papa's Cinema" was pronounced dead, and New German Cinema was born.

But by the early '90s, Oberhausen's star had faded. The once-radical spirit among German directors and producers had long since dissipated. And with the opening up of Soviet bloc countries, Oberhausen lost the distinction of being the only Western short film festival with connections to Eastern Europe.

In recent years, the festival has been struggling to reestablish and redefine its international profile. Oberhausen has several competition sections, including International Competition, German Competition, Children's Cinema and Filmothek (for young filmmakers) as well as an array of special film program sections. In 1997, these included "American Comedies of the Silent Movie Era," "The Long Night of Short Films—The '70s" and " 'Europe in Shorts'—Short Films from Europe."

During Angela Haardt's eight-year term as festival chief (she left in 1997), symposiums were organized on topics such as globalization and migration, film in advertising and the role of the media in the Gulf War. A special focus on "Hyper-media" in 1997 looked at the relationship between technological developments and nonlinear narrative forms.

Germany's largest short film market takes place parallel to the festival. Filmmakers whose films are not accepted into competition can nonetheless apply for screenings and inclusion in the market's German/English catalog.

Under the leadership of newly appointed festival topper Lars Henrik Gass, the festival is moving in 1998 from its former quarters in the Luise-Albrecht-Halle to a theater in the city's pedestrian zone. The market will be housed in a nearby museum.

—*Miriam Hils*

San Francisco International Film Festival (41st)

1521 Eddy St.
San Francisco, CA 94115
Phone: (415) 929-5000, ext 110
Fax: (415) 921-5032
Contact: Cathy Fischer
Web site: www.sfiff.org
Dates: Apr. 23–May 7

Akira Kurosawa, Andrezej Wajda, Satyajit Ray, Michelangelo Antonioni, Luchino Visconti: These artists were virtually unknown in the U.S. when the newborn San Francisco International Film Festival, the first "international" festival in the Americas, introduced their work in December 1957. The most famous names to appear that year were Mary Pickford, who had never before appeared at a festival, and Shirley Temple Black, who presented the Golden Gate Awards for best director and best film to Ray for his *Pather Panchali.*

The festival was founded by the mustachioed Irving (Bud) Levin, a theater owner who had been visiting European festivals and showing foreign films at his theaters for years. In 1956, he had helped organize an Italian film festival at the suggestion of Italian consul general Pierluigi Alvera. Its success, featuring Fellini's prize-winning *La Strada*, prompted Alvers to propose that Levin start an international festival, which began under the sponsorship of the San Francisco Arts Commission.

Levin hired film buff Albert Johnson, a student at the University of California, to help with the programming. Now a University of California professor of film, Johnson was brought on board full time in 1968 when the Chamber of Commerce began to sponsor the festival under the direction of Claude Jarman, who had won an honorary Oscar when he was thirteen for his performance in *The Yearling.* He served as executive director from 1968 to 1979.

Johnson proposed retrospectives with film clips, innovations that later were copied by many other festivals. First interviewees were John Ford, Walt Disney, Bing Crosby, King Vidor and William Wellman. Unprecedented tributes were given to Lillian Gish and Elizabeth Bergner.

Although Levin had hoped that San Francisco would get FIAPF "A" accreditation as the fifth competitive festival after Berlin, Cannes, Edinburgh and Venice, he ran into opposition from the Motion Picture Academy, which feared the awards were stealing the limelight from the Oscars. When Levin left in 1964, there were no more feature film prizes. Since then, the festival has reflected the input of several other programmers, moved to five different venues from the single-screen Metro theater to the multiplex AMC Kabuki and grown from 15 features submitted by twelve countries to 217 productions from forty-one nations in 1997. Documentaries, video productions, animation and experimental films continue to vie for recognition in the Golden Gate Awards competition, headed by Brian Gordon. It attracted 1,525 entries from sixty-two countries in 1997.

Over the festival's four decades, a host of classics has been shown including Luis Bunuel's *Viridiana* (1961); Ján Kadár and Elmar Klos' *The Shop on Main Street* (1966); Jiri Menzel's *Closely Watched Trains* (1968); Francois Truffaut's *The Wild Child* (1971); Vittorio de Sica's *The Garden of the Finzi-Continis* (1971); Louis Malle's *Murmur of the Heart* (1971); Martin Scorsese's *Mean Streets* (1973); Akira Kurosawa's *Dersu Uzala* (1976); Fellini's *La Strada* (1976); Paolo and Vittorio Taviani's *Padre Padrone* (1977); Francesco Rosi's *Christ Stopped at Eboli* (1981); Agnieszka Holland's *Angry Harvest* (1986); Chen Kaige's *Yellow Earth* (1986); Zhang Yimou's *The Story of Qui Ju* (1993) and Charles Burnett's *To Sleep with Anger* (1993).

Other highlights included Krzysztoff Kieslowski's extraordinary *Decalogue* (1990), the witty true encounter between British actress Coral Browne and British spy Anthony Burgess in John Schlesinger's ebullient *An Englishman Aboard* (1984) and the reappearance of the Soviet Union's long-shelved *Commissar* (1989), directed by Alexandre Askoldoc. And several years before Mike Leigh won the Cannes festival's Palme d'Or for *Secrets and Lies*, San Francisco saw *High Hopes* (1989) and many of his other satirical takes on the British class system.

In the highly political late '60s, audiences went wild with excitement over Constantin Costa-Gavras's *Z* (1969), a powerful attack on the Greek colonels. They gave a standing ovation to Haskell Wexler's prophetic *Medium Cool* (1969), which juxtaposed fiction and fact to show how the media manipulated the messages at the tumultuous Democratic National Convention in Chicago in 1968. A notable dissent was expressed in '66 when Shirley Temple Black quit the board of directors in protest against what she saw as the "pornography for profit" in Mai Zetterling's *Night Games*.

—Judy Stone

Munich International Documentary Film Festival (13th)

Trogerstr. 46
81675 Munich, Germany
Phone: (49-89) 470-3237
Fax: (49-89) 470-6611
Contact: Gudrun Geyer
Dates: Apr. 24–May 3
Deadline: Feb. 20

Shows 16mm and 35mm only and documentaries. FIAPF recognized.

Philadelphia Festival of World Cinema (7th)

3701 Chestnut St.
Philadelphia, PA 19104
Phone: (215) 895-6593
Fax: (215) 895-6562

Contact: Linda Blackaby
E-mail: pfwc@libertynet.org
Web site: www.libertynet.org/-ihouse
Dates: Apr. 29–May 10
Deadline: Jan. 12

Featuring more than 100 films of many genres, both features and shorts, from American independents to international cinema, with a "Set in Philadelphia" screenwriting competition. Noncompetitive.

The Ohio Independent Film Fest (10th)

2258 W. 10th St.
Cleveland, Ohio 44113 USA
Phone: (1-216) 781-1755
Contact: Bernadette Gillota
E-mail: OhioIndieFilmFest@juno.com
Dates: Apr. 30–May 3 98
Deadline: Mar. 15

Small festival geared toward short films.

Avignon/New York Film Festival

Alliance Francaise/French Institute
22 E. 60th St.
New York, NY 10013 USA
Phone: (1-212) 343-2675
Fax: (1-212) 343-1849
Dates: late Apr.
Deadline: late Feb.

Boston International Festival of Women's Cinema

1126 Boylston St., Ste. 201
Boston, MA 02215
Phone: (617) 536-1540
Fax: (617) 536-3576
Contact: Anne Marie Stein
Dates: mid-April
Deadline: mid-January

Cape Town International Film Festival (22nd)

University of Cape Town
Private Bag, Rondebosch 7700

Cape Town, South Africa
Phone: (27-21) 238-257/8
Fax: (27-21) 242-355
Contact: James A. Polley
E-mail: filmfest@hiddingh.uct.ac.za
Dates: Apr.
Deadline: late Jan.

Features of artistic quality, independents, and historical/contemporary documentaries. Noncompetitive. FIAPF recognized.

Cartoons on the Bay (3rd)

c/o Sacis, Via Teulada 66
00195 Roma, Italy
Phone: (39-6) 374-981
Fax: (39-6) 370-1343
Contact: Alfio Bastiancich
E-mail: bastiancich@mail.sacis.it
Web site: www.sacis/cartoonsbay/
Dates: Apr. (Exact dates TBD)
Deadline: Jan. 21

International festival of animation including films, TV series and fairy tales. Competitive.

Filmfest DC (12th)

P.O. Box 21396
Washington, DC 20009
Phone: (202) 724-5613
Fax: (202) 724-6578
Contact: Anthony Gittens
E-mail: Filmfestdc@aol.com
Web site: www.capaccess.org/filmfestdc
Dates: late Apr.
Deadline: late Jan.

Celebrating the best in world cinema including special events. Noncompetitive.

Gen Art Film Festival (3rd)

145 W. 28th St., Ste. 116
New York, NY 10001 USA
Phone: (1-212) 290-0312
Fax: (1-212) 290-0254
Contact: Ian Gerard
E-mail:genart@media.net
Dates: late April

Early deadline: Dec. 15
Late deadline: Feb. 15

Focuses on emerging American independents.

MAY

Golden Prague International TV Festival

Czech Television, International Relations
Karel Hory
Prague 140 70
Czech Republic
Phone: (42-2) 6113-4028 or 6113-4405
Fax: (42-2) 6121-2891
Contact: Jiri Vejvoda
Dates: May 4–7
Deadline: Feb. 20

Presents TV programs in the field of serious music. Competitive.

Rochester International Film Festival (40th)

Box 17746
Rochester, NY 14617
Phone: (716) 288-5607
Fax: (716) 271-3970
Contact: Josephine Perini
Dates: May 6–9
Deadline: Mar. 1

Held at International Museum of Photography and Film. Focuses on short films.

Augsburg Short Film Festival (7th)

Filmburo Augsburg
Schroeckstr. 8
86152 Augsburg, Germany
Phone: (49-821) 153-077
Fax: (49-821) 349-5218
Contact: Erwin Schletterer
Dates: May 7–10
Deadline: Feb. 25

International competition for fiction, animation and documentary shorts. Competitive.

the variety guide to film festivals

Cannes International Film Festival (51st)

99 Blvd. Malesherbes
75008 Paris, France
Phone: (33-1) 4561-6600
Fax: (33-1) 4561-9760
Contacts: Gilles Jacob (director),
Jerome Paillard (market)
E-mail: festival@festival-cannes.fr
Web site: www.festival.cannes.com
Dates: May 13–24
Deadline: mid March

The world's most famous film festival, screening world cinema, with a market. Competitive. FIAPF recognized.

It's too big, it's too crazy, it's too arrogant, and everyone says they dread even the thought of going there every year. But go they still do, and the deals and headlines still get larger. No fest has even come close to rivaling the Grande Dame of them all—Cannes.

Renowned as an event where taste and tack manage to cohabit for eleven days every May, Cannes is still perceived in the popular imagination as a place where producers loll on yachts, starlets whip off their bikini tops, the great and the good ascend red-carpeted stairs to snooze through some arty masterpiece, and critics burrow like moles through a mountain of celluloid. All that is still partly true, to varying degrees, though less so than in the fest's more showbizzy days of the '50s and

'60s. Since the '80s, and especially in the '90s, Cannes has become more of a hard-nosed business arena, where a deal rather than a D-cup now makes the front page, over-stressed buyers scurry the Croisette with mobiles glued to their ears, and there's no such thing as a free dinner.

Cannes is unique in being at least five parallel universes rolled into one: the black-tie evening screenings in the Palais, gawked at by the starstruck and attended by people who hardly ever go to the movies; round-the-clock screenings for the press (from 8:30 A.M. to past midnight), themselves segregated by different-colored passes (white, through pink and blue, down to yellow); market screenings for buyers in *salles* ranging from the poky to the luxurious; the star-interview circuit; and private power meals in discreet locations up in the hills or out of town between execs who wouldn't be caught dead in the film-going melee at sea level. Few Cannes attendees ever get the chance or time to experience more than a couple of these parallel universes—making the oft-repeated question "How was it for you this year?" an exercise in nonsequiturs.

Cannes in its present form is really only two decades old, from when current Official Selection head Gilles Jacob took over in 1978, remolding structural changes introduced by his predecessor, Maurice Bessy. Prior to that, it was a very different affair. After a failed start in 1939, scuppered by the outbreak of World War II, Cannes was finally launched in the fall of 1946 and only became an annual event, held in the spring, beginning in 1951. Until 1972 it was basically a bunch of movies selected by national committees rather than by the festival itself, initially on a quota system based on the number of pix produced by a country during the previous year. During the '50s, the event became as much a political battleground (particularly between the U.S. and Soviets, with Western Europe pincered in between) as a celebration of cinema.

Its present structure started to evolve in 1969 with the parallel mini-fest, the sixteen-to-seventeen-title Directors' Fortnight—begun in response to younger cineastes shuttering the previous-year's event two-thirds of the way through. Longtime Official Selection head Robert Favre Le Bret encouraged the Fortnight's creation as a way of ensuring a trouble-free 1969 fest;

more recently it has become, under longtime head Pierre-Henri Deleau, a constant thorn in Jacob's side for hot titles, and almost indistinguishable from Jacob's not-quite-good-enough-for-competition sidebar, Un Certain Regard (about twenty titles). Also still holding its own as an arena for new talent is the fourth section of the fest, the Critics' Week, headed by Jean Roy and begun in 1962.

Dominating everything, however, is the Competition, a collection of two dozen movies that has been built by the press into a de facto temperature reading for the health of international cinema. Jacob has steered this mighty ocean liner with aristocratic (and autocratic) skill, making tiny course corrections here and there, and balancing Hollywood glitz with traditional Euro-auteurist demands. Sometimes the mix works, sometimes it doesn't—Jacob says he's always hostage to what filmmakers produce, and vintage years rarely run in succession—but it never fails to generate miles of newsprint and weeks of animated discussion.

Despite the event's uncluttered official name—Festival International du Film—that disdains even a geographical location, it is too often overlooked that Cannes is a thoroughly French affair, exclusively programmed by French movie buffs with an unshakable belief in their solitary defense of the holy flame of cinema. It's that simple conviction, rather than the glamour, deals or hoopla, that still gives Cannes its unique flavor.

—*Derek Elley*

Seattle International Film Festival (24th)

801 E. Pine St.
Seattle, WA 98122
Phone: (206) 324-9996
Fax: (206) 324-9998
Contact: Darryl Macdonald
E-mail: mail@seattlefilm.com
Web site: www.seattlefilm.com
Dates: May 14–June 7
Deadline: Mar. 1

Featuring more than 180 features and shorts. Competitive for director and American independent.

Running for a whopping twenty-five days in its peak calendar years, the Seattle International Film Festival is the world's *longest* fest. It's also the largest in the U.S., with about 180 features getting 340 or so screenings. Highlights include juried awards for American Independents and New Directors' Showcase, with the latter singling out first or second pics by up-and-comers, usually Europeans. The fest also ends with a popular vote, in six categories, collectively called Golden Space Needle Awards. (It's one of five North American fests in which a film can compete for the Independent Spirit Awards without a distributor attached.)

Programming divisions include a broad swath of world cinema, a reputable documentary section, a wigged-out midnight series, kidflicks, archival themes, and the long-running Secret Festival, which patrons—including press and bizzers—attend with no foreknowledge, and only by signing a vow of silence. On the other hand, the fest has also launched whole pics on the Internet, being the first to do so with a cybercast of *Party Girl* in 1995.

SIFF founders Darryl Macdonald and Dan Ireland started with exhib roots deep in Vancouver, B.C., running the now-defunct Rembrandt Theatre until its close in the early '70s. The mavens moved south of the border in 1975, taking over Seattle's Moore Egyptian, 1,600-seat vaudeville house built at the beginning of the century. The next year, they started SIFF, which consisted entirely of eighteen films in as many days—each showing twice!

The fest limped along for the first few years but drew attention by launching *The Rocky Horror Picture*

Show, which spun off its first showing for an additional twenty-six
weeks. By the end of the decade, the
event had gained a reputation as an
excellent water-tester, accessing
world premiers of *Alien* and *The
Empire Strikes Back*. It also helped
parlay troubled pics like *The Stunt
Man* and *One False Move* into cult
triumphs. More recently it helped
jump-start youngsters such as Sal
Stabile with his *Gravesend* debut.
Other world and North American
bows have included *Braveheart*,
Emma, *Brother from Another
Planet*, *Dazed and Confused*, *The
Wedding Banquet*, *La Bamba*, *Kiss
of the Spider Woman* and *Trainspotting*.

There have been a few stum-
bles, starting with some confusion
over the exact age of the event.
Much of this stems from SIFF's
skipping its thirteenth year; fate
wasn't fooled by calling it the four-
teenth, since projectors broke down
at opening premiere of *The Mod-
erns*, with director Alan Rudolph
and other notables squirming in the
house.

Smoother going have been substantial tributes to directors such as
Michael Powell, Bertranc Tavernier, Louis Malle and Bernardo
Bertolucci. The fest toppers' partic-

ular interest in Paul Verhoeven and
other Dutch players led them to
open an import office in L.A., with
Ireland moving there full-time in
1980. He eventually worked for
Vestron, in acquisitions, maintain-
ing his "programmer emeritus"
status while developing his own pic-
making career. Ireland got to premiere first effort, *Whole Wide World*,
at his home fest in 1996. Meanwhile, Macdonald had side jobs
programming the Vancouver fest
from 1988 through 1991, Palm
Springs through 1993, and the
Hamptons through '96. Currently,
he's narrowed his focus to SIFF and
to building a film institute intended
to anchor Northwest pic-making
with archives and production facilities.

The fest has also goosed local
bizzers, with inner-city outreach
programs, a spin-off Women-in-
Film Festival (in January) and a
Filmmakers' Forum during the fest,
with roundtables and hands-on
workshops—the '97 version handed
cameras to a half-dozen young directors and told them to make a
complete short by the end of the
fest.

While press and buyers have
increased over the years, the fest is
most remarkable for its rabid civil-

ian following, with Seattlelites (130,000 in 1997) taking annual vacations during the event—although pics don't actually screen on weekdays until 5 P.M. This loyalty isn't lost on Hollywood marketeers, who can study response to fare that stakes out large middle ground between edgy indie fare and big-budget juggernauts. Positioned right after Cannes, the SIFF consistently snags hot titles just before they're bought by distributors. Of course, this small window also makes for major traffic headaches and many last-minute substitutions.

—*Ken Eisner*

Viper (International Film, Video and Multimedia Festival) (18th)

P.O. Box 4929
CH-6002 Lucerne, Switzerland
Phone: (41-1) 450-6262
Fax: (41-1) 450-6261
Contact: Conny E. Voester
E-mail: viper@dial.eunet.ch
Web site: www.viper.ch
Dates: May 19–24
Deadline: Feb. 15

Presents experimental and innovative film, video and multimedia projects. Competitive.

Inside Out Lesbian and Gay Film and Video Festival (8th)

401 Richmond St. West, Suite 456
Toronto, Ontario
M5V 3A8, Canada
Phone: (416) 977-6847
Fax: (416) 977-8025
Contact: Deanna Bowen

Dates: May 21–31
Deadline: Feb. 20

Screens more than 150 films and videos from North America, Europe and Australia. Noncompetitive.

International Film Festival of Slavonic and Orthodox Peoples

'Zolotoi Vityz
Vasiljevskaja st 4, ap 174
Moscow, 123056, Russia
Phone: (7-095) 254 2646/117 2264/255 9053
Fax: (7-095) 254 2646/117 2664/255 9053
Contact: Tatiana Varskaya
Dates: May 24–Jun 4
Deadline: TBD

Competitive.

Krakow International Short Film Festival (35th)

Ul. Pychowicka 7
30-364 Krakow, Poland
Phone: (48-12) 672-340 or 671-355
Fax: (48-12) 671-552
Contact: Wit Dudek
Dates: May 29–June 2
Deadline: Jan. 31

Shows documentary, fiction, experimental and animation shorts (under 35 minutes). Competitive. FIAPF recognized.

Toronto Worldwide Short Film Festival (4th)

60 Atlantic Ave., Ste. 110
Toronto, Ontario
M6K 1X9, Canada
Phone: (416) 535-8506
Fax: (416) 535-8342
Contact: Brenda Sherwood
E-mail: twsff@idirect.com
Web site: www.torontoshort.com/film/festival
Dates: May 31–June 6
Deadline: March 1

Short-film festival with the major marketplace in North America for shorts. Categories include drama, animation, documentary, experimental and children's. Competitive.

Newport International Film Festival

150 W. 82nd St., Ste. 5D
New York, NY 10024
Phone: (401) 245-0121
Fax: (401) 245-5011
Contacts: Christine Schomer, Nancy Donahue
E-mail: newportff@aol.com
Dates: May 31–June 7
Deadline: Apr. 1

Presents American and international independents, including shorts, documentary and animation. Takes place in Newport, R.I. Competitive.

Troia International Film Festival (14th)

Forum Luisa Todi
Av. Luisa Todi, 65
2902 Setubal Codex
Troia, Portugal
Phone: (351-65) 525-908
Fax: (351-65) 525-681
Contact: Mario Ventura Henriques
Web site: www.inis.pt/inis/festroia
Dates: late May/early June
Deadline: late February

Focuses on countries with annual production of fewer than 21 features. Competitive. FIAPF recognized.

International Film and Video Festival

The Athens Center for Film and Video
P.O. Box 388 Athens, Ohio 45701
USA
Phone: (614) 593-1330
Fax: (614) 593-1328
E-mail: Bradley@ouvaxa.cats.-ohiou.edu

Dates: May
Deadline: TBD

Silver Images Film Fest

Terra Nova Films
9848 S. Winchester Ave.
Chicago, Illinois 60643 USA
Phone: (773) 881-6940
Fax: (773) 881-3368
Contact: Al Stein
Date: May
Deadline: Jan. 15

Hudson Valley Film Fest

40 Garden St.
Poughkeepsie, NY 12601
USA
Phone: (914) 473-0318
Fax: (914) 473-0082
Contact: Denise Kasell
E-mail: hvfo@vh.net
Dates: May 98
Deadline: TBD

JUNE

U.S. International Film and Video Fest

841 N. Addison Ave.
Elmhurst, Ill 60126-1291 USA
Phone: (630) 834-7773
Fax: (630) 834-5565
Contact: J.W. Anderson
E-mail: FILMFESTIVALandMOBIU-SAYWARD@compuserv.com
Dates: Jun 3–4
Deadline: Mar 1

Competitive.

International Film Festival Cinevision (7th)

Museumstr. 31
6020 Innsbruck, Austria
Phone: (43-512) 580-723
Fax: (43-512) 581-762
Contact: Helmut Groschup

Dates: June 4–8
Deadline: Feb. 1

Presents new films from and about Africa, Asia and Latin America. Noncompetitive.

Shots in the Dark (8th)

Broadway Media Centre
14–18 Broad St.
Nottingham, NG1 3AL, U.K.
Phone: (44-115) 952-6600
Fax: (44-115) 952-6622
Contact: Gill Henderson
Web site: broadway@bwymedia.demon.co.uk
Dates: June 4–14
Deadline: Mar. 31

Showcase for thrillers, film noir and mysteries, including a strong preview program with retrospectives and screenwriting events. Noncompetitive.

Bellaria Film Fest

Viale Paole Guidi 108
1-47041
Bellaria, Italy
Phone: (39-541) 347 186
Fax: (39-541) 349 563
Contact: Enrico Ghezzi
Dates: June 5–9
Deadline: Apr. 15

Competitive.

Huesca Film Festival

Avda, Parque
1 piso
E-22002 Huesca, Spain
Phone: (34-74) 212582
Fax: (34-74) 210065
Contact: Jose Maria Escriche
E-mail: huescafest@fsai.es
Dates: June 5–13
Deadline: Apr. 1

Competitive.

Balticum Film and TV Festival (9th)

Skippergade 8
DK-3740 Svaneke, Denmark
Phone: (45) 7020-2002
Fax: (45) 7020-2001
Contact: Bent Nørby Bonde
E-mail: balticmediacentre@bmc.dk
Web site: www.dk-web.com/bmc
Dates: June 6–12
Deadline: Feb. 15

Documentary competition for Baltic producers, European Film School and features. Competitive.

Banff Television Festival (19th)

1516 Railway Ave. Canmore,
Alberta, T1W 1P6, Canada
Phone: (403) 678-9260
Fax: (403) 678-9269
Contact: Pat Ferns
E-mail: info@banfftvfest.com
Web site: www.banfftvfest.com
Dates: June 6–13
Deadline: February

Midnight Sun Film Festival (13th)

Malminkatu 36
00100 Helsinki, Finland
Phone: (358-9) 685-2242
Fax: (358-9) 694-5560
Contact: Peter von Bagh
Dates: June 10–14
Deadline: March 31

Combination of director retrospectives, brand-new films and silent movies with live music. No shorts. Noncompetitive.

International Electronic Cinema Festival (11th)

Rue du Theatre 5
1820 Montreux, Switzerland
Phone: (41-21) 963-3220
Fax: (41-21) 963-8851
Contact: R. Crawford
E-mail: message@symposia.ch
Web site: www.montreux.ch/symposia/

Dates: June 10–15
Deadline: Mar. 3

Presenting the best productions of high-definition television. Held this year in Chiba, Japan. Competitive.

Human Rights Watch International Film Festival (9th)

485 5th Ave., 3rd Floor
New York, NY 10017
Phone: (212) 972-8400
Fax: (212) 972-0905
Contact: Bruni Burres
E-mail: burresb@hrw
Web site: www.hrw.org/iff
Dates: June 11–25
Deadline: Jan. 10

Showcase for films related to human rights subject matter. Documentary, fiction and animation of any length. Noncompetitive.

Showbiz Expo West

Reed Exhibition Co.
383 Main Ave.
Norwalk, CT 06851
Phone: (203) 840-5888 (exhibiting);
(800) 840-5688 (attending)
Fax: (203) 840-9888 (exhibiting);
(203) 840-9688 (attending)
Contact: Dave Bonaparte
Dates: June 12–14

The entertainment production industry's most comprehensive trade event.

Florida Film Festival (7th)

1300 S. Orlando Ave.
Maitland, FL 32751
Phone: (407) 629-1088
Fax: (407) 629-6870
Contact: Matthew Curtis
E-mail: filmfest@gate.net
Web site: www.enzian.org
Dates: June 12–21
Deadline: Mar. 20

Features films from around the world, yet focusing on American independent filmmakers. Competitive.

Cinema Expo International

244 West 49th St., #200
New York, NY 10019
Phone: (212) 246-6460
Fax: (212) 265-6428
Contact: Jimmy and Robert Sunshine
Dates: June 15–18

Europe's leading convention for film exhibition.

Norwegian Short Film Fest

Filmens Hus
Dronnigens Gate 16
N-0152 Oslo Norway
Phone: (47-22) 47 46 46
Fax: (47-22) 47 46 90
Contact: Turunn Nyen
Web site: www.nfi.no/krtf/welcome.html
Dates: June 16–20
Deadline: Mar. 15

Competitive.

La Rochelle International Film Festival (26th)

16 rue Saint Sobin
75011 Paris, France
Phone: (33-1) 4806-1666
Fax: (33-1) 4806-1540
Contact: Jean Loup Passek
Dates: June 16–July 6
Deadline: end of April

International showcase for full-length features including retrospectives and tributes. Noncompetitive.

La Rochelle, a historic fortress town on the Atlantic coast of France, has become home to one of the country's most successful annual gatherings. More than seventy thousand tickets are issued during a frenetic ten days in early July. When one considers that the town's population is a mere seventy-five thousand, that's a formidable attendance figure.

The secret lies in two attributes: a formula, and a passion. The formula comprises tributes to a handful of auteurs, both the quick and the dead, with honorees—if alive—almost invariably on hand, mingling with the film buffs in theater lobbies and restaurants alike. Of course, La Rochelle screens a selection of recent quality films (under the rubric "The World as It Is"), as well as the odd all-night session of horror movies, or a special silent film presentation with piano accompaniment. But it's the tributes that count, and that leads to discoveries for local audiences and subsequent distribution in France. The mix is eclectic, from Boorman to Risi, from Dassin to Kieslowski, from Mollberg to Weir. The passion belongs to Jean-Loup Passek and his loyal team who since the festival's inception in 1973 have worked like Trojans to ensure a high level of programming and a warm welcome to visitors.

Passek, responsible for the world's finest film dictionary at Larousse, also runs the Cinema department at the Georges Pompidou Center in Paris. Poet and jazz enthusiast, he has dwelt outside the mainstream of French film culture these past three decades, and continues a defiant struggle against the ravages of television and the new media. Everyone attending La Rochelle will run into him and his enthusiasm for each and every one of his programs. And for the few hours not devoted to screenings, there is always a succulent fish meal to remember to be found at the Restaurant La Marmite in the Old Port.

—*Peter Cowie*

Hamburg International Short Film Festival (14th)

Kurzfilmagentur Hamburg e.V.
Friedensallee 7
22765 Hamburg, Germany
Phone: (49-40) 3982-6122
Fax: (49-40) 3982-6123
Contact: Markus Schaefer
E-mail: kfa@shortfilm.com
Dates: June 17–21
Deadline: Mar. 1

Shows international and no-budget shorts including a variety of special programs. Competitive.

San Francisco International Lesbian and Gay Film Festival (22nd)

c/o Frameline
346 Ninth St.
San Francisco, CA.94103
Phone: (415) 703-8650
Fax: (415) 861-1404
Contact: Michael Lumpkin
E-mail: Frameline@aol.com
Web site: www.framline.org
Dates: June 19–28
Deadline: Mar.14

Screens international lesbian and gay films and videos. Noncompetitive.

Cardiff International Animation Fest

18 Broadwick St.
GB-London W1V1FG, UK
Phone: (44-171) 494-0506
Fax: (44-171) 494-0807
Contact: Jane Williams
Dates: June 23–28
Deadline: TBD

Hong Kong International Film Market (2nd)

Hong Kong Trade Development Council
38/F, Office Tower Convention Plaza
1 Harbour Rd., Wanchai
Hong Kong
Phone: (852) 2584-4333
Fax: (852) 2824-0249
Contact: Jenny Koo
E-mail: ernest.chan@tdc.org.hk
Dates: June 24–26

A market to promote and sell Hong Kong movies, Chinese-langauge films and TV programs.

Il Cinema Ritrovato (12th)

Via Galliera 8
40121 Bologna, Italy
Phone: (39-51) 237-088
Fax: (39-51) 261-680
Contact: Gian Luca Farinelli
Web site: www2.comune.bologna.it/bologna/cineteca
Dates: June 26–July 5
Deadline: Mar. 28

Focuses on film restoration and cinema history. Noncompetitive.

Vila do Conde International Short Film Festival and Market (6th)

Auditorio Municipal
Praca da Republica
4480 Vila do Conde, Portugal
Phone: (351-52) 641-644
Fax: (351-52) 642-871

Contact: Rui Maia
E-mail: isffviladoconde@mail.telepac.pt
Dates: June 30–July 5
Deadline: Apr. 17

Showcase for recent international and Portuguese shorts including special exhibitions and retrospectives. Short Film Market attached. Competitive.

London Jewish Film Festival (13th)

National Film Theatre, South Bank
London, SE1 8XT, U.K.
Phone: (44-171) 815-1323/4
Fax: (44-171) 633-0786
Contact: Adrian Wooton
E-mail: jane.ivey@bfi.org.uk
Web site: www.bfi.org.uk
Date: June
Deadline: Mar. 15

Showcase for films dealing with Jewish identity and experience. Noncompetitive.

International Television Festival Cologne Conference (8th)

c/o Adolf Grimme Institut
Im Mediapark 5B
50670 Cologne, Germany
Phone: (49-221) 454-3280
Fax: (49-221) 454-3289
Contact: Lutz Hachmeister
E-mail: info@cologne-conference.de
Web site: www.cologne-conference.de
Date: June
Deadline: Mar.

A festival and market combined, including cult TV, retrospectives and seminars. Competitive.

Festival du Nouveau Cinema de Montreal (27th)

3668 Boulevard St. Laurent
Montreal, Quebec
H2X 2V4, Canada
Phone: (514) 843-4725
Fax: (514) 843-4631
Contact: Claude Chamberlan

E-mail: montrealfest@fcmm.com
Web site: www.fcmm.com
Date: June
Deadline: Mar.

Cinema, video and new-media festival. Noncompetitive, with monetary prizes awarded in certain sections.

Pesaro Film Festival (34th)

Via Villafranca, 20
00185 Roma, Italy
Phone: (39-6) 445-6643
Fax: (39-6) 491-163
Contact: Adriano Apra
E-mail: pesarofilmfest@mclink.it
Web site: www.abanet.it/pesaro/
cinema.html
Date: mid-June
Deadline: Mar. 31

Showcase for new directors and emerging cinemas, with features, shorts, documentaries, animation and experimental works on film and video. Noncompetitive.

**International French Film Festival
Tübingen-Stuttgart (15th)**

Osterbergstr.9
72074 Tübingen, Germany
Phone: (49-7071) 56960
Fax: (49-7071) 569696
Contact: Dieter Betz
E-mail: filmtage.tubingen@t-online.de
Web site: www.cityinfonetz.de/
filmtage/oo.html
Date: June (Exact dates TBD)
Deadline: March

Features and shorts from all Francophone countries including recent films, homages and retrospectives. Competitive.

Bradford Animation Festival (3rd)

National Museum of Photography,
Film and TV
Pictureville, Bradford
BD1 1NQ, U.K.
Phone: (44-1274) 773-399, ext. 241
Fax: (44-1274) 770 217

Contact: Chris Fell
Web site: www.hmsi.ac.uk/nmpft/
Date: June (Exact dates TBD)
Deadline: Mar.

Showcase for international animation films. Competitive.

Vue Sur Les Docs (9th)

Doc Services
3, Square Stalingrad
13001 Marseille, France
Phone: (33-4) 91 40 18 92 27
Fax: (33-4) 9184-3834
Contact: Delphine Camolli
E-mail: docfilmfest-
mars@hotmail.com
Web site: www.doc-film-fest-
marseilles.fr
Date: June (Exact dates TBD)
Deadline: Mar.

International documentary film festival. Competitive.

Prix Italia (50th)

c/o RAI, V. le Mazzini 14
Rome, 00195 Italy
Phone: (39-6) 3751-4996
Fax: (39-6) 361-3401
Contact: Paolo Battistuzzi
E-mail: prix-wg@rai.it
Date: June
Deadline: mid-May

International competition for radio and television programs in documentary, fiction and music. Competitive.

**Sydney International Film Festival
(45th)**

P.O. Box 950
Glebe, NSW 2037, Australia
Phone: (61-29) 660-3844
Fax: (61-29) 692-8793
Contact: Paul Byrnes
E-mail: sydfilm@ozonline.com.au
Web site: www.sydfilm-fest.com.au
Date: June (Exact dates TBD)
Deadline: Mar.

Forum for international features, documentaries, shorts, animation, experimental and video along with retrospectives and tributes. Competitive for Australian shorts only. FIAPF recognized.

The Sydney International Film Festival is a spinoff from Australia's film society movement. In 1952, Representatives of New South Wales film societies participated in the first Australian Film Festival in the Melbourne suburb of Olinda, and when it became clear that their Victorian colleagues wanted to retain a festival in the Melbourne area thereafter—rather than alternate with Sydney—the NSW film society people formed a committee to launch the first Sydney festival in June 1954, at the University of Sydney.

Only nine features were screened that first year (among them, Roberto Rossellini's *Germany Year Zero* and Jacques Tati's *Jour de Fête*), but the event was a success. Over the next few years it gradually expanded and made a small profit every year save in 1958 (when, as a one-time experiment, it moved from June to October).

There was, in the beginning, no government support of the event, and virtually no sponsorship. Money was raised solely from ticket sales, and much of the work was done by volunteers. In 1962, the festival board appointed Ian Klava as its first full-time director, but the event was so modest that Klava had to work from his home for most of the year and only rented an office and hired a secretary for three months around the festival period.

In 1962, the festival—still held at various university venues—screened nineteen features and a clutch of shorts, all of them noncompetitive, including Claude Chabrol's *Le Beau Serge,* Jerome Hill's *The Sand Castle* and Kaneto Shindo's *The Island,* as well as entries from Poland, Hungary, Czechoslovakia and the Soviet Union.

By the mid-'60s, the festival was facing a serious problem because of draconian censorship laws that refused to allow any special consideration for the event's noncommercial status. When it became obvious that films loaned to the festival were regularly seized and cut by the film censors (victims included Hiroshi Teshigahara's *Woman of the Dunes* and Akira Kurosawa's *Yojimbo*) the festival Board launched a campaign against film censorship in Australia.

Klava resigned after the 1965

festival and was replaced by David Stratton (Editor's Note: the author of this profile) who led the anticensorship campaign. For the next five years, there were fierce confrontations between the film censors and the federal government on the one hand and the festival on the other; but eventually a compromise was reached and, by 1970, festival films were screened censor-free. This enabled the festival to screen, in succeeding years, such controversial films as Dusan Makavejev's *W.R. Mysteries of the Organism* and Nagisa Oshima's *In the Realm of the Senses* uncut, but the festival's campaign also resulted in far more liberal censorship for commercial screenings, just in time for the arrival of titles like *A Clockwork Orange* and *Last Tango in Paris.*

In 1967, the festival moved from the university to the suburban Wintergarden cinema in Rose Bay, a 2,000-seater; and in 1974 the event moved downtown to Greater Union's venerable 2,500-seat flagship State Theater, where it remains to this day.

Alongside screenings of contemporary films, the festival began to organize retrospectives. Josef von Sternberg attended screenings of his films in 1967, and Rouben Ma-

moulian performed similar chores a few years later.

As the festival's reputation grew internationally, more and more filmmakers attended with their work, among them directors Satyajit Ray, Dusan Makavejev, Michelangelo Antonioni, Jerzy Skolimowski, Istvan Szabo, Paul Bartel, Lindsay Anderson and Peter Greenaway. Actors, including Warren Beatty and Giancarlo Giannini, also made the pilgrimage to Australia for the festival.

In 1973, the festival established a competition for Australian short films and the following year screened the world premiere of Peter Weir's first feature, *The Cars That Ate Paris.* In 1975, the festival opened with an Australian film, Ken Hannam's *Sunday Too Far Away* and arranged a comprehensive retrospective of Australian cinema, which sparked considerable local interest at a time when the film industry was reasserting itself after years in the wilderness.

Since that time, the festival has always been an important launching pad for local productions. In 1974, the festival also established an offshoot, the Traveling Film Festival, an event in which festival entries that had secured theatrical distribution were screened in country towns across Australia.

—*David Stratton*

Sochi International Film Festival (5th)

c/o 35 Arabat St.
121835 Moscow, Russia
Phone: (7-095) 241-0772 or 248-0911
Fax: (7-095) 248-0966
Contact: Mark Rudinstein
Dates: June (Exact dates TBD)
Deadline: Mar.

International competition and panorama of world cinema. Competitive. Takes place alongside the Open Russian Competition for CIS.

St. Petersburg International Film Festival

12 Karavannya St.
191099 St. Petersburg, Russia
Phone: (7-812) 235-2660
Fax: (7-812) 235-2660
Contact: Mikhail Litvyyakov
Dates: June (Exact dates TBD)
Deadline: Mar.

Mystfest (Mystery Film Festival) (19th)

Centro Culturale Polivalente
Piazza della Repubblica, 31
Cattolica, Italy
Phone: (39-541) 967-802 or 968-214
Contact: Fapolo Fabri
E-mail: mystfest@cattolica.net
Web site: www.cattolica.net
Dates: June 4–12
Deadline: March

Showcase for mystery films. Competitive. FIAPF recognized.

Art Film (6th)

Konventna
811 01 Bratislava, Slovakia
Phone: (42-7) 531-1679
Fax: (42-7) 531-9372

Contact: Peter Hledik
Dates: June (Exact dates TBD)
Deadline: March

Presenting recent films and documentaries about art including a student film section. Competitive.

Zagreb International Festival of Animated Film

Koncertna Direkcija Zagreb
Animafest
41000 Zagreb, Kneza
Nislava 18, Croatia
Phone: (385-1) 410-134/410-128
Fax: (385-1) 410-134/443-022
Contact: Iva Stipetic
E-mail: animafest.z@carnet.hr
Dates: June (Exact dates TBD)
Deadline: April 1

Munich Film Festival (15th)

Internationale Munchener
Filmwochen GmbH
Kaiserstrasse 39
80801 München, Germany
Phone: (49-89) 38 1904-0
Fax: (49-89) 38 1904 26
Contact: Eberhard Hauff
Dates: late June
Deadline: early May

A forum for German and international film. Noncompetitive. FIAPF recognized.

International Film Festival Cinematograph

CineVision C/O Cinematograph
Museumstrasse 31
A-6020
Innsbruck, Austria
Phone: (43-512) 580723
Fax: (43-512) 581762
Contact: Dr. Helmut Groschup
e-mail: cinema@
nomad.transit.or.at
Dates: June
Deadline: April 5

Films that are from or about Africa, Asia or America. The selection is strictly by invitation only.

Newark Black Film Festival

The Newark Museum
49 Washington St. P.O. Box 540
Newark, NJ 07101-0540 USA
Phone: (201) 596-6550
Fax: (201) 642-0459
Contact: Jane Stein
Dates: June
Deadline: Mar. 1

Competitive. Films by black filmmakers and films featuring the history and culture of black people in America and elsewhere.

JULY

Taormina International Film Festival (28th)

Via Pirandello 31
98039 Taormina, Italy
Phone: (39) 9422-1142
Fax: (39) 9422-3348
Contact: Enrico Ghezzi
Web site: www.taormina.aol.it
Dates: early July
Deadline: April 15

International features.

L'Age D'or Prize

Rue Ravenstein 23
B-1000 Brussels, Belgium
Phone: (32-2) 507 8370
Fax:(32-2) 513 1272
Contact: Gabrielle Claes
Dates: July 1–15
Deadline: April 17

Karlovy Vary International Film Festival (33rd)

Panska 1, Prague 1
110 00, Czech Republic
Phone: (420-2) 2423-5413
Fax: (420-2) 2423-3408
Contact: Eva Zaoralova

E-mail: iffkv@tlp.cz
Web site: www.tlp.cz/internet/iffkarlovy_vary
Dates: July 3–11
Deadline: Apr. 15

Feature film and documentary competition, sections for Western and Eastern films and a Forum of Independent Filmmakers. Competitive.

The Karlovy Vary International Film Festival has changed radically since the breakup of the former Soviet Union and the free market transitions of its East Euro satellite nations in 1989. Founded in the famed Czech Republic spa town of Karlovy Vary (roughly two hours west of Prague) in 1946, the fest was held annually until 1958, when it began alternating on a biannual basis with Moscow. While its peak of popularity was probably the '60s, when Czech cinema was enjoying its greatest period of international acclaim, the fest, which was painfully privatized in 1994, has moved from being a showcase for Soviet-controlled East Bloc filmmakers to a more open fest that introduces American indie films and the top Euro art films as well as the best of the East Euro cinema.

In 1995, KV faced its greatest challenge with the upstart and now-defunct Prague International Film Festival. For two years, the Prague Fest claimed title to the critical

FIAPF "A" certification and created a rancorous split amongst filmmakers, producers, sponsors and government supporters of the film arts. The Prague Fest, however, collapsed after its second year, while Karlovy Vary seemed to strengthen both its programming and its private-enterprise base of operations. Many observers of the two competing fests noted that the challenge forced KV to drop its opposition to American filmmaking and sharpen its logistics and financial footing.

The contrast between 1994 and 1997 was dramatic; the former was plagued with uninspired programming, a paucity of high-quality new East Euro film offerings, a lack of celebrity sparkle and myriad logistical snafus. In '97, other than a computer malfunctioning sending the ticketing operation into chaos, the affair was almost too precisely organized, while the lineup of films, both Western and Eastern, yielded several gems, and the celebrity turnout had brightened considerably, with a Milos Forman tribute and appearances from international stars such as Christopher Walken, Jeffrey Wright, Ellen Burstyn, Steve Buscemi, Seymour Cassel, Julia Or-

mond, Armin Muhler-Stahl and Klaus Maria Brandauer.

In a setting that is bucolic and friendly, nestled snugly in the mountains near the border of Germany, the Karlovy Vary fest unspools over eight days amid the storybook atmosphere of a city that boasts visitors over the centuries from Beethoven to Goethe to Thomas Mann. More than 140 films are featured, from retrospectives of major filmmakers to sidebars on the American indie scene.

The fest's competition is FIAPF sanctioned, putting it in the front ranks of award-presenting fests, including Venice, Cannes and Berlin. There is also a documentary film competition and a sidebar of new East Euro films, as well as sections specifically devoted to student films, the latest in Czech cinema and films produced for Czech television.

While the fest is making strides to secure its status as a key Euro fest, it still needs to make progress in establishing a serious film market that would draw more major international film business professionals. The fest has benefited from programming chief Eva Zaoralova's sharp selections in the last two years; the '96 jury picked the Georgian film *A Chef in Love* for its top award, and the '97 competition winner was France's *Ma Vie en Rose*, both of which have gone on to international box office success.

Press coverage is, not surprisingly, strongest in the East Euro territories, although the '97 fest drew heavy attention Stateside from an unusual source; American radio personality Howard Stern was so proud of his film *Private Parts* winning the Audience Award at that year's fest that for months he almost daily boasted of the victory and tried to promote his film for the Academy Awards on the basis of its Karlovy Vary showing!

—*Steven Gaydos*

Festival du Court Metrage en Plein Air de Grenoble (21st)

4, rue Hector Berlioz
38000 Grenoble, France
Phone: (33-4) 76 54 43 51
Fax: (33-4) 76 51 24 43
Contact: Michel Warren
Dates: July 7–11
Deadline: end of May

Presents new and old talents, with both indoor and open-air screenings. Competitive.

Galway Film Fleadh

Cluain Mhuire, Monivea Road
Galway, Ireland
Phone: (353-91) 751-655
Fax: (353-91) 770-746
Contact: Antony Sellers
E-mail: gafleadh@iol.ie

Dates: July 7–12
Deadline: end May

International festival for features and shorts, with lively debates and audience awards.

Outfest '98 (16th)

8455 Beverly Blvd., #309
Los Angeles, CA 90048
Phone: (213) 951-1247
Fax: (213) 951-0721
Contact: John Cooper
E-mail: outfest@aol.com
Web site: www.outfest.com
Dates: July 10–19
Deadline: April 20

Showcase for films for and by gay men and lesbians. Competitive.

Montevideo International Film Fest for Children and Young People

Lorenzo Carnelli 1311
11200 Montevideo, Uruguay
Phone: (598-2) 495 795/482-460
Fax: (598-2) 404 572
Contact: Richard Casas
e-mail: cinemuy@
chasque.apc.org
Dates: Jul. 14–28
Deadline: May 15

Competitive.

Asian American International Film Festival

Asian Cinevision
37 E. Broadway, 4th Floor
New York, NY 10002
Phone: (212) 925-8685
Fax: (212) 925-8157
Contact: Bill Gee
E-mail: acvinnyc@aol.com
Dates: July 17–Aug. 7 (weekends)
Deadline: April 25

Four weekends of films (short and feature length) by Asian or Asian American filmmakers. The first and oldest festival of its kind. Noncompetitive.

Rio Cine Festival (14th)

Praca Mahatma Gandhi 2
GR402 RJ 20018-900, Brazil
Phone: (55-21) 262-8870 or 240-2262
Fax: (55-21) 262-8870 or 240-2262
Contact: Vilma Lustosa
Dates: July 23–30
Deadline: April 10

Brazilian shorts (competitive), features (noncompetitive) and international seminars. Attached market.

Fantasy Filmfest (International Film Festival for Science Fiction, Horror and Thriller) (12th)

Rosebud Entertainment Berlin
Wittelsbacherstr. 26
10707 Berlin, Germany
Phone: (49-30) 861-4532
Fax: (49-30) 861-4539
Contact: Schorsch Muller
E-mail: rosebud_entertainment@t-online.de
Web site: home.t-online.de/home/rosebud_entertainment
Dates: July 29–Aug. 28
Deadline: June 2

Traveling showcase (Munich, Berlin, Frankfurt, Stuttgart, Cologne, Hamburg) for all genres of fantasy, horror and thriller films. Noncompetitive.

Brisbane International Film Festival (7th)

P.O. Box 909
Brisbane 4001, Australia
Phone: (61-7) 3220-0333
Fax: (61-7) 3220-0400
Contact: Anne Demy-Geroe
E-mail: brisfilm@ thehub.com.au
Web site: biff.thehub.com.au
Dates: July 30–Aug. 9
Deadline: May 20

Showcase for world cinema with a special focus on the Asia-Pacific region. Noncompetitive.

Jerusalem Film Festival

P.O. Box 8561
Jerusalem, 91083, Israel
Phone: (972-2) 672-4131
Fax: (972-2) 673-3076
Contact: Lia van Leer
E-mail: jer_cine@intern.net.il
Web site: www.cine.jer.org.il
Dates: July (Exact dates TBD)
Deadline: Apr. 20

Shows the best of international, Israeli and Mediterranean cinema, with sidebars including Avant Garde, New Directors and Jewish Themes. Competitive.

The biggest film event in Israel, the Jerusalem Film Festival, beats out the only slightly smaller Haifa fest in September mainly with its awe-inspiring location just outside the King David tower, in the shadow of the old city walls. Outdoor screenings on ten pleasant July evenings take place in the amphitheater.

Fest director Lia van Leer, who founded the Jerusalem Cinematheque and Israeli Film Archive with her late husband, Wim, has adeptly steered this very personal festival through occasionally rough political waters and combined public with private financing in a high-quality event.

Juries and judging abound in Jerusalem, and since each prize carries a highly sought cash award, the competition is serious business. Honors include a prize for the best Israeli screenplay, which is offered by the Lipper Foundation of New York; a Mediterranean Cinema prize; the "In the Spirit of Freedom Award" for films focusing on human rights; Films on Jewish Themes Award; and the Wolgin Award Competition for Israeli Feature and Documentary Films.

—*Deborah Young*

Wellington Film Festival (27th)

P.O. Box 9544
Te Aro, Wellington, New Zealand
Phone: (64-4) 385-0162
Fax: (64-4) 801-7304
Contact: Bill Gosden
E-mail: enzedff@actrix.gen.nz
Web site: www.enzedff.co.nz
Dates: July
Deadline: April 30

New Zealand's leading film festival, screening New Zealand premieres of diverse films and videos. Noncompetitive.

Cambridge Film Festival (21st)

8 Market Passage
Cambridge, CB2 3PF, U.K.
Phone: (44-1223) 578-944
Fax: (44-1223) 578-956
Contact: François Ballay
E-mail: festival@cambarts.co.uk
Dates: July
Deadline: May 30

International panorama, with retrospectives, discussions and exhibitors' conference. Noncompetitive.

Auckland International Film Festival (30th)

P.O. Box 9544
Wellington, New Zealand
Phone: (64-4) 385-0162
Fax: (64-4) 801-7304
Contact: Bill Gosden
E-mail: enzedff@actrix.gen.nz
Web site: www.enzedff.co.nz
Dates: July
Deadline: April 30

International showcase twinned with the Wellington Film Festival. Noncompetitive.

Moscow International Film Festival (21st)

Khikhlovsky Per. 10/1
109028 Moscow, Russia
Phone: (7-95) 917-0944 or 917-8628
Fax: (7-95) 916-0107
Contact: Sergei Soloviev, Aleksandr Abdulov
Dates: July (Exact dates TBD)
Deadline: Apr. 15

Presents about 20 international features including the screening of films from the former republics of the Soviet Union and a tribute to Russian cinematography. Competitive.

From 1959, the Moscow International Film Festival had been the key showcase event for communist cinema. In the '90s it has proved slow to adapt to political changes—and, more important, financing problems—though in 1997, the twentieth anniversary fest showed the first signs of a move in a positive direction.

Moscow was traditionally held on a biannual basis, alternating with the Eastern bloc's other main fest, Karlovy Vary. Main prizes were awarded to pics either from the home territory or from fraternal socialist nations: the 1963 victory for Fellini's *8 1/2* was the exception that proved the rule, a decision apparently made at Kremlin Politburo level. With the festival being the only opportunity for Soviet viewers to catch a glimpse of cinema from beyond the Iron Curtain, Moscow became renowned for its packed houses and audience attention.

The recent heyday for Moscow came at the end of the '80s, when Western interest in Gorbachev's perestroika brought high-profile visitors to the Soviet capital for the first time in decades. The appearance of previously banned or unreleased Soviet pics such as Tenghiz Abuladze's *Repentance* also helped to put Moscow back on the creative map.

Financing difficulties hit Moscow at the beginning of the '90s, forcing organizers, previously guaranteed almost unlimited state backing, to look elsewhere for funds. After an unprecedented last burst of state generosity, which put an estimated $10 million the way of the 1995 fest, event organizers were savaged in local press and film cir-

cles for their profligacy: Russian filmmakers, deprived of even basic state funds for production, could only look on with envy at such huge sums being lavished on a showcase event.

The fest's frequency became an issue, too. After 1995, Moscow was due to become an annual event, though the 1996 fest never got beyond the drawing board—uncertainties over presidential elections scheduled for the same period, plus finance problems, put a firm nail in its coffin. Preparations for 1997 went ahead on an absolutely ad hoc basis, with pic selection compressed into a few months and government money transferred only weeks before the fest unspooled. As a result recent programming has been characterized more by a desperate get-whatever's-still-available policy rather than any wider international slant. U.S. representation is still usually weak (a legacy of U.S. studios' blockade of Russia in the early '90s), with Europe and Asia traditionally better represented.

Running over ten or eleven days at the end of July, Moscow is not the easiest fest for foreign visitors. Some become loyal regulars, others leave frustrated by bureaucratic hiccoughs. Faced by an increasingly chaotic city infrastructure and language difficulties, outsiders are often left with a quasi-nightmare experience of endlessly changing schedules and venues, mitigated only by the natural kindness of their Russian hosts. Recent years have also shown an unwelcome trend toward a two-tier guest list scenario, in which top star guests are wined and dined with government notables, while other invitees fend for themselves the best they can.

The 1997 fest stood out from its recent predecessors for a brighter atmosphere, with the event centered on the newly restored central Pushkinsky cinema and ticket sales coming in much higher than expected (though, somewhat typically, organizers proved absolutely unable to release any exact figures). With the competition program acknowledged as weak, fest interest moved toward generous sidebar action, including director and country retrospectives, student programs and an impressive ex-USSR panorama. Whatever else it may not be, Moscow remains the main meeting point for film colleagues from around the far-flung boundaries of the once-great Soviet film space.

Clinging only very tenuously to its FIAPF "A" status, the festival lacks any serious film market, and this detracts from its international role, while consolidation of the rival Open Russian International Fest in June (better known by its traditional title, Kinotavr) has seen many foreign pics and guests bypassing the Moscow July event for the easier atmosphere of Sochi's Black Sea riviera.

Locals may argue volubly as to Moscow's successes, shortcomings and future. Suggestions range from outright cancellation to a move toward a noncompetition format. For most involved, the fest's most urgent goal is just to keep going at all. With local TV and theater distribution markets slowly picking up, there are signs that postcommunist Russia is at last showing itself a potentially significant partner on the international scene. As it emerges, the Moscow fest should still be around to showcase it.

—*Tom Birchenough*

Giffoni Film Festival (27th)

Piazza Umberto I
84095 Giffoni, Valle Piana
Salerno, Italy
Phone: (39-89) 868-544
Fax: (39-89) 866-111
Contact: Claudio Gubitosi
E-mail: giffoni@peoples.it

Web site: www.giffoniff.it
Dates: July (Exact dates TBD)
Deadline: Apr. 10

*Competitive children's festival, with a
jury of kids. Also co-organizes the
collateral event, Shadow-Line Festival, in Salerno, programmed by Peppe
D'Antonio, and other events in the region from January through May.*

**Melbourne International Film
Festival (47th)**

1st Floor, 207 Johnston St.
Fitzroy, Victoria 3065, Australia
Phone: (61-3) 9417-2011
Fax: (61-3) 9417-3804
Contact: Sandra Sdraulig
E-mail: miff@netspace.net.au
Web site: www.cinemedia.net/miff
Dates: July–August
Deadline: April

*Presents international features, shorts,
documentaries, animation and experimental films. Competitive for shorts.
FIAPF recognized.*

Australia's two original film festivals, held in Melbourne and Sydney, have common origins. Both
grew from Australia's burgeoning
postwar film society movement, and
both were inspired by the Edinburgh Film Festival, an event
founded by Scotland's film societies.

In 1950, at a meeting of the
Australian Council of Film Societies in the Sydney beachside suburb
of Newport, it was decided to establish an Australian Film Festival
which would alternate between the
two largest Australian cities.

The first Australian Film Festival was held in January 1952, in
the Melbourne suburb of Olinda,
and was attended by film society
delegates from Sydney as well as
their Melbourne counterparts.

The success of this event en-
couraged the Victorian Federation
not to support the 1953 event in
Sydney; the Olinda festival is now
considered to be the first Melbourne
Film Festival. Included in the pro-
gram of that first event were Jean
Cocteau's *Beauty and the Beast* and
Charles Crichton's *The Lavender
Hill Mob.*

The 1953 festival was more ambitiously staged but operated at a
deficit, and the future of the event
was in doubt until 1954, when Erwin Rado was appointed director. A
prewar refugee from Hungary, Rado
was perfect for the job—he was a
man of taste and culture and also a
first-class administrator.

Rado moved the festival first to
a series of venues on the Melbourne
University campus (with financial
support from the university's film
society) and later to a variety of independent suburban cinemas in the
Melbourne area before settling, in
1962, at the cavernous, three
thousand-seat Palais in the beach-

side suburb of St. Kilda, where it remained for twenty years.

Recognized by FIAPF in 1958, the festival gradually expanded until it was screening more than one hundred features and shorts; an international competition for short films was established.

For the next twenty-five years, the festival screened (usually in conjunction with the Sydney Film Festival, which was also held in June) Australian premieres of the cream of international cinema, with the work of Akira Kurosawa, Satyajit Ray, Michael Cacoyannis, Luis Buñuel, Andrzej Wajda and Michelangelo Antonioni regularly represented.

By the time Rado retired in 1979, the festival had become firmly established as a major arts event in Australia. His place was taken by Geoff Gardner, who moved the event from the Palais to a more intimate venue. Gardner directed three festivals, and when his replacement, Mari Kuttna, died suddenly while preparing her first festival in 1983, Rado returned, until his death in 1988.

After that, the festival experienced a turbulent period, moving venues with bewildering regularity, changing directors with alarming

frequency, and suffering from serious budget shortfalls in the late '80s. Today, under executive director Sandra Sdraulig, the festival, which now takes place in the heart of the city, is once again on solid ground.

In 1997, the festival shifted from its traditional June time slot and now takes place over seventeen days in late July and early August, enabling Sdraulig to invite films that have premiered at Cannes in May. That same year a program of nearly two hundred films, discussions, forums and retrospectives was attended by more than 67,000 people.

—*David Stratton*

Wine Country Film Festival (12th)

Box 303
Glen Ellen, CA 95442
Phone: (707) 996-2536
Fax: (707) 996-6964
Contact: Stephen Ashton
E-mail: wcfilmfest@aol.com
Web site: www.winezone.com
Dates: July–August
Deadline: late Apr.

Annual showcase for features, shorts, documentaries and animation in 16mm, 35mm and video formats. Competitive.

AUGUST

Palm Springs International Short Film Festival (4th)

1700 E. Tahquitz Canyon Way, #3
Palm Springs, CA 92262
Phone: (760) 322-2930
Fax: (760) 322-4087
Contact: Craig Prater
Web site: www.psfilmfest.org
Dates: Aug. 5–9
Deadline: June 1

Short films from around the world, seminars and student programs. Competitive. FIAPF recognized.

Locarno International Film Festival (51st)

Via della Posta 6
6600 Locarno, Switzerland
Phone: (41-91) 751-0232
Fax: (41-91) 751-7465
Contact: Marco Muller
E-mail: pardo@tinet.ch
Web site: www.pardo.ch
Dates: Aug. 5–15
Deadline: May 31

International showcase for the year's major new films, competition for emerging directors and New Cinema displaying innovative trends in style and content. Competitive. FIAPF recognized.

Locarno is the Euro egghead fest that can't quite bring himself to wear a funny hat now and then. Though it has built a distinguished rep over half a century for showcasing the best of art-house cinema and launching many names, its development in the late '90s remains hamstrung by the shadow of showier Venice (a few weeks later) and its very correct, Swiss notions of cul-

tural imperatives. In the present-day rough and tumble of the international fest circuit, Locarno is fighting hard to keep a place at the main table among its more extroverted cousins.

Like several of Europe's most distinguished fests, Locarno was started just after World War II with tourism, not just film culture, on its mind. The idea of a group of local tourist agencies, the fest bowed in 1946 with a fifteen-pic program that included Roberto Rossellini's *Rome, Open City*, Sergei Eisenstein's *Ivan the Terrible* and Billy Wilder's *Double Indemnity*. The U.S. majors were heavily repped.

In an uncanny parallel to Venice's beginnings the previous decade, the festival held evening screenings in the sloping, two thousand-seat natural arena of the gardens of the Grand Hotel, the luxurious Mittel Europa–like hostelry that still dominates the town. The early events were just as important for their parties and dinners as for their films (hardly a taxing schedule), but during the '50s the fest developed a reputation for encouraging serious art-house fare, daring to program Soviet bloc films (at a time when Cannes was still wary), encouraging Third World cinema and generally fostering a culture of film appreciation in one of West Europe's least filmically developed countries.

In the late '50s, Locarno started to define its niche—young filmmakers and first works, seasoned by more audience-friendly fare in the evenings to bolster the box office. Tensions between art and commerce grew during the '60s, when *al fresco* evening screenings in the town's six thousand-seat Piazza Grande were introduced; and when Moritz de Hadeln (current head of Berlin) took over, the fest expanded its programming to become more of a general, international event. In broad terms, Locarno has remained the same since then, though subsequent directors Jean-Pierre Brossard, David Streiff and current head Marco Muller have tweaked the formula. (Muller recently persuaded FIAPF to let him include more than just first- and second-time directors in the Official Competition.)

Organization is close to Swiss-clock perfect—unlike nearby Venice's—with the only stress factor being whether the evening screening in the Piazza will be rained out due to temperamental weather. The fest's retros are often the jewel in its crown, immaculately programmed and opening up the past works of directors alive or dead (in recent years, Abbas Kiarostami, Youssef Chahine, Kato Tai) for often striking reevaluation.

Muller (formerly with Pesaro and Rotterdam) has waged an aggressive battle to heighten Locarno's profile as a platform for both U.S. indies and major studio titles, and has been more successful with the latter. For new Italian movies, Venice remains a powerful draw. Attempts to build an associated market have yet to get off the ground: Buyers treat it more as a pleasant vacation/meeting spot than a place to make real discoveries or deals.

Muller's sinologist background has at times paid off: Hong Kong director Wong Kar-wai's *Chung King Express* bowed in Locarno in 1994, and largely established the director's rep in the West. However, with China, Muller's still picking up the pieces after daring to screen the banned *Beijing Bastards* the previous year.

—Derek Elley

Gramado Cine Video (5th)

(The Gramado Festival of Brazilian and Latin Cinema)
R. Evaristo da Veiga, 21-Sala 606
20.031-040 Rio de Janeiro, RJ, Brazil

Phone: (55-21) 240-7804
Fax: (55-21) 537-2898
Contact: Antonio Urano
E-mail: urano@ax.apc.org
Dates: Aug. 10–13
Deadline: July 15

Market with focus on Latin America, particularly Brazil, Argentina, Uruguay and Paraguay.

Maybe it's hard to imagine snow falling over a Brazilian city. It's harder to imagine that most restaurants in this town serve fondue and fresh trout for dinner—and that you can walk home in the wee hours without the slightest chance of being disturbed.

The town is Gramado, nestled in the mountains of the southern state of Rio Grande do Sul, not far from the borders of Argentina and Uruguay. The history of Brazil's most charming film festival starts there, twenty-five years ago.

At that time, a group of film critics from the south—led by the late Paulo F. Gastal—received government support to run a small festival that in its first three years awarded national filmmakers like Arnaldo Jabor (*Toda Nudez Sera Castigada*), Hugo Carvana (*Vai Trabalhar Vagabundo*) and Nelson Pereira dos Santos (*O Amuleto de Ogun*). The festival was then taking place during the Southern Hemisphere summer, and the celebrities of Brazilian cinema could all be seen lounging by the pool of the Serra Azul Hotel.

In the late '70s the festival came under the direction alternately of Esdras Rubin and Enoir Zorzanelo. Buoyed by the municipal government, Gramado continues to see its leadership alternate between these two according to whichever party is in power. Yet Gramado has maintained a fairly consistent design. It was, for example, the first fest to give space to filmmakers shooting in Super 8; today, it continues this tradition.

Gramado welcomes the most important Brazilian features made every year. As a showcase for domestic product, it has surpassed the Brasilia Film Festival, their one-time rival. In the early '90s, following Brazilian film's worst-ever crisis (production fell to almost zero after President Collor nixed state agency Embrafilme), Gramado decided to take films from elsewhere in Latin America, and also Spain and Portugal. The fest awarded pics like *Tecnicas de Duelo*, by Colombia's Sergio Cabrera, *Un Lugar en el Mundo*, by Argentina's Adolfo Aristain, and *Amnesia*, by the Chilean Gustavo Justiniano.

As Brazilian production has begun to boom again recently, Gramado has separated its awards into Brazilian and Latin American categories. About seven films compete in each, and an additional ten or so noncompeting films (retrospectives, etc.) round out the slate. Audiences now pay more attention to the accomplishments of local directors. The crowds in fact, never left this lovely German-influenced town, where blond, blue-eyed children ask for autographs from anybody getting into the Festival Palace, which is the town's only 35mm theater.

—*Nelson Hoineff*

Odense International Film Festival (13th)

Vindegade 18
5000 Odense C, Denmark
Phone: (45) 6613-1372
Fax: (45) 6591-4318
E-mail: Mag4kult@inet.uni-c.dk
Dates: Aug. 11–15
Deadline: May 1

Showcase for fairy-tale and original shorts whose content is experimental or imaginative. Competitive.

Chichester Film Fest

New Park Film Centre
New Park Rd.
Chichester, Sussex PO191XN, UK
Phone: (44-1243) 784 881
Fax: (44-1243) 539-853
Contact: Roger Gibson
Dates: Aug. 15–Sept. 1
Deadline: End of June

Edinburgh International Film Festival (52nd)

Filmhouse
88 Lothian Road
Edinburgh, EH3BZ, Scotland
Phone: (44-131) 228-4051
Fax: (44-131) 229-5501
Contact: Lizzie Francke
E-mail: info@edfilmfest.org.uk
Web site: www.edfilmfest.org.uk
Dates: Aug. 16–30
Deadline: May 5

International premieres, plus NBX, the only showcase of every British film produced annually. Competitive.

Edinburgh is the feisty little Scottish veteran that still wears its hair long and doesn't give a hoot what others think. When the event celebrated its fiftieth anniversary in 1996, it cheekily billed itself as the world's oldest, *continuous* film festival: technically true—both Venice and Cannes started prior to Edinburgh, but had early hiccups— but no one missed the point as the mighty Cannes began cranking up for its silver anniversary nine months hence.

Still run on a shoestring, still championing the indie and the outré, and still managing to combine its intensely local, Scottish character with an international perspective on moviemaking, Edinburgh just won't give up, even when it's on its knees. Held every August, when the Scottish capital is awash with its huge arts and music festival, it's a fest that, like all the great ones, intimately reflects the city in which it is held. Rough, tough and still with a no-necktie campus feel, it's a celebration of celluloid that's eagerly lapped up by young locals—and anyone else who cares to make the trip.

When it was started in 1947 by the Edinburgh Film Guild as a showcase for documentaries (a genre close to the Scottish filmmaking tradition), no one expected it to last very long, especially at that time of the year. (The event overlapped into September, when Venice—and at that time, Cannes—were going head-to-head.) The advisory committee included Basil Wright, Paul Rotha and H. Forsyth Hardy. The turning point came in the mid-'60s, under the brief tenure of David Bruce, when features became the main focus (pics by Polanski, Makavejev, Lean), and under director Murray Grigor (1967–72) the festival directly reflected the madcap, energized film culture of the time, where commercial movies mixed with foreign art films and Euro-hyped Hollywood B-meisters like Sam Fuller (who got a bagpipe welcome at the airport in 1969!) and Roger Corman.

Those years, and the subsequent period under Lynda Myles (1973–80), were Edinburgh's glory days, championing figures like Scorsese, Cronenberg, Jarman, Lynch and Jonathan Demme with a collegiate, film-buff glee. Jim Hickey's reign during the '80s came at a difficult time, when U.K. cinema attendances were plummeting and other fests were mushrooming, but Edinburgh just about remained on course and maverick enough in its programming (and retros) to make a mark on the new era.

During the '90s, when fests progressively became more institutionalized and reliant on sponsorship to maintain profile, Edinburgh wobbled badly but finally in 1995 found a young director, Mark Cousins, with the energy, knowledge and passion to revive its traditional '60s/'70s spirit in modern terms. There's every sign that current director, critic Lizzie Francke, who took over in 1997, will keep that alive. (Though the competition for titles in the fall fest logjam is now tougher than ever, Francke effectively managed to launch the British Renaissance at her first event.)

Under Cousins and now Francke, Edinburgh has gradually been developing a Britpic trade showcase—New British Expo—on a budget that's mostly nickels and dimes, as well as managing to pull celebrity filmmakers for talk-throughs of their works (dubbed Scene by Scene). Though the fest is noncompetitive and sans glitzy prizes, there's still a reservoir of goodwill by international filmers toward the event for its buffish passion, willingness to take risks and its quirky mix of the commercial, political and trashy. Edinburgh is one of the few fests that, even in its fifties, feels as if it's always in its first year.

—*Derek Elley*

Norwegian International Film Festival (25th)

P.O. Box 145
5501 Haugesund, Norway
Phone: (47-52) 734-430
Fax: (47-52) 734-420
Contact: Gunnar J. Lovvik
E-mail: haugfest@online.no
Dates: Aug. (Exact dates TBD)
Deadline: May 20

Highlights a selection of films for the upcoming season. Noncompetitive. FIAPF recognized.

Portobello Film Festival (2nd)

The Seventh Feather, Dalgano Way
London, W10 5EL, U.K.
Phone/fax: (44-181) 964-8747
Contact: Angeli Macfarlane
Dates: Aug.
Deadline: end of June

Cutting-edge independent film and video. Noncompetitive.

Hiroshima International Animation Festival

4-17 Kako-machi
Naka-ku, Hiroshima 730
Japan
Phone: (81-82) 245-0245
Fax: (81-82) 245-0246
Contact: Sayoko Kinoshita
E-mail: hiroanim@urban.or.jp
Web site: http://www.city.hiroshima.jp
Dates: Aug. 20–24
Deadline: Apr. 21

Competitive.

The Hiroshima International Animation Festival, typically a biannual event, is the largest animation festival in the world in terms of films entered and one of the premiere events for animators.

Hiroshima first launched the festival with the aim of broadening international understanding. The festival started when the Association Internationale du Film d'Animation proposed to Hiroshima holding a festival to mark the fortieth anniversary of the atomic bombing of the western Japanese city. Organizers believed that Japan, with its rich animation tradition, and Hiroshima with its mission of peace, would bring a unique flavor to the festival.

Animation is a thriving industry in Japan. While the live-action motion picture business has been in a slump the past two decades, animated films and TV shows dominate Japan's entertainment landscape. The top-earning picture in Japanese history, *Mononoke Hime* (The Princess Mononoke), is an animated work from Hayao Miyazaki. The film took in about $140 million at the domestic box office and toppled Steven Spielberg's *E.T. The Extra-Terrestrial* as the number-one movie in Japan.

The Hiroshima Fest was held for the first time in 1985 and marked the first time that a major international film festival had been held in Japan. Since then the festival has been held in 1987, 1990, 1992 and 1996. The number of entries has increased from 451 at the first festival to 1,102 in 1996. In 1996, 348 films were shown at the festival, which recorded attendance of just under 30,000.

Special screenings include the latest animation works from specific countries as well as retrospectives on some of the great animators of the world. Hiroshima is a comprehensive animation festival, consisting of competition, special screenings, workshop, symposia, exhibits and more. Over the past few events, Hiroshima festival of-ficials have tried to get more animators from Asian nations to participate in the event.

Hiroshima, destroyed by a U.S. atomic bomb at the end of World War II, conducts a number of festivals, symposia and other events to promote international peace and understanding. The rebuilt city, with seven rivers running through it, is home to one of the most scenic metropolitan areas in Japan. The festival is a nonprofit venture run under the auspices the Hiroshima municipal and prefectural governments. There are five award categories and cash prizes awarded to winning films. At the '97 festival, Britain had the most films entered (170), with Japan and the U.S. rounding out the top three.

—Jon Herskovitz

São Paulo International Short Film Festival (9th)

Rua Cristiano Viana 907
05411-001 Sao Paulo, SP, Brazil
Phone: (55-11) 852-9601
Fax: (55-11) 852-9601
Contact: Zita Carvalhosa
E-mail: spshort@ibm.net
Web site: www.estacao.ignet.com.br/kinoforum/saoshortfest
Dates: Aug. 20–30
Deadline: May 20

Promotes a greater exchange between Latin American and international production, and the development of the short film. Noncompetitive.

The Guardian Edinburgh International Television Festival (23rd)

24 Neal St.
London, WC2H 9PS, U.K.
Phone: (44-171) 379-4519
Fax: (44-171) 836-0702
Contact: Charlotte Ashton
E-mail: geitf@festival.demon.co.uk
Dates: Aug. 28–31

A discursive forum for TV program makers and broadcasters with international speakers. No screenings.

Espoo Cine Film Festival (9th)

P.O. Box 95
02101 Espoo, Finland
Phone: (358-9) 466-599
Fax: (358-9) 466-458
Contact: Timo Kuismin
Web site: www.kaapeli.fi/-lumo/
Festivaalit/Espoo
Dates: August
Deadline: by invitation only

European cinema, U.S. independents and highlights from other continents, mixing art and entertainment. Non-competitive.

Venice International Film Festival

La Biennale di Venezia
San Marco, Ca'Giustinian
30124 Venice, Italy
Phone: (39-41) 521-8711
Fax: (39-41) 523-6374
Contact: Felice Laudadio
Dates: late August (Exact dates TBD)
Deadline: May 25

Presents international cinema including a panorama of recent Italian productions. Competitive. FIAPF recognized.

One of the heavyweight trio that dominates the European festival circuit, the Venice International Film Festival occupies the middle ground between the hustle of Cannes and the sobriety of Berlin. International press and industryites unfailingly gripe about its high prices and often maddening disorganization, but the world's oldest film festival remains a major draw, not least of all for its enviable location.

Founded by Count Giuseppe Volpi in 1932 to extend the tourist season in the city's elegant Lido seaside resort, the fest began as an elitist event for well-heeled guests at the Hotel Excelsior, with forty films from nine different countries unspooling in the gardens after dinner each evening. While the core of big spenders still crowds the Excelsior and its swanky sister hotel, the Des Bains, the fest now attracts a broader range from impoverished film students to studio execs and A-list stars.

Taking its place alongside parallel events of the Biennale arts exposition devoted to visual arts, music, poetry and later theater, the fest was a notable initiative for its time in that film was then still in its infancy and had not yet acquired the cultural cachet to be grouped together with the more established arts. But despite skepticism, the event was an instant success, expanding substantially in its 1934 sophomore edition before becoming an annual event the following year.

While it is commonly believed that the festival began as a propaganda machine for Mussolini's regime, that came somewhat later. During the rise of Fascism, the regime had quickly become savvy to the power of the media, and film in particular. Its hands-on role in running the fest began with the construction, in 1937, of Venice's permanent home, the Palazzo del Cinema. As Italy's links to Nazi Germany were fortified, the fest became a nationalistic event honoring primarily Italian and German films (including Leni Riefenstahl's *Olympiad*) in its first competitive editions prior to and during World War II.

That said, its importance right from the outset as an international showcase is undeniable. Robert Flaherty's *Man of Aran* was the first foreign film to win an official prize at Venice in 1934, while other early competition lineups boasted directors such as Frank Capra, René Clair, Marcel Carne, Howard Hawks, King Vidor, George Cukor and Jean Renoir.

The festival may no longer be the propagandistic tool it was during Fascism, but it has remained a source of controversy due to the political nature of directorial appointments and the tendency of right-wing or leftist Italian filmmakers—depending on who is in power at the time—to point the finger of political bias as a reason for their exclusion.

The fest has had a checkered history over the years, becoming noncompetitive during the decade that followed the revolutionary ferment of 1968. But Venice gradually reinforced its international standing throughout the 1980s and '90s under the direction of Carlo Lizzani, Guglielmo Biraghi, and especially, Gillo Pontecorvo. From 1992 through '96, the veteran *Battle of Algiers* director was instrumental in strengthening the profile of the U.S. majors and stars at the festival and in establishing Venice as a key European launchpad for fall releases.

Current chief Felice Laudadio toned down the star wattage and U.S. presence for his debut year in 1997, with his first program focusing largely on smaller films by lesser-known names. While many observers noted the selections seemed more suited to a second-string event than to one of Europe's big three, future editions may take a different shape as the rookie director finds his feet. His biggest challenge will be to bring a clear identity to an event that, with the often random proliferation of sidebars and special sections over the past ten years, has suffered from a lack of focus.

Despite a marked increase in acquisitions activity during recent years, attempts to set up a parallel market at the fest have not come to fruition. Reforms of the Biennale were due for government approval in 1998, looking to make the venerable event, along with its infamous bureaucracy, more flexible.

—*David Rooney*

Austin Gay and Lesbian International Film Festival (11th)

P.O. Box L
Austin, TX 78713
Phone: (512) 476-2454
Fax: (512) 495-9824
Contact: Ted Smith
Web site: www.agliff.org
Dates: Aug. 28–Sept. 10
Deadline: May 30

Showcase of gay- and lesbian-themed films. Competitive.

Montreal World Film Festival (22nd)

1432 de Bleury St.
Montreal, Canada, H3A 2J1
Phone: (514) 848-3883
Fax: (514) 848-3886
Contact: Serge Losique
E-mail: ffm@interlink.net
Web site: www.ffm-montreal.org

Dates: August–September
Deadline: July 5

Aims to encourage understanding between nations and promote meetings in North America between cinema professionals from around the world. Competitive. FIAPF recognized. Has attached film, TV and video market.

As the Montreal World Film Festival moves into its third decade, it is becoming increasingly clear that the Canadian fest is carving out its own distinctive niche far from the Hollywood mainstream.

Other festivals cater more to the studio pics, while Montreal focuses almost exclusively on art-house fare from all around the globe, and the fest's schedule is heavy on films that will have few opportunities to screen elsewhere in North America. One of the strengths of the Montreal festival is the fact that the bilingual city has always been a keen supporter of pics from other territories, and audiences here are among the most open-minded on the continent. This translates into big public support for virtually all the programming at the festival—nearly 350,000 moviegoers turned out for the twentieth-anniversary edition of the fest in 1997, making it one of the best-attended film fests in North America.

One of the quirks of the fest is

that the pics start unspooling daily at 9 A.M., and it's not uncommon to see hefty lineups along Ste. Catherine Street early on weekday mornings during the event. The schedule is anchored by the official competition, in which pics take a run at nabbing a number of trophies including the Grand Prix des Amériques. But one of the fest's problems has always been the difficulty in landing A-list titles for the competition given that it runs at almost the same time as the Venice festival. Other sections include the Hors Concours out-of-competition category, which usually features fairly high-profile offerings, many of which have previously screened at Berlin and Cannes; the regular Latin American sidebar; and the Cinema of Today and Cinema of Tomorrow sections, which are largely devoted to the work of up-and-coming auteurs.

The ambitious program—which generally includes around 220 features—is rounded out by the Panorama Canada category, which gives a boost to Canuck productions; a slot for films made-for-television; and the Canadian Student Film Festival. Each year, the festival presents a section devoted to pics from one country. In

1997, the recent output from Iran was in the spotlight. The Hollywood superstars tend not to make the trek to Montreal, making the fest something less than a star-studded gathering. But the festival's always-upbeat president and founder Serge Losique likes to say that the films are the real stars at his festival and, given the increased competition in the art-film arena, the U.S. acquisitions executives are realizing they can't miss out on Montreal for fear of losing a foreign gem to one of their competitors.

There has been more buying activity than usual in Montreal over the past couple of years and business was on the upswing in 1997, notably with Miramax picking up the Grand Prix winner, *The Children of Heaven*, from Iranian director Majid Majidi. The Montreal festival also includes a film and television market, which is designed in large part to help Canadian producers and distributors sell their wares internationally. The fest takes place in the heart of downtown Montreal in the area surrounding the Place des Arts complex, and all the theaters are within walking distance of the fest headquarters at the Complexe Desjardins Hotel.

—*Brendan Kelly*

Dublin Lesbian and Gay Film Fest

125 Melvin Rd.
Dublin 6W, Ireland
Phone: (353-1) 492-0597
Fax: (353-1) 670-6377
Contact: Kevin Sexton
Dates: August
Deadline: June 1

Underground Film Fest

2501 N. Lincoln Ave. Ste. 278
Chicago, Ill. 60614 USA
Phone: (1-312) 866-8660
Fax: (1-312) 489-3468
E-mail: clark@interaccess.com
Date: Aug (Exact dates TBD)
Deadline: May

Yugoslav Film Festival

JUK Herceh-Fest
Dvorana Park
Njgoseva bb
85340 Herceg-Novi, Bosnia
Phone: (381-82) 52 098
Fax: (381-82) 52 004
Contact: Zoran Zivkovic
Dates: Aug.
Deadline: July 15

Competitive.

SEPTEMBER

Oldenburg International Film Festival (4th)

Gottorpstr. 6
26122 Oldenburg, Germany
Phone: (49-441) 25659
Fax: (49-441) 26155
Contacts: Torsten Neumann, Thorsten Ritter
E-mail: riter@filmfest-oldenburg.de
Web site: www.filmfest-oldenburg.de
Dates: Sept. 3–7
Deadline: June 30

Focus on independent film. Recent guests include Alex Cox, Frank Oz and James B. Harris. Noncompetitive.

Telluride Film Festival (25th)

53 S. Main Street, #212
Hanover, NH 03755
Phone: (603) 643-1255
Fax: (603) 643-5938
Contact: Bill Pence
E-mail: tellufilm@aol.com
Web site: www.telluridemm.com/filmfest.html
Dates: Sept. 3–7
Deadline: July 4

One of the major showcases for new and independent film from around the world. Noncompetitive.

For most of the people who return to it year after year, and even for those who might have been there only once, the Telluride Film Festival represents the rarest jewel in the crown of their festival-going experience. Set in a former mining town 9,000 feet up in the Rocky Mountains in southwestern Colorado, Telluride is unquestionably elite and exclusive. It is expensive to get there as well as to attend. Its population of about a thousand doubles while the festival is on. But it is also, paradoxically, the most open, democratic and collegial of festivals, in addition to being one of the best programmed and run. Most of all, it is one of the most surprising, since the lineup of films and events is never announced to attendees until they arrive. You just have to have faith.

But that faith is always well rewarded, which is why Telluride has been one of the most influential festivals in the world almost since its inception twenty-five years ago. Co-directors Bill Pence and Tom Luddy spend the entire year canvassing the world for films they like and, because the festival runs only four days (always on Labor Day weekend), they can afford to be very choosy. Unlike most festivals, Telluride is not forced to fill dozens or even hundreds of slots across a couple of weeks, and the only thing people consistently complain about is that the festival is deliberately designed to make it impossible to see everything; you're forced to make choices.

And choices there always are. The only standard Pence and Luddy apply is excellence; otherwise, there are no limitations on where a film came from or when it was made. In addition to screening the latest pictures of interest from all over the world (there are normally at least a half dozen world premieres and many more North American ones), Telluride specializes in resurrecting and celebrating legendary figures from film history, not in the manner of mere fans but in the most intelligent, appreciative way.

No doubt the defining Telluride moment was the 1979 tribute to Abel Gance. Then all but forgotten in his native France, not to mention in the United States, the frail ninety-year-old giant of silent cinema was persuaded to make the arduous voyage to this remote town with the odd name. But it was there that his reputation began its rehabilitation. Shown on a specially constructed outdoor screen, his masterpiece *Napoleon* was presented to a shivering but thrilled crowd while Gance himself surveyed the scene from his hotel window. Based on the reaction in Telluride, the restored *Napoleon* then went on to conquer the world.

One could argue that Telluride is the ultimate cinephile festival. It has honored—in person—everyone from Leni Riefenstahl, Gloria Swanson, Michael Powell, Luis Trenker, Emilio Fernandez, James Stewart, Hal Roach, André de Toth, Cy Endfield and John Alton to Werner Herzog, Jack Nicholson, Chuck Jones, Sterling Hayden, Andre Tarkovsky, Andrzej Wajda, Robert Altman and Klaus Kinski. On top of that, since Telluride is basically built on either side of a single street, guests are utterly accesssible, making chance encounters and involved conversations the norm rather than the exception. Every year, its mix of bracing mountain air, creative international personalities and top-tier films serves to restimulate participants, to remind them of why they developed a passion for cinema in the first place.

Although any number of celebrated or breakthrough films have debuted there—*My Dinner with André, El Norte, Fitzcarraldo, Blue Velvet, El Mariachi, The Crying Game, Ed Wood* and *Sling Blade* are just a few—Telluride has managed to keep its emphasis firmly on the artistic side of things and minimize the "industry," or market mentality that seems to have overtaken even the most well-meaning of other festivals. The festival does nothing to court distributors, publicists or the press and, other than the filmmakers themselves and those few rich folks who invest more than $1,000 in a fest pass, there are no VIPs, only dedicated film lovers who are all there for the same reason. The jewel-box Sheridan Opera House remains the heart of the festival, but the large new Max Theater has made it much easier for everyone who wants to see a hot title to do so.

Telluride created the international cliché of the tiny, unheard-of community suddenly becoming famous by putting on a film festival. Unlike any of its imitators, however, Telluride has endured due to its cultured tastes, unique setting, refusal to succumb to the temptation to grow, and adherence to its founding principles.

—Todd McCarthy

Toronto International Film Festival (22nd)

2 Carlton St., #1600
Toronto, Ontario, M5B 1J3, Canada
Phone: (416) 967-7371
Fax: (416) 967-9477
Contact: Piers Handling
E-mail: tiffg@torfilmfest.ca
Web site: www.bell.ca/filmfest
Dates: Sept. 4–13
Deadline: June 27

A celebration of cinema featuring hundreds of films and filmmakers from Canada and abroad. Noncompetitive. FIAPF recognized.

The Toronto International Film Festival has it all. It has consistently attracted the hot films, courted the leading lights and up-and-comers and secured the sponsorship of private donors and government to put on the film event of the Americas.

"It's one-stop shopping," said October Films president Bingham Ray. "There are lots of new films, the industry is here and it's convivial. Toronto is the festival you want all others to be and they're not."

Annually assembling close to three hundred features, the September showcase is one of the largest and most popular public festivals in the world. The city virtually shuts down for eleven days; liquor laws change, people take off work and festival fever invades in a way that few venues can equal. Its vast array of programs attracts top international filmmakers, buyers and deal makers even though it has steadfastly refused to establish an official market. For the press—close to one thousand strong in 1997—it's "the stop" to see the world's best movies and to interview established stars and cutting-edge talents.

Toronto began virtually as a lark in 1975 when three local entrepreneurs, William Marshall, Dusty Cohl and Henk Van de Kolk, figured they could put on a show that would rival even Cannes. It turned out to be the right place at the right time, clicking with locals from opening day. The organizers had a keen sense of how to get headlines and stole both the media and the industry.

Unlike other festivals, Toronto has largely eschewed prizes and values a program created by a staff rather than a single sensibility. Star vehicles mingle with arcanities, and the audience eats it all up.

"I learned a long time ago never to buy a film based on the crowd reaction at Toronto," said vet acquisitions exec Jeff Lipsky. "They love everything."

Aside from an abundance of riches, the frustrations of Toronto are the sorts of things most other events would kill to have. As it programs right up to the last minute, it's been plagued by ticketing dilemmas and long lines at the box office. As a result, the industry/press screening sked is as jampacked as the public showings, and the two components have been able to coexist amicably.

Program director Piers Handling says that because of the festival's size and diverse attendance, one can actually create one's *own* festival. And he's right. For the public, it's two weeks of indulgence in many movie menus, the industry can go on a feeding frenzy of new films, and the critics are able to canonize some hitherto unknown personality.

—*Leonard Klady*

Figueira da Foz International Film Festival (26th)

Apartado do Correios 50407
1709 Lisboa Codex, Portugal

Phone: (351-1) 812-6231
Fax: (351-1) 812-6228
Contact: Jose Vieira Marquez
E-mail: jose.marques@ficff.pt
Web site: www.ficff.pt
Dates: Sept. 4–14
Deadline: July 5

Aims at discovering new talents as well as unknowns. Attached independent film market. Competitive.

Brainchild of festival director Jose Vieira Marques, the Figueira da Foz International Film Festival evolved out of a series of annual "Film Encounters" that began in Portugal in the early 1950s, linked to the International Christian film movement. Marques also was closely tied to the Portuguese film club network, which during the fascist era attempted to introduce spectators to films that were banned to the general public. The formal inauguration of the festival in 1972, which established it as the leading film event in the country, was further dynamized by the 1974 Portuguese Revolution.

In the intervening years, the town of Figueira da Foz has grown from a small fishing port to a popular holiday resort, but the festival has maintained its "cinema of resistance" outlook. The festival is openly committed to developing the public's "critical sense" and offering "an alternative to the traditional market of cinema spectaculars." Each year the festival includes a Portuguese and international retrospective, plus special sections for Portuguese cinema, children's films, documentaries and shorts. The festival showcases an average of 189 films and 30 videos drawn from twenty-six countries.

The main selection is dominated by newcomers and offbeat European and Stateside independent cinema—the fruit of Vieira Marques's touring of the international festival circuit, on behalf of Figueira da Foz and also as a journalist. Jury prizes reflect a dedication to nonmainstream voices. In 1996 the top award went to the Portuguese production *Ma's Sin*, by French-born director Saguenail, and in 1997 to the French film *Marius et Jeanette*

The festival boasts an attractive setting—including Portugal's largest beach, sea-front cafes, a busy casino, bustling nightclubs and an informal atmosphere in which filmmakers can easily rub shoulders. But although Figueira da Foz is Portugal's oldest film festival, it has been increasingly challenged during recent years by Fantasporto, Troia and Vila do Conde. Detractors accuse the festival of being overly esoteric and extremely disorganized.

U.S. independent film director Peter Hall was severely critical of the festival organizers after his film *Delinquent* was awarded a prize in the 1996 edition but he received only the $4,000 prize money and never had a clearly planned list of screenings. The cultural representative of the local town council, Melo Biscaia, recently suggested, "If it were possible to alter the tone of the festival a little, include some more commercial films, and invite a few film personalities, we could energize the event. . . . The festival is no longer a pole of resistance as it was before the 1974 Revolution."

The festival will inevitably evolve over the coming years, but is certain to maintain its commitment to the independents. In 1998, the schedule includes retrospectives on Argentine director Fernando Solanas and Portuguese producer-director Antonio da Cunha Telles.

—*Martin Dale*

Festival of Fantastic Films (9th)

Sacha's Hotel, Tib Street
Manchester, U.K.
Phone: (44-161) 929-1423
Fax: (44-161) 929-1067
Contact: G.R. Lane Young
E-mail: 101341.3352@compuserve.com

Web site: savvy.com/-festival
Dates: Sept. 5–7
Deadline: June 10

Fantasy, sci-fi, horror. Competitive.

Deauville Festival of American Film (24th)

36 rue Pierret
92200 Neuilly-sur-Seine, France
Phone: (33-1) 46-40-55-00
Fax: (33-1) 46-40-55-39
Contacts: Lionel Chouchan, A. Halimi
E-mail: publics@imaginet.fr
Dates: Sept. 5–14
Deadline: Aug. 15

Showcase for U.S. features and independent films. Competitive. FIAPF recognized.

The demilitarized zone in the ongoing Gallic war against American Cultural Imperialism is a picturesque resort town in Normandy, not far from the historic beaches whence the Allied forces parlayed D-Day into victory. Every September since 1975, the Deauville Festival of American Cinema has declared a truce and welcomed American movies—from the mega-budgeted *ID4* to the micro-budgeted *In the Company of Men*—to a balmy stretch of sand facing the English Channel.

While the year-round big-screen offerings in many foreign lands qualify as all-American by default, Deauville claims the distinction of being the only lineup of all-American fare held beyond U.S. borders. English is cheerfully spoken and projected (making Deauville a promising destination for Anglo-Saxons who like the idea of being on the Continent while feeling free to ignore the subtitles), and Gallic audiences gladly immerse themselves in special effects (from the studios) and dysfunctional families (from the American indies).

As time goes by, an event that once thrived on tributes to Elizabeth Taylor and Lana Turner is finding stars with their glamour quotient harder to come by. (Which is not to imply that 1997 honoree John Waters isn't glamorous in his own inimitable way.) Deauville still attracts marquee names, but it has branched out since 1995 by adding a competition that awards two trophies to contestants from a field of ten recent indies.

The action is all concentrated within a very small circuit of hotels and theaters just a few blocks from the train station. Because fest founders André Halimi and Lionel Chouchouan are well connected in media circles, and because, when it comes to moviegoing, the fall in France is analogous to summer in the U.S. with packed movie houses across the country, an avalanche of national Deauville coverage helps boost recognition throughout Europe for studio and indie product alike (TV commercials for movies are not permitted in France but feature stories are allowed).

Big-name stars have graced Deauville from the start and continue to attend the fest, although vets perennially complain that there aren't as many celebs as there used to be. That said, Tom Hanks, Harrison Ford, Sean Penn, Kevin Costner, Tom Cruise, John Travolta, Clint Eastwood, Sylvester Stallone and Morgan Freeman have all put in appearances in recent years.

Thanks to the largesse of the Lucien Barriere hotel chain, journalists are treated to several nights in swell accomodations—which helps soothe frazzled nerves brought on by covering a ten-day fest which has a press office that is notoriously casual about providing useful or accurate information. Dealing directly with publicists generally yields better results; Gallic reporters and a smattering of film scribes from the rest of Europe value Deauville as an opportunity to stock up on celeb profiles for months to come. The 1997 edition hosted world preems of Tom DiCillo's *The Real Blonde* (the director's *Living in Oblivion* won the very first Grand Prix) and Gary Fleder's Morgan Freeman thriller, *Kiss the Girls*, along with a spate of worthy indies.

Although press and VIPs get priority treatment that sometimes squeezes out the rank-and-file viewers, Deauville has always prided itself on serving the general public. Regular folks can buy tickets on a per-film basis or invest in a pass that may or may not be amortized. If there's room, patient fans are allowed into the balcony of the Casino for press conferences. Not a bad way to see Billy Crystal (*Forget Paris*, 1995) or Eddie Murphy (*The Nutty Professor*, 1996) crack wise to a small house for free.

It's sheer coincidence that the Deau in Deauville is pronounced "dough"—a handy commodity to have if one wants to book a room at a waterfront palace. But film buffs on a budget can stay in the adjacent and less elegant Trouville and will be happy to know that, unlike those in Cannes, local eateries do not ratchet up their prices.

Although not condoned by hotel management, anyone who buys a drink at their cozy lobby bars or manages to loiter by the entrances has an excellent chance of snapping

a photo or nabbing an autograph from the likes of Ron Howard, David Mamet, Patrick Stewart, Parker Posey or Kevin Smith.

Deauville has also instituted an annual tribute to an outstanding American producer. The first three honorees were Irwin Winkler, Arnon Milchan and Arnold Kopelson. It's a long way to go to pitch an idea, but you never know.

—*Lisa Nesselson*

Boston Film Festival (13th)

P.O. Box 516
Hull, MA 02045
Phone: (617) 925-1373
Fax: (617) 925-3132
Contact: Mark Diamond
Dates: Sept. 5–18
Deadline: July 15

Presents 50 features, U.S. independents, documentaries and shorts. Noncompetitive.

Since its founding as an independent showcase in 1985, Boston has gone through numerous twists and turns to become a worthwhile stop on the northeastern fall fest circuit that starts with Montreal and Toronto and ends in New York.

In its second year, local exhibitor USACinemas arranged for a few major attractions to try to draw attention to the fledgling fest and by 1987 had totally taken it over. From then through 1993, Boston offered the only film festival in the world operated entirely by a major chain exhibitor. (USA was bought by Loews in 1988.) A. Alan Friedberg, head of USA and later Loews chairman until 1992, committed the business to fostering the event, even going so far as to donate the festival profits to local arts groups.

That ended in 1993 when Loews announced that it would continue to sponsor the festival and provide its downtown theaters (the Cheri and the Copley Place) for fest screenings but would no longer organize it. Film booker Mark Diamond and publicist Susan Fraine, who had been with the fest while working for USA and Loews, decided to take it over themselves. They have been running it ever since and also operate the Palm Beach Festival. (They spent several years running the Palm Springs Festival as well.)

Boston appeals to filmmakers because it is noncompetitive and, somewhat unusual for a fest, committed to making all entries available for review by the local press before the fest showings. This has encouraged smaller, independent filmmakers to submit their movies, in the hope that good reviews in Boston might lead to fest bookings and even distribution somewhere down the road.

For major studio and indie releases, the Boston fest provides good word of mouth as well as a way to get the reviews early. As it is a prominent art film market, a distributor with an iffy opening date in Boston might push harder knowing that a glowing review in the *Boston Globe* will be reprinted (and expanded) upon the film's regular release.

Fest size has varied over the years, although the current two-week run in September with about fifty films on the schedule seems to have become the standard. Since 1995, the festival screenings have expanded to Landmark Theatres' Kendall Square venue across the river in Cambridge.

Diamond and Fraine have taken a festival that was often predicted to be on its final legs and firmly established it as an independent presence, winning support from the industry and from filmgoers alike. As one sign of its establishment on the scene, the fest finally received some state funding in 1997—its thirteenth year—with Massport joining the various business sponsors of the fest.

—*Daniel M. Kimmel*

Latin American Film Festival (8th)

79 Wardour St.
London, W1V 3TH, U.K.
Phone: (44-171) 434-3357
Fax: (44-171) 287-2112
Contact: Eva Tarr
Dates: Sept. 5–18
Deadline: June 30

Lineup of contemporary feature films, shorts and documentaries from Latin America. Noncompetitive.

Tacoma Tortured Artists Film Festival

Club Seven Studios
728A Pacific Ave.
Tacoma, WA 98402 USA
Fax: (253) 627-1525
Contact: James Hume
Dates: Sept. 6, 12, 13
Deadline: July 31

Alexandria International Film Festival (13th)

9 Oraby St.
Cairo 11111, Egypt
Phone: (20-2) 574-1112 or 578-0042
Fax: (20-2) 768-727
Contact: Ahmad Al Hadary
Dates: Sept. 8–14

Showcase for Mediterranean cinema as well as international films. Competitive.

Fantoche (2nd)

Ottikerstrasse 53
8006 Zurich, Switzerland
Phone: (41-1) 361-4151
Fax: (41-1) 364-0371
Contact: Otto Alder
E-mail: fantoche@access.ch
Web site: www.fantoche.ch
Dates: Sept. 9–14
Deadline: June 15

Recent animated films in competition, plus sidebars including comics and animation, student work, retrospec-tives and Internet animation. Competitive.

Fantastisk Film Festival (3rd)

Box 1693
221 01 Lund, Sweden
Phone: (46-46) 120-001
Fax: (46-46) 146-582
Contact: Magnus Paulsson
E-mail: www.info@fff.se
Web site: www.fff.se
Dates: Sept. 10–14
Deadline: Aug. 8

Presents films of the unimaginable including sci-fi, horror and cult movies. Competitive.

Copenhagen Film Fest

C/O FSI, Vesterbrogade 35
1620 Copenhagen V Denmark
Phone: (45-33) 25 25 01
Fax: (45-33) 25 57 56
Contact: Jonna Gensen
Dates: mid Sept.
Deadline: May 30

Competitive. Focuses on European cinema, films from the Third World, and U.S. independents, and includes the Gay and Lesbian Film Fest.

International Broadcasting Convention (18th)

IBC Office, Savoy Place
London, WC2R 0BL, U.K.
Phone: (44-171) 240-3839
Fax: (44-171) 240-3724
Contact: Tony Lawes
E-mail: show@ibc.org.uk
Web site: www.ibc.org.uk/ibc/
Dates: Sept. 12–16
Deadline: June 4

Convention, exhibition and conference, with a wide-screen festival.

Fukuoka International Film Festival— Focus on Asia (7th)

c/o Fukuoka City Hall
1-8-1, Tenjin, Chuo-Ku

Fukuoka 810, Japan
Phone: (81-92) 733-5170
Fax: (81-92) 733-5595
Contact: Tadao Sato
Dates: Sept. 12–21
Deadline: June 24

Top quality films from Asia, spot-lighting Taiwanese films in 1997. Noncompetitive.

One of the main events on the Asian film circuit, the Fukuoka International Film Festival is aimed at honoring some of the best movies coming from Asia, featuring films by directors from Kazakhstan to Singapore. The twenty to thirty movies in the festival attract about fifteen thousand people. Films entered in Fukuoka often go on to dominate art-house theaters in Asia.

Organizers say the festival's purposes are to introduce the best Asian films to the world, deepen understanding of Asian films, provide cultural interchange among Asian nations through film, and to uncover and foster new film talent. The Fukuoka Festival started in 1991 and organizers invite actors, directors and film experts from across Asia to participate in the events, which include question-and-answer sessions and panel discussions. At the first festival, twenty-three films from ten countries were shown and attendance was 10,724.

In 1997, in spite of a major typhoon striking during the festival, the fest did see sixty-four overseas delegates visiting the festival, the largest number in its brief history.

The festival is unique in Japan because of its exclusive focus on Asian films. All films are shown in their native language, with English and Japanese subtitles. There were three categories of films in '97: the Excellent Films of Asia, a Taiwanese film collection and a sponsored program on Japanese films depicting modern images of Asia. Taiwanese directors Lee Hsing, Chang Pei-Cheng and Wan Jen were on hand for the festivities.

The city of Fukuoka, which backs the festival, is working to keep available an archive of Asian films. The city's main library has a Film Archives Section, which acquires mostly Asian cinema. The library has a film storage vault, a 246-seat theater, a mini-theater and AV booths for people who want to see films in the collection. As of March 1997, the archives section had acquired 470 titles for preservation.

—*Jon Herskovitz*

Independent Feature Film Market (19th)

104 W. 29th St., 12th floor
New York, NY 10001

Phone: (212) 465-8200
Fax: (212) 465-8525
Contact: Valerie Sheppard
Web site: www.ifp.org
Dates: Sept. 14–21
Deadline: Mid-May

Market devoted to emerging U.S. independent films and filmmakers.

Cinema tout ecran (3rd)

Maison des Arts du Grutli
16 rue du General-Dufour
Case postale 5305
1211 Geneva, Switzerland
Phone: (41-22) 328-8554
Fax: (41-22) 329-6802
Contact: Leo Kaneman
E-mail: info@cinema-tout-ecran.ch
Web site: cinema-tout-ecran.ch
Dates: Sept. 15–21
Deadline: end of July

Showcase for high quality TV films. Competitive.

International Short Film Festival of Drama (3rd)

Ag Yarvoras 9,
66100 Drama, Greece
or: Emm Benaki 71
10681 Athens, Greece
Phone: (30-521) 47575; (30-1) 330-0309
Fax: (30-521) 33526; (30-1) 330-2818
Contact: Antonis Papadopoulos
Dates: Sept. 15–21
Deadline: June 13

Showcases shorts including fiction, documentaries, student films, experimental and animation. Competitive.

Cinefest: The Sudbury Film Festival (9th)

218-40 Elm St.
Sudbury, Ontario
P3C 1S8, Canada
Phone: (705) 688-1234
Fax: (705) 688-1351
Contact: Tammy Frick

Dates: Sept. 16–21
Deadline: Aug. 15

More than 100 Canadian and international films, shorts, documentaries, animation, children's films and Midnight Madness. Competitive.

Breckenridge Festival of Film (17th)

P.O. Box 718
Breckenridge, CO 80424
Phone: (970) 453-6200
Fax: (970) 453-2692
Contacts: Julie Bullock, Terese Keil
E-mail: filmfest@brecknet.com
Web site: www.brecknet.com/BFF/home.html
Dates: Sept. 18–21
Deadline: June 30

Films, receptions, tributes and film education activities. Noncompetitive.

International Student Animation Festival of Ottawa (1st)

2 Daly Ave.
Ottawa, Ontario, K1N 6E2, Canada
Phone: (613) 232-8769
Fax: (613) 232-6315
Contact: Chris Robinson
E-mail: oiaf@ottawa.com
Web site: oiaf.ottawa.com
Dates: Sept. 18–21
Deadline: July 1

Animation festival that showcases and encourages student work. Competitive. FIAPF recognized.

Temecula Valley International Film Festival (3rd)

27645 Jefferson Ave., #104A
Temecula, CA 92590
Phone: (909) 699-6267
Fax: (909) 308-1414
Contact: Jo Moulton
Web site: www.temecula.org
Dates: Sept. 18–21
Deadline: June 14

Presents feature-length romantic com-edies as well as shorts and student films of other genres. Competitive.

Yugoslav Animated Film Fest

Dom Kulture/Photo kino/klub
Cacak, 32000 Cacak, Bosnia
Phone: (381-32) 23508
Contact: Slobodan Pajic
Dates: Sept. 18–21
Deadline: Sept. 1

Athens International Film Festival—Opening Nights (3rd)

Benaki 5 & AG Nectarioy Str.
15235 Athens, Greece
Phone: (30-1) 606-1428
Fax: (30-1) 601-4137
Contact: George Tziotzios
Dates: Sept. 18–25
Deadline: July 1

Showcase for American independents as well as shorts, documentaries and a panorama of world cinema. Non-competitive.

The British Short Film Festival (9th)

Room A214, BBC TV Centre
56 Wood Lane
London, W12 7SB, U.K.
Phone: (44-181) 743-8000, ext. 62222
Fax: (44-181) 740-8540
Contact: Amanda Casson
Dates: Sept. 18–25
Deadline: June 9

Sole specialized short film fest in the U.K. Screens film and video. Compet-itive.

Forum Festival

Groesslingova 32, 81109
Bratislava, Slovakia
Phone: 521 5035
Fax: (42-7) 37 88 290
Contact: Martin Smatlak
Dates: Sept. 18–25
Deadline: TBD

Competitive.

San Sebastian International Film Festival (45th)

Plaza de Oquendo, s/n
20004 San Sebastian, Spain
Phone: (34-43) 481-212
Fax: (34-43) 481-218
Contact: Diego Galan
E-mail: ssiff@mail.ddnet.es
Web site: www.ddnet.es/
san_sebastian_film_festival/
Dates: Sept. 18–27
Deadline: July 31

Reviews most recent worldwide pro-ductions and recovers classic trea-sures. Competitive.

While political infighting and un-certainty regarding the direction of the event threatened to relegate the San Sebastian International Film Festival to permanently marginal status in the 1980s and early '90s, Spain's premiere film meet has staged a remarkable comeback in recent years, reestablishing itself as one of the key appointments of Eu-rope's fall fest calendar.

Framed by rolling hills not far south of the French border and set along the bay of La Concha, San Se-bastian is the queen of the Basque bathing resorts. Its magnificent lo-cation, mild climate and superlative cuisine have made it a fashionable vacation spot that eschews the flashy glamour of the south of France. The town's film festival was founded in 1953 by a group of ten local businessman in order to prolong tourism beyond the traditional summer season.

From its inaugural edition, composed of nineteen films from eight countries, the fest was a resounding success. Its substantial budget and solid local-industry support helped establish a winning formula of premieres, parties, lavish dinners and visits from major international stars, starting with Gloria Swanson in 1954. Even today, directors such as Claude Chabrol confess to accepting an invitation to the fest as a good excuse to visit the gastronomically renowned (and astronomically priced) restaurants in the hills overlooking the town.

Under the direction of Diego Galan since 1995—returning from an earlier stint in the late '80s—the fest has successfully taken the tarnish off its glitz factor while at the same time steadily strengthening its feature competition, popularizing its retrospectives and securing a handful of international premieres each year. These have included Bob Rafelson's *Blood and Wine*, Pedro Almodovar's *The Flower of My Secret*, Bertrand Tavernier's *Captain Conan*, Jean-Paul Rappeneau's *The Horseman on the Roof*, Claude Cha-

brol's *Rien ne va plus* and Adrian Lyne's controversial *Lolita*.

Alongside the competitive main section, San Sebastian's extensive Zabaltegi (Open Zone) sidebar, introduced in its present form in 1985, has developed into a lively window for work by new filmmakers and pics rendered ineligible for competition due to appearances in previous fests.

First and second features from this section and the competition vie for the $170,000 New Directors prize (formerly the Euskal Media Prize), one of the richest cash awards of any fest in the world. Recent recipients have included Scott Silver's *Johns* from the U.S., Chinese director Ning Ying's *For Fun*, Paddy Breathnach's *Ailsa* and the same Irish director's *I Went Down*.

The fest's Donostia career award goes to a seasoned star each year, invariably yielding major media coverage. And while recent honorees may not quite have been a match for the ninety minutes of bitchy repartee from a chain-smoking Bette Davis in her last public appearance at the fest in 1989, visitors such as Lauren Bacall, Robert Mitchum, Lana Turner, Susan Sarandon and Michael Douglas have more than satisfied the paparazzi.

Another popular feature unique to San Sebastian is the event screenings at the 3,500-seat Anoeta Velodrome arena, ranging from *Trainspotting* to Alex de la Iglesia's *Perdita Durango* to *Singin' in the Rain*, while the *Made in Spanish* section provides a useful recap of the year's best productions from Spain and Latin America. The fest also packs houses with its Hollywood retrospectives. These lately have included William Wellman, Gregory La Cava, James Whale, Tod Browning and Mitchell Leisen.

A strategic platform for the launch of films in one of Europe's most important markets, San Sebastian receives saturation Spanish coverage. Its position on the heels of Venice, Montreal and Toronto makes it a battle to attract substantial numbers of international press— especially North Americans, who clearly favor the Canadian event— but the fest is slowly building on its fast-growing attendance from across Europe and farther afield.

Immediate expansion beyond the fest's existing dimensions is limited by the screening facilities available. But construction has begun and is expected to be completed by 1999 on the town's new Cultural and Congress Center. With a main theater seating 1,850 and a second 580-seat screen, along with conference rooms, stores, exhibition spaces and eateries, the new venue will take the place of the regal but rather cramped Victoria Eugenia Theater that currently serves as the fest's centerpiece.

—*David Rooney*

Rio de Janeiro Film Festival (9th)

Rua Voluntarios da Patria, 97
Botafogo, Rio de Janeiro
22270-000, RJ, Brazil
Phone: (55-21) 537-1145 or 537-0222
Fax: (55-21) 539-1247
Contact: Adhemar Oliveira
E-mail: ilda@ax.apc.org
Web site: www.estacao.ignet.com.br/
Dates: Sept. 18–29
Deadline: July 7

Presents a panorama of this year's worldwide productions. Noncompetitive.

Helsinki Film Festival: Love and Anarchy (10th)

Unioninkatu 10
Fin-00130 Helsinki, Finland
Phone: (358-9) 629-528
Fax: (358-9) 631-450
Contact: Mika Siltala
E-mail: r&a@cultnet.fi
Web site: love-and-anarchy.cultnet.fi
Dates: Sept. 19–25
Deadline: June 30

Daring and controversial titles and themes. Noncompetitive. FIAPF recognized.

Atlantic Film Festival (17th)

CBC Radio Building, 2nd floor
5600 Sackville St.
Halifax, Nova Scotia, B3J 3S9,
Canada
Phone: (902) 422-3456
Fax: (902) 422-4006
Contact: Gordon Whittaker
E-mail: aff@screen.com
Web site: www.screen.com/
atlanticfilm.html.cochran.com
Dates: Sept. 19–27
Deadline: June 15

Presents films from the Atlantic region and Canada as well as international work from countries bordering the Atlantic Ocean. Competitive.

Umea International Film Fest (12th)

P.O. Box 43
90102 Umea, Sweden
Phone: (46-90) 133-388
Fax: (46-90) 777-961
Contact: Thom Palmen
E-mail: film.festival@ff.umea.se
Web site: www.ff.umea.se
Dates: Sept. 19–27
Deadline: Aug. 8

Focuses on new features and documentaries. Shorts welcome. Noncompetitive.

EuropaCinema and TV (14th)

Via XX Settembre 3
00187 Rome, Italy
Phone: (39-6) 4201-1184, 4200-0211
Fax: (39-6) 4201-0599
Contact: Monique Veaute
Dates: Sept. 20–26
Deadline: June 30

Screens films from European countries that are representative of young and emerging trends. Competitive.

Sportel (8th)

Worldwide Sales and Marketing:
Vital Communications

6040 Boulevard East, #27C
West New York, NJ, 07093
Phone: (201) 869-4022
Fax: (201) 869-4335
Contact: Liliane and William Vitale
E-mail: vitcom_usa@aol.com
Dates: Sept. 21–24

International TV program market devoted exclusively to sport. Competitive.

Screens on the Bay (4th)

Sacis, Via Teulada 66
00195 Rome, Italy
Phone: (39-6) 379-981
Fax: (39-6) 370-1393
Contact: Giovanna Maccagno
E-mail: maccagno@sacis.it
Web site: www.sacis.it
Dates: Sept. 22–24

Convention.

International Festival of the Alpine Film (28th)

FIFAD Case Postale 144
1865 Les Diablerets, Switzerland
Phone: (41-24) 492-3358
Fax: (41-24) 492-2348
Contact: Pierre Simoni
Dates: Sept. 22–28
Deadline: July 12

Focuses on the identity of life in the mountains, including sports and environmental issues. Competitive.

Festival de Cine de Bogota (14th)

Calle 26, #4-92
Santa Fe de Bogota, Colombia
Phone: (57-1) 282-5196
Fax: (57-1) 342-2872
Contact: Henry Laguado
Dates: Sept. 22–Oct. 1
Deadline: July 1

Films by new directors (first three films). Competitive. FIAPF recognized.

Aspen Filmfest (19th)

110 E. Hallam, #102
Aspen, CO 81611
Phone: (970) 925-6882
Fax: (970) 925-1967
Contact: Laura Thielen
E-mail: celdred@aspenfilm.org
Web site: www.aspen.com/filmfest
Dates: Sept. 23–28
Deadline: July 11

Showing American independents and foreign features, documentaries and shorts, including tributes and special presentations. Noncompetitive.

LUCAS—International Children's and Young People's Film Festival (23rd)

c/o Deutsches Filmmuseum
Schaumainkai 41
D-60596 Frankfurt, Germany
Phone: (49-69) 2123-8835
Fax: (49-69) 2123-7881
Contact: Walter Schobert
E-mail: filmmuseum@stadt-frankfurt.de
Dates: Sept. 23–Oct. 3
Deadline: June 15

Showing current international film productions for children and young people, with a video-infomation market. Competitive. FIAPF recognized.

Mipcom Junior Youth Programming Screenings (5th)

Reed Midem Organization
BP 572, 11 rue du Colonel Pierre Avia
75726 Paris Cedex 15, France
Phone: (33-1) 4190-4580
Fax: (33-1) 4190-4570
Contact: André Vaillant
Web site: www.mipcom.com
Dates: Sept. 24–25
Deadline: Aug. 19

Youth film and TV market.

International Film Camera Festival "Manaki Brothers"—Bitola (18th)

"8-mi Mart" Nr. 4
91000 Skopje, Macedonia
Phone: (389-91) 211-811
Fax: (389-91) 211-811
Contact: Delcho Mihajlov
Dates: Sept. 24–28
Deadline: Sept. 10

Competitive festival, focusing on the work of cinematographers. Named after the first Balkan cameraman, Milton Manaki.

Riminicinema International Film Festival (10th)

Via Gambalunga 27
47037 Rimini, Italy
Phone: (39-541) 22627
Fax: (39-541) 24227
Contact: Gianfranco Miro Gori
E-mail: riminicinema@comune.rimini.it
Web site: comune.rimini.it/rimini.cinema/rco.htm
Dates: Sept. 24–28
Deadline: July 30

Showing independent films focusing on the relationships between different cultures and languages. Competitive. FIAPF recognized.

Filmfest Hamburg (5th)

P.O. Box 500 480
22704 Hamburg, Germany
Phone: (49-40) 3982-6210
Fax: (49-40) 3982-6211
E-mail: 0403904040-0007@+-online.de
Contact: Josef Wutz
E-mail: filmfest-hamburg@t-online.de
Web site: www.cinemaxx.de
Dates: Sept. 24–Oct. 2
Deadline: July 14

Showcase for independent features and international films, including an East Asia special focus. Noncompetitive. FIAPF recognized.

Netherlands Film Festival (17th)

P.O. Box 1581
3500 BN Utrecht, Netherlands
Phone: (31-30) 273-4526
Fax: (31-30) 231-3200
Contact: Jacques van Heijningen
E-mail: ned.filmfest@inter.nl.net
Web site: www.netherlandfilm.nl
Dates: Sept. 24–Oct. 3
Deadline: July

Presents the best of Dutch film and TV drama including documentaries and shorts, incorporating Holland Film Meeting. Competitive.

Resfest Digital Film Festival

San Francisco Palace of Fine Arts
109 Minna Street, Ste. 390
San Francisco, CA 94105
Phone: (415) 567-9052
Fax: (415) 567-9056
Website: www.resfest.com
Dates: Sept. 24–25
Deadline: July

Nextframe (formerly the UFVA Student Film and Video Festival

Department of Film and Media Arts
Temple University
Philadelphia, PA 19122 USA
Phone: (1-215) 923-03532
Fax: (1-215) 204-6740
Contact: Dennis Doyon
E-mail: HYPERLINK mailto:
ufva@vm.temple.edu ufva@
vm.temple.edu
Web site: www.temple.edu/ufva
Dates: Sept. 26–28
Deadline: May 3

Competitive.

Ourense Film Festival (2nd)

Apartado 664
32080 Ourense, Spain
Phone: (34-88) 215-885
Fax: (34-88) 215-885
Contact: Eloy Lozano
E-mail: ney@bitmailer.net
Web site: www.sister.es/ourense.htm

Dates: Sept. 26–Oct. 2
Deadline: July 20

Showcase for independent cinema, with seminars and retrospectives. Competitive.

Festival International du film Francophone (12th)

Rue des Brasseurs 175
5000 Namur, Belgium
Phone: (32) 8124-1236
Fax: (32) 8122-4384
Contact: André Ceuterick
E-mail: fiff@pericles.namur.be
Dates: Sept. 26–Oct. 4
Deadline: Aug. 15

Promoting French-language features, shorts and documentaries. Competitive. FIAPF-recognized.

Mipcom (13th)

Reed Midem Organization
P.O. Box 572
11 rue du Colonel Pierre Avia
75726 Paris Cedex 15, France
Phone: (33-1) 4190-4580
Fax: (33-1) 4190-4570
Contact: André Vaillant
Web site: www.mipcom.com
Dates: Sept. 26–30

International film and program market for TV, video, cable and satellite.

Films From the South (7th)

Dronningensgt. 16
0152 Oslo, Norway
Phone: (47-22) 822-480 or 822-481
Fax: (47-22) 822-489
E-mail: filmsor@filmenhus.no
Web site: www.filmsor.filmenhus.no/
Dates: Sept. 26–Oct. 5
Deadline: Aug. 1

Showcase for films from Latin America, Africa and Asia, including features, documentaries and shorts. Noncompetitive.

Black Filmworks (23rd)

405 14th St., Ste. 515
Oakland, CA 94612
Phone: (510) 465-0804
Fax: (510) 839-9858
Contact: Dorothy J. Karvi
E-mail: bfhfi@aol.com
Dates: Sept. 26–28; Oct. 4–5
Deadline: Aug. 1

New York Film Festival (35th)

70 Lincoln Center Plaza
New York, NY 10023
Phone: (212) 875-5638
Fax: (212) 875-5636
Contact: Richard Pena
E-mail: filmlinc@dti.net
Web site: www.filmlinc.com
Dates: Sept. 26–Oct. 12
Deadline: July 11

Twenty-five to 30 features and shorts screened without categories, with public screenings at Lincoln Center's Alice Tully Hall. Noncompetitive.

When the New York Film Festival was launched as the second major U.S. festival, after San Francisco, in 1963, the timing could not have been more opportune. The vogue for foreign films among sophisticated urbanites was at its zenith and the surge of artistically exciting works from a variety of countries was increasing at a near-astonishing rate. The highbrow interest in international film culture would only grow bigger in the years to come, and the New York festival rode this wave with great skill and growing influence through the '60s and into the '70s.

Going into that first festival in September 1963, no one, least of all skeptical members of the film trade, expected much. But the festival wowed everyone, first by landing the unknown director of one of its entries (Roman Polanski, for *Knife in the Water*) on the cover of *Time* magazine, then by presenting a sterling program of pictures: *The Exterminating Angel*, *The Servant*, *The Fiancés*, *Muriel*, *The Trial of Joan of Arc*, *An Autumn Afternoon*, *Harikiri*, *Point of Order*, *I Live in Fear* and *Hallelujah the Hills*, just for starters.

From the outset, festival founder Amos Vogel and his programming director, Richard Roud, aimed to present to New York tastemakers for the first time the finest foreign films the season had to offer, and there was an abundance in those days. They determined to keep the festival exclusive by limiting it to twenty to twenty-five films, and since they conceived of it explicitly as an artistic event rather than a business conclave, even they had to be surprised by its success as an unofficial market. At the second festival, which included such future classics as *Before the Revolution*, *Woman in the Dunes*, *Band of Outsiders*, *A Woman Is a Woman*,

Lilith, Diary of a Chambermaid, and *King and Country* sales were made for domestic distribution.

Staged at the then-new Lincoln Center for the Performing Arts, which symbolically put film on an equal artistic footing with classical music, opera, dance and theater, the festival became a major cultural event virtually as soon as it appeared. Although Roud came to be criticized in retrospect as being overly Eurocentric and, specifically, Francophile (he lived in Paris most of the year), the fact remains that Europe was where most of the action was during the festival's first decade and that the New York festival fairly represented the swirl of cinematic activity taking place in those years in France, Italy, the U.K. and Eastern Europe. The Japanese masters were also regularly on hand and, if anyone was comparatively neglected during those first few years, it was the Americans, who slipped in with just a sampling of socially conscious and/ or arty features such as *All the Way Home, Nothing but a Man* and *Mickey One.*

Responding to criticism of this policy, the festival booked its first studio-produced opening night attraction, *Bob and Carol and Ted and Alice,* in 1968, and shortly thereafter hit the jackpot with its premieres of such early '70s landmarks as *The Last Picture Show* and *Mean Streets.* However, the festival's most famous moment was unquestionably its world premiere screening of *Last Tango in Paris* in 1972. It was Roud's close personal relationship with Bertolucci that made this possible in the first place, and while Roud was sometimes attacked for predictably showing almost anything by such favorites (and friends) as Godard, Truffaut, Wenders, Blier and Fassbinder, he was for the most part justified in doing so on any number of counts.

But nothing stays the same and, by the mid-'80s, the map of the international cinema, as well as the function of film festivals, had fundamentally changed. The old auteurs who were still working were mostly past their prime; the creative hot spots had shifted away from Europe to such distant areas as Australia, South America and, especially, Asia, where Roud, who refused to fly, never visited; and the plethora of exciting new film festivals in North America began to threaten New York's hitherto unquestioned preeminence. The trend now was toward mammoth festivals, offering a smorgasbord of upwards of 150 to 200 pictures, that served the increasingly diverse interests and populations of major urban centers, a trend best represented by the Toronto festival, which was also becoming very popular with the Hollywood studios.

In 1987, immediately after the New York festival's twenty-fifth anniversary, Roud was unceremoniously fired, even though the event's popularity was running as high as ever, with tickets selling at 99 percent of capacity. Richard Pena, the highly knowledgeable director of the film program at the Chicago Art Institute, was brought in to replace him, and festival programming soon took on a more diverse, globally flavored character.

A decade later, the festival retains an air of refined exclusivity due to its limit of roughly two dozen titles and the persistence of the New York media in treating it as though it still carried the same importance that it did twenty-five years ago. Its most vociferous detractors maintain that the festival today serves as little more than a glamorous setting for the cultural elite (i.e., members of the Film Society of Lincoln Center) to see prestige films a few days before they open in regular theaters,

and it's a fact that a very high percentage of New York's entries already have U.S. distributors before they play the festival. It is also true that, due to its limited slate, the festival serves the general population of New York filmgoers much less than do the festivals in at least a dozen other major North American cities.

Although the programming under Pena and his selection committee is largely intelligent, the New York festival, due to its size, can't begin to represent all that is happening globally in the cinema in any given year. Several of its main films are always drawn from the Cannes Film Festival four months before and, even then, most of these titles will already have been shown in Toronto; very rarely is New York able to present more than two or three significant world premieres. The explosion of interest in American independent cinema, amply reflected by such festivals as Sundance, the Hamptons, South X Southwest and New York's own New Directors/New Films, is another area that the festival has been able to represent in only a token manner. The time has long since passed when the New York Film Festival was a place where discoveries are made.

Due to its limitations, the question has been raised over the years as to whether the festival could be profitably transformed by becoming a competitive event that would attract more original pictures, or by expanding in size to embrace more films and better cater to the huge number of film enthusiasts in Manhattan alone for whom the festival is a largely inaccessible event due to ticket shortages for the general public. Thus far, it has resisted the temptation of going in either direction and, given the guaranteed audience for the films it does present, there has been no compelling reason to do so. But at this point the festival remains important more because it takes place in New York than because of the films it shows.

—*Todd McCarthy*

Vancouver International Film Festival/ Film & TV Trade Show (16th)

1008 Homer St., #410
Vancouver, B.C., V6B 2X1, Canada
Phone: (604) 685-0260
Fax: (604) 688-8221
Contact: Alan Franey
E-mail: viff@viff.org
Web site: viff.org/viff/
Dates: Sept. 26–Oct. 12
Deadline: July 15

Presenting 300 films from 50 countries with special focus on East Asian, *Canadian and nonfiction features. Noncompetitive.*

Touted as the third largest fest in North America—based on about 400 screenings of more than 220 features—Vancouver also has third place on the food chain, coming right after Montreal and Toronto. Alan Franey, the fest's topper since 1988, has made a virtue of late skeding and relatively low funding by picking up pics finished at year-end and concentrating on writers and directors instead of stars.

With its Dragons & Tigers competition, the fest boasts the biggest Asian-cinema display outside that continent, with notable tie-in events around such auteurs as Ishii Sogo and Beat Takeshi; the latter got a major exhibition of his paintings in 1996, alongside a retrospective of his hard-boiled flicks. The D&T series has helped spur the nascent Eastern independent scene, with People's Republic of China underground efforts like *Beijing Bastard* getting an international push. Main Asian programmer Tony Rayns has, however, created controversy with his overall skew toward gay-themed and avant-toned content.

Other international independent fare, like Michael Hoffman's *Some Girls* and Tony Gatlif's *Gypsy* have taken off at the VIFF, and the fest's uncompromising attitude has attracted major figures, such as Polish maestro Krzysztof Kieslowski, who showed up in 1994 for his last major tribute. Vancouver was also a home to the late Allan Francovich, the muckraking documaker (*On Company Business*) whose disturbing pics were regularly featured in the nonfiction section, one of the largest in the world, and one of the few that offers a cash prize to juried award-winners. The fest is also marked by its commitment to presenting silent films with live orchestras, usually in gala settings.

Other highlights have included a 1993 reunion for the Canuck "SCTV" troupe, and a recent look at work of the Hollywood blacklisters. The ongoing Best of Britain section also offers cutting-edge UK stuff.

The VIFF was founded in 1982 by exhibitor Leonard Schein, who at that time ran the Ridge rep house and has since founded the successful Festival Cinemas independent chain (which recently bought two venues in Toronto). Schein left in '86 for a short stint topping the Toronto International Film Festival. His job was filled by Hannah

Fisher, who raised more dollars and spent them bringing new glitz to the event, with old-line stars like Shirley MacLaine and Sarah Miles flown in. A board tussle followed, with Franey—who had run his own first-run house, the Vancouver East Cinema, and programmed pics for the 1988 Calgary Olympics—ending up in control, to largely favorable effect. (Fisher went on to helm the Floating Film Festival, which cruises the Caribbean in January.)

The fest, which covers 40 percent of its costs through box office and splits the rest between government and corporate support, has grown prudently, with about 130,000 tickets sold in 1997—part of a steady increase in attendance of 10 percent each year over the past decade. Films show at about eight venues, all of which are in the downtown core, except for the west side's Ridge, which is also the largest room.

A film and television forum, with a day set aside for young local filmmakers, was added four years into the VIFF's life, and has been run by Melanie Friesen for most of this decade; it generally runs during the second weekend.

—*Ken Eisner*

Ottawa International Animation Festival (12th)

2 Daly Ave.
Ottawa, Ontario, K1N 6E2, Canada
Phone: (613) 232-8769
Fax: (613) 232-6315
Contact: Chris Robinson
E-mail: oiaf@ottawa.com
Web site: oiaf.ottawa.com
Dates: Sept. 29–Oct. 4
Deadline: July 1

World's second largest animation festival, featuring retrospectives, professional development workshops and a trade fair. Competitive. FIAPF recognized.

Lesbian Film Festival Berlin

c/o Sandra Collins
Feurigstr. 61
10827 Berlin, Germany
Phone/fax: (49-30) 788-6487
Contact: Sandra Collins
Dates: Sept. 30–Oct. 5
Deadline: July 15

Showing films by, about and for lesbians. Noncompetitive.

Isfahan International Festival of Film and Video for Children and Young Adults (13th)

Farhang Cinema
Dr. Shariati Ave.
Gholhak, Tehran 19139, Iran
Phone: (98-20020) 888-890
Fax: (98-20020) 267-082
Contact: Ezzatollah Zarghami
Dates: Sept.
Deadline: July

Promoting film and video production for children and encouraging intellectual confrontation between children and adults. Competitive.

OCTOBER

Festival du Film Britannique de Dinard (8th)

2 Boulevard Feart
35800 Dinard, France
Phone: (33-2) 9988-1904
Fax: (33-2) 9946-6715
Contact: Thierry de la Fourniere
Dates: Oct. 2–5
Deadline: July 31

Screens British films, with an English-French producers meeting.

Idyllwild International Film Festival (2nd)

P.O. Box 3319
Idyllwild, CA, USA 92549
Phone: (1-909) 659-7733
Fax: (1-909) 659-7735
Contact: Fritz Schwab
E-mail: info@filmcafe.com
Web site: www.filmcafe.com
Dates: Oct. 2–5
Deadline: Sept. 1
Competitive.

Mill Valley Film Festival (20th)

38 Miller Ave., #6
Mill Valley, CA 94941
Phone: (415) 383-5256
Fax: (415) 383-8606
Contact: Mark Fishkin
E-mail: finc@well.com
Dates: Oct. 2–12
Deadline: June 20

Includes Videofest, Interactive Mediafest and Children's Film Fest. International. Noncompetitive. FIAPF recognized.

Established in 1978 to salute the plentiful reservoir of filmmaking talent in northern California, the Mill Valley Film Festival has grown upward and outward over its first twenty years.

In 1978, it was a decidedly homespun, three-day weekend that managed to lure 2,500 people to the local Oddfellows Hall, a bottleneck with seats. By 1997, it was an eleven-day event drawing an audience of more than 40,000 for more than one hundred film programs, in venues within Mill Valley and in neighboring theaters. Today it presents a respectable, eclectic, cross-section of world, American and independent cinema, as well as the nation's longest ongoing festival of new video works.

The list of Mill Valley's nearly fifty subjects for its in-person tributes gives an idea of the festival's growth and focus. The '70s and early '80s celebrated locals Philip Kaufman, John Korty, Waldo Salt and Bill Graham; cinematographer Robert Surtees, Jeanne Moreau, Tony Richardson, Idrissa Ouedraogo and Brenda Fricker have also been honored.

The noncompetitive festival is produced by the private, nonprofit Film Institute of Northern California, which also sponsors year-round educational seminars, community-outreach programs and national and international exchanges. Integrated with the community since its first weekend, when volunteers from the high school drama department provided at least one-quarter of the workforce, it is a festival that, perhaps more than most, has mirrored the passions and the excesses of its city and of Marin County.

Mill Valley is consistently tagged as one of the nation's most affluent, mostly liberal communities. It's to the festival's credit that it has persevered beyond its laid-back beginnings to build a reputation as a serious fest. Across the Golden Gate Bridge, the San Francisco Film Festival, founded in 1957, was already a major international force by 1978.

For Mill Valley to create its own identity, it had to find its own strengths. From its second year, the festival was canny enough to include a focus on new media, at a time when that technology seemed remote, impractical and inscrutable to the general public. That would seem almost prescient, when the next twenty years saw the development of George Lucas's nearby Industrial Light & Magic, and the on-again, off-again fortunes of Frances Ford Coppola's Zoetrope, giving Mill Valley access to the cache of technical talents who prefer the hills of Marin County to the hills of Hollywood. It's not uncommon for ILM to come out of its labs to do a festival program of some of its less-guarded secrets, and MV runs well-attended, hands-on workshops: James L. Brooks, Jim Abrahams and Harold Ramis in a comedy-writing seminar and veteran scenarist Salt on screenwriting, for example.

Not many U.S. festivals have Mill Valley's physical setting: a handsome, redwood-shaded "village" within sight of Mt. Tamalpais and fifteen minutes across the Golden Gate from San Francisco. Perhaps only Telluride rivals it visually, and it was Telluride's first year that gave MV's young film-lover founders the idea of launching something similar in northern California.

Die-hard twenty-year MV veterans still remember the memorable films that defined the festival's early days: *Payday* (whose screenwriter Don Carpenter lived next door to the movie house), *Alambrista*, *River's Edge*, *Stand and Deliver*, even Oldrich Lipsky's *Adele Hasn't Had Her Supper Yet*—and the presence of Krzysztof Zanussi, Peter Weir, Les Blank and Haskell Wexler, whose maverick work seemed

particularly fitting in this setting. In recent years, Mill Valley has provided the local launch for many major art house films: *The Piano*, *Prizzi's Honor*, *Short Cuts*, *Reservoir Dogs*, *Shine*, *My Left Foot* and *Secrets and Lies*.

—*Sheila Benson*

Warsaw Film Festival (13th)

P.O. Box 816
00950 Warsaw 1, Poland
Phone: (48-22) 471-826
Fax: (48-22) 644-1184
Contact: Stefan Laudyn
E-mail: filmfest@free.polbox.pl
Dates: Oct. 2–12
Deadline: June 30

Showcase for international features, 35mm only. Noncompetitive.

Los Angeles Short Film Fest

289 S. Robertson Blvd., #270
BH, CA 90211 USA
Phone: (1-213) 221-9247
Contact: Tammy Glover
E-mail: info@lo-con.com
Dates: Oct. 3–5
Deadline: TBD

Competitive.

Bite the Mango Film Festival (3rd)

National Museum of Photography, Film and TV
Pictureville, Bradford, BD1 1NQ, U.K.
Phone: (44-1274) 773-399, ext. 262
Fax: (44-1274) 770-217
Contact: Cary Sawhney
Web site: www.nmsi.ac.uk/nmpft/
Dates: Oct. 3–10
Deadline: Sept. 1

Celebrates international black and Asian film and TV. Noncompetitive.

Continental Film Festival (1st)

Phone: (213) 876-0975
Fax: (213) 876-0975
Contact: Jorge Ameer
E-mail: ajprod@primenet.com
Dates: Oct. 5–10

American independent film festival overseas. Competitive.

Prix Europa (11th)

SFB (Sender Freies Berlin)
14046 Berlin, Germany
Phone: (49-30) 3031-1619
Fax: (49-30) 3031-1610
Contact: Susanne Hoffmann
E-mail: prix-europa.@t-online.de
Dates: Oct. 5–12
Deadline: June 1

Now merged with the Prix Futura, this event shows films produced for TV including fiction, nonfiction, miniseries and programs for young people. Also hosts a European Radio and TV competition.

Asia Pacific Film Fest

c/o Motion Pictures Producers Association of Korea, Inc.
16-6 Pildong
2KA Choong-Ku Seoul, Korea
Phone: (82-2) 278-3297
Fax: (82-2) 278-3298
Contact: Kim Chae Huan
Dates: Oct. 6–9
Deadline: July 1

Competitive.

Flanders International Film Festival— Ghent (24th)

1104 Kortrijksesteenweg
9051 Ghent, Belgium
Phone: (32-9) 221-8946
Fax: (32-9) 221-9074
Contact: Jacques Dubrulle, Walter Provo

E-mail: filmfestival@infoboard.be
Web site: rug.ac.be/filmfestival/Welcome.html
Dates: Oct. 7–18
Deadline: mid-August

Focusing on "The Impact of Music on Film." Competitive. FIAPF recognized.

During the last quarter century, the Flanders Film Festival in Ghent has proved one of the most efficient and well attended in Europe, and certainly the preeminent such event in Belgium. Ghent belongs among the Continent's most appealing medieval cities, a jewel in the crown of ancient Burgundy and already by the thirteenth century a remarkably rich and powerful center for the manufacture of cloth.

The festival originated with an unerring focus on music in film. There were tributes to composers such as Georges Delerue and roundtable discussions and concerts conducted by well-known Hollywood tunesmiths. That tradition continues, but today the international jury selects its winners from a palette of features from around the world (many of them without a Belgian distributor). Shorts have their place, as do retrospective tributes. Since 1985, the Flanders Film Festival has given significant money prizes to competing films with the top winner taking home around $30,000. A recent innovation has been a major symposium on a theme of European interest, such as the problems facing would-be producers and distributors in smaller countries.

Attendance runs to an enthusiastic seventy thousand. Jacques Dubrulle, the director over the past decade, has taken this festival to its present status, with most screenings held in a multiplex beside a canal not far from the center of the city. Stars and directors like the relaxed atmosphere of Ghent and tend to stay more than the usual twenty-four hours. Hotels overlook cobbled streets with a view of the historic three hundred-foot-high bell tower, and there is a punctual shuttle service between hotels and theaters.

—*Peter Cowie*

Popcorn: Filmfest Stockholm '97 (1st)

c/o Atmosphere Media
Lastmakargatan 14–16
SE-111 44 Stockholm, Sweden
Phone: (46-8) 611-0320
Fax: (46-8) 611-0290
Contact: Petter Mattsson
Dates: Oct. 8–12
Deadline: Aug. 22

New festival showcasing international independents. Competitive.

Sitges International Film Festival of Catalonia (30th)

c/o Rossello, 3-E
08008 Barcelona, Spain

Phone: (34-3) 415-3938
Fax: (34-3) 237-6521
Contact: Alex Gorina
E-mail: cinsit@arrakis.es
Dates: Oct. 9–18
Deadline: July 31

Official competitive section for fantasy films and noncompetitive section for nonfantasy films. FIAPF recognized.

The 1997 edition of the Sitges Film Festival involved a name change: Previously the Sitges International Festival of Fantasy Film, the festival now includes the word *Catalonia* in its title, confirming it as this Spanish region's leading festival.

Sitges was founded in 1968 as the Festival of Fantasy and Terror, at a time when the strongly centralist politics of the Franco regime made it hard—particularly in the autonomous regions of Spain—for such potentially subversive initiatives to succeed. The ideological roots of the festival lay in antigovernment riots which had taken place in the town in 1967 and which had been suppressed by the police. Although there was no direct connection between the two events, the disturbances were still fresh in memory. A pleasant Mediterranean location, a consequent popularity with tourists and a reputation as an artistic center made Sitges the natural site for the new festival, under the direction of Antonio Rafales.

Until 1982, the festival survived on private funding. That year, with the fiscal future looking uncertain, the Catalan government intervened and restructured it, injecting much-needed funds and knocking the word *terror* out of the title in the process.

Sitges values the weird, wonderful and downright kitsch: in 1986, for example, when *Blue Velvet* took Best Film, the Best Actress award went to Caroline Williams for *The Texas Chainsaw Massacre II.* The 1997 overhaul, though not interfering with the management structure, led to a reorganization of the festival's sections with the aim of giving it a broader film base. Although its flagship section, "Fantastic," with its Maria statuette award, will continue to attract fantasy filmmakers—as it has the likes of David Cronenberg and David Lynch in the past—there is a new section, "Gran Angular," decided by a people's vote. The "Seven Chances" section is the festival's Critics' Week, with seven international critics choosing seven movies, one a day throughout the festival.

The Catalan Audio-Visual Conference, which is also new, has screenings of, and debates on, local Catalan product which all too often fails to register outside the region. There is also the regular round of retrospectives and tributes. With Spanish cinema's creative power on the rise through the '90s, Sitges can now provide a viable home base for films across all genres.

Running for ten days in October, with the Mediterranean temperatures at their balmiest, the Sitges festival has three thousand seats, screens more than one hundred films and pulls audiences of sixty thousand. Press and media coverage is still pretty much restricted to Spain, but the festival aims to increase its international profile after what festival director Alex Gorina calls its "relative isolation," by consolidating its connections with the Euro festival circuit. Gorina points to two visits as particularly memorable in the festival's history: that of Fay Wray—the big monkey is the festival symbol—and MichaelPowell's1989appearance—the last festival appearance made by the director before his death.

—*Jonathan Holland*

Chicago International Film Festival (33rd)

32 West Randolph St., Ste. 600
Chicago, IL 60601

Phone: (312) 425-9400
Fax: (312) 425-0944
Contact: Michael J. Kutza
E-mail: filmfest@wwa.com
Web site: www.chicago.ddbn.com/
filmfest/
Dates: Oct. 9–19
Deadline: July 25

Oldest international competitive fest in North America. Screens features, shorts, animation, documentary and student films, with tributes and retrospectives. Competitive.

The Chicago International Film Festival is one of the oldest fests in the U.S. and one of the longest-running competitive unspoolings in North America. It's weathered four decades of ups and downs and big chills, as might be expected when you program two weeks in October in Chicago. But two key factors have remained constant since its inception: the event continues under the stewardship of Michael Kutza, and its famous, sexually provocative annual posters are still shot by renowned photographer Victor Skrebneski.

The origins of the event date back to Kutza's college days when he was in search of a venue to show his student films. Apart from San Francisco, the U.S. fest circuit was a virtual desert, so he sent off his short films to such exotic-sounding locales as Cork and Krakow and Cannes. Scraping together nickels

and dimes, he landed at the Cannes fest in 1962 and returned with the notion of creating a similar event in the Windy City.

He hustled and put the first edition together with favors and sweat, including the assistance of silent screen star Colleen Moore. Chicagoans were taken with the novelty and it held a prominent spot on the international fest circuit for years, introducing Hugo Awards for shorts, specialized films, industrials and documentaries, in addition to the higher-profile feature prizes.

With the proliferation of fests in the 1970s and '80s, Chicago saw some of its luster fade, and Kutza got the brunt of media criticism for its seeming erosion of prestige. His blunt handling of local press saw him become the fest director "you love to hate," with critics mercilessly taking pokes at his film selections, tributes, "misleading" catalogue descriptions, venues and tardy start times. Until recently, it appeared he could do no right.

Two years ago, an attempted Kutza coup by several fest board members failed miserably, leading one city cultural observer to the conclusion that, good or bad, Kutza and the Chicago fest were synonymous. The event's strengths remain in programming European cinema and the work of veteran filmmakers. Though attempts have been made to beef up the selection of American independents and films from emerging nations, they've been thwarted by competition and a seeming lack of interest from a core audience that prefers films with subtitles. The Windy City film showcase also benefits from Kutza's penchant to go for the glitz, endearing him to patrons and raising the hackles of purists.

There's no denying the Chicago Film Festival's impact on the viewing tastes of the metropolis and on getting the ball rolling for other cinema showcases in North America. Chi town has one of the most active alternative film screening skeds with no fewer than a half dozen regular outlets whose programmers, at the very least, grudgingly point to the veteran festival as the kickoff point for developing an audience with broad and eclectic tastes

—*Leonard Klady*

Chicago International Children's Film Festival (14th)

Facets Multimedia
1517 W. Fullerton Ave.
Chicago, IL 60614
Phone: (773) 281-9075
Fax: (773) 929-5437
Contact: Rebekah M. Cowing
E-mail: kidsfest@facets.org
Web site: www.facets.org

Dates: Oct. 9–31
Deadline: May 30

Focus on nonviolent, humanistic films and videos that celebrate global culture. Competitive.

Iowa Independent Film and Video Fest

c/o Christopher Martin, Electronic Media Division
University of Northern Iowa
Cedar Falls, Iowa 50614-0139 USA
Phone: (1-319) 273-2788
Fax: (1-319) 273-7356
Contact: Christopher Martin
E-mail: martinc@uni.edu
Web site: www.uni.edu/martin/iifv.html
Dates: Oct. 10–11
Deadline: Sept. 5

Competitive.

International Filmfestival Mannheim-Heidelberg (46th)

Collini-Center, Galerie
68161 Mannheim, Germany
Phone: (49-621) 102-943
Fax: (49-621) 152-316
Contact: Michael Koetz
E-mail: ifmh@mannheim-filmfestival.com
Web site: www.mannheim-filmfestival.com
Dates: Oct. 10–18
Deadline: July 1

Aims to discover young talented independent filmmakers from all over the world. Competitive. FIAPF recognized.

Pusan International Film Festival (2nd)

Yachting Center, Room 208
#1393, Woo 1-dong
Haeundae-ku, Pusan
612-021 Korea
Phone: (82-51) 747-3010/11

Fax: (82-51) 747-3012
Contact: Kim Ji-Seok
E-mail: piffoo@chollian.dacom.co.kr
Web site: www.piff.or.kr
Dates: Oct. 10–18
Deadline: July 16

Presents Korean, Asian and international cinema including retrospectives, special events and seminars.

Raindance Film Showcase (5th)

81 Berwick St.
London, W1V 3PF, U.K.
Phone: (44-171) 287-3833
Fax: (44-171) 439-2243
Contact: Elliot Grove
E-mail: indiefilm@easynet.co.uk
Dates: Oct. 10–18
Deadline: Sept. 1

Presents independent films and videos. Competitive.

Athens Film Fest

P.O. Box 1631 Athens, Georgia
30603 USA
Phone: (1-706) 613-7669
Fax: (1-706) 613-0959
Contact: Juanita M. Giles
E-Mail: gafilm@negia.net
Dates: Oct. 11–18
Deadline: Aug. 15

Competitive.

Pordenone Silent Film Festival (16th)

Le Giornate del Cinema Muto
c/o La Cineteco del Friuli
Vio Osoppo, 26
33013 Gemona (UD), Italy
Phone: (39-432) 980-458
Fax: (39-432) 970-542
Contact: David Robinson
E-mail: codelli@interware.it
Web site: 194.184.27.63/gcm/
home.html
Dates: Oct. 11–18
Deadline: July 20

Showcase for silent cinema. Noncompetitive.

Cinekid (11th)

Engel & Engel
Weteringschans 249
1017 XJ Amsterdam, Netherlands
Phone: (20) 624-7110
Fax: (20) 620-9965
Contact: Dorien van de Pas
Dates: Oct. 11–19
Deadline: June 30

International film and television event for children and young adults. Competitive.

Cork International Film Festival (42nd)

Hatfield House, Tobin Street
Cork, Republic of Ireland
Phone: (353-21) 271-711
Fax: (353-21) 275-945
Contact: Michael Hannigan
E-mail: ciff@indigo.ie
Web site: www.corkfilmfest.org/ciff/
Dates: Oct. 12–19
Deadline: July 11

Shows everything from features to shorts, including retrospectives, master classes and seminars. Competitive for shorts.

Hot Springs Documentary Film Festival (6th)

817 Central Ave., Malco Theater
Hot Springs, AR 71901
Phone: (501) 321-4747
Fax: (501) 321-0211
Contact: Patricia Dooley
E-mail: hsdff@hotspringsar.com
Web site: www.hotspringsar.com/hsdff/
Dates: Oct. 12–19
Deadline: May 31

Dedicated to advancing the documentary genre as a meaningful art form, plus new and classic award-winning foreign films. Noncompetitive. FIAPF recognized.

London Premiere Screenings (1st)

c/o 23-24 George St.
Richmond, Surrey, TW9 1HY, U.K.
Phone: (44-181) 948-5522
Fax: (44-181) 332-0495
Contact: Tim Etchells
Dates: Oct. 13–17

U.K. distributors screen films to buyers.

Sheffield International Documentary Festival (4th)

The Workstation
15 Paternoster Row
Sheffield, S1 2BX, U.K.
Phone: (44-114) 276-5141
Fax: (44-114) 272-1849
Contact: Brent Woods
E-mail: shefdoc@fdgroup.co.uk
Web site: www.fdgroup.co.uk/neo/sidf/
Dates: Oct. 13–19
Deadline: June 13

Film and television festival dedicated to documentary films. Noncompetitive.

Hollywood Film Festival (1st)

433 N. Camden Dr., Ste. 600
Beverly Hills, CA 90210
Phone: (310) 288-1882
Fax: (310) 475-0193
Contact: Carlos de Abreu
Web site: www.hollywoodfilmfestival.com
Dates: Oct. 14–19
Deadline: Aug. 30

Film and new-media festival featuring awards for features, shorts, animation, documentaries, CD-ROM, online services and computer games.

Hamptons International Film Festival (5th)

3 Newtown Mews
East Hampton, NY 11937
Phone: (516) 324-4600
Fax: (516) 324-5116
Contact: Bruce Feinberg
E-mail: hiff@peconic.net
Web site: www.peconic.net
Dates: Oct. 15–19
Deadline: Aug. 8

Showing American independents, international documentaries, shorts and restored/preserved films. Competitive.

The Hamptons International Film Festival is still very much one of the new kids on the American film-fest block and continues to live under the long shadow of the powerhouse Sundance festival. But given the explosion of U.S. independent product, there is still no shortage of independent producers keen to have their films unspool at the Hamptons event: the festival received seven hundred submissions in 1997.

The key section in the Hamptons is the Golden Starfish competition, which features ten American independent films vying for the Golden Starfish and other awards. This is the part of the programming most watched by acquisitions executives. Over the past few years, the competition has yielded a couple of noteworthy indie titles, including Daniel J. Harris's edgy *The Bible and Gun Club* in 1996 and Darren Stein's inspirational *Sparkler* in 1997.

But the Hamptons continues to

have trouble drawing top-level execs to the event, and the 1997 edition was dogged by criticism that there simply weren't enough big-time industryites on hand for the fest. Part of the problem may simply be timing: the small festival kicks off almost immediately after the New York Film Festival and comes on the heels of the busy fall fest season that includes Montreal, Toronto and Venice. The other problem that has plagued the Hamptons is the seemingly endless series of changes in the upper levels of the event's executive ranks.

One of the draws of the Hamptons is unquestionably the location. It takes place in the picturesque Long Island resort town of East Hampton, and a large part of the cachet of the festival comes from the pleasant, upscale surroundings and the mystique of an area that is known as a summer playground for Hollywood stars and bigwigs. It is always an agreeable event for the journalists and film biz folks who make the trek since the scaled-down, laid-back approach leaves room for lots of interaction with visiting filmmakers and producers, providing a welcome contrast to the hectic pace of the bigger, more established festivals.

The festival also features a Contemporary International Cinema section, an international documentary competition, and a short-film competition. There is usually an archival film category and, in 1997, this section included a special screening of a restored print of Norman Jewison's *In the Heat of the Night*. The spotlight country in 1997 was Spain, which was showcased in a six-pic sidebar titled "Viva Espana," and the fest also paid tribute to three international directors in 1997, French documentary director Nicholas Philibert, Spain's Julio Medem and Argentina's Alejandro Agresti.

—Brendan Kelly

British Film Festival

8 Passage Digard
F-50100 Cherbourg, France
Phone: (33-33) 93 38 94
Fax: (33-33) 01 20 78
Contact: Yolande Forafo
Dates: Oct. 15–21
Deadline: July 18

Showcases new British features and shorts as well as classics and lesser-known films.Competitive.

Valencia Film Festival(18th)

Fundacion Municipal de Cine
Plaza del Arzobispo, 2 Bajo
46003 Valencia, Spain
Phone: (34-6) 392-1506
Fax: (34-6) 391-5156
Contact: Luis Fernandez
Dates: Oct. 15–23
Deadline: June 20

Aims to encourage a greater understanding between people and cultures, especially in the Mediterranean area. Competitive.

Neighbors — Haifa International Film Festival (13th)

142 Hanassi Ave.
Haifa 34633, Israel
Phone: (972-4) 838-3424
Fax: (972-4) 838-4327
Contact: Pnina Blayer
Dates: Oct. 16–21
Deadline July 30

Featuring Mediterranean and Israeli cinema, international panorama, shorts and documentaries. Competitive for Mediterranean features.

San Juan Cinemafest (9th)

P.O. Box 9020079
San Juan, 00902 Puerto Rico
Phone: (809-787) 721-6125
Fax: (809-787) 724-4187
Contact: José Artemio Torres
Dates: Oct. 16–26
Deadline: Aug. 31

Showcase for both regional and world cinema including features, shorts, videos, documentaries and animation. Competitive. FIAPF recognized.

Leeds International Film Festival (11th)

The Town Hall, The Headrow
Leeds, LS1 3AD, West Yorkshire, U.K.
Phone: (44-113) 247-8389
Fax: (44-113) 247-8397
Contact: Liz Rymer
Dates: Oct. 16–31
Deadline: Aug. 1

Thematic, issue-based program including premieres, previews and seminars. Noncompetitive.

Viennale (Vienna International Film Festival) (35th)

Stiftgasse 6
1070 Wien, Austria
Phone: (43-1) 526-5947
Fax: (43-1) 523-4172
Contact: Hans Hurch
E-mail: office@viennale.or.at.
Web site: www.viennale.or.at.
Dates: Oct. 17–29
Deadline: mid-August

Features, documentaries, shorts and director tributes. Noncompetitive. FIAPF recognized.

Although the Vienna International Film Festival launches relatively few world premieres, the twelve-day fest shines on both the human and artistic planes. Local audiences are assiduous and enthusiastic (93 out of 244 screenings sold out in 1997). A more competent and cheerful press office or ticket-selling staff would be hard to come by in all of Western Europe.

During the actual event, the fest is headquartered in the imposing Vienna Hilton. Films unspool at five cinemas, including the exquisite wood-paneled Metro near the Stefansdom cathedral and the Urania, a freestanding theater appended to a vintage observatory. An able pool of multilingual moderators steers Q & A sessions with actors and directors. Foreign vistors will find they can get by easily in English.

Vienna, with its abundance of opera, concerts, theater and world-class museums, does not lack high-caliber cultural distractions, and that's been part of a problem the Viennale has done its bit to remedy. Until recently, movies were second-class citizens, right down to the realm of cultural criticism.

Now, thanks to the younger batch of scribes, local audiences seem genuinely excited about cinema, particularly the offerings at the Viennale. Documentaries, however lengthy or obscure, draw loyal crowds. Ticket sales are impressive, with interested viewers showing up for "difficult" fare at all hours. The 1997 edition boasted 70 percent capacity for the five-film tribute to Albert Brooks in his morosely funny—and unsubtitled—English-language glory.

The Viennale is also devoted to international cinema's heritage. In 1997 a Rossellini retrospective at the Austrian Film Museum spanned the entire month of October, and the fest offered a two-day orgy of pix featuring recently deceased legends Bob Mitchum and Jimmy Stewart.

There's something endearing about a fest that cheerfully discloses the ratio of tickets purchased (86.4 percent) to comps (13.6 per-cent). Audience satisfaction is tracked with survey cards at every screening (average score: 1.9 on a scale of 1 to 5, with "1" the best). The main program offers an average of 130 features from over 25 countries. The Viennale also publishes an exhaustive catalogue (250 pages, bilingual German/English) complete with critical essays as well as attractively illustrated guides to each year's major thematic retrospective.

—*Lisa Nesselson*

São Paulo International Film Festival (21st)

Al. Lorena 937, CJ. 303
01424-001 São Paulo, Brazil
Phone: (55-11) 883-5137
Fax: (55-11) 853-7936
Contact: Leon Cakoff
E-mail: info@mostra.org.
Web site: www.mostra.org.
Dates: Oct. 17–31
Deadline: Sept. 1

Introducing new international film-makers and films. Competitive. FIAPF recognized.

In 1977, when Brazil was enduring its military dictatorship and many films could not be shown in the country, Leon Cakoff, a young film critic working for the São Paulo Museum of Art (MASP), created an international film series to celebrate the thirtieth anniversary of the institution.

Pictures like *Lucio Flavio, Passaqeiro da Agonia*, by Hector Babenco, earned popular acclaim at the event and encouraged a second edition of the showcase, or "Mostra," for the following year.

Against all odds, Cuban films were brought to São Paulo for the fest. The Brazilian government had determined that no official contact could be established with Cuba, but still, *La Ultima Cena*, by Tomas Gutierrez Alea, received the public's award. The event was already finding its vocation: to focus on maverick auteurs and little-explored national cinemas. Among directors introduced here were Pal Gabor, Dusan Makavejev, Emir Kusturica and Ylmar Guney, who was granted a release from jail in order to attend the São Paulo fest but instead went to Switzerland to edit the Cannes Palm d'Or winner *Yol*. In 1984, the São Paulo fest disassociated from MASP and became independent. The name was slightly changed to the São Paulo International Film Festival, but the structure remained the same: noncompetitive and devoted to fostering the interest of local distributors and exhibitors in independent filmmaking. The public award was joined by a critics' award. In 1989, the São Paulo fest was recognized by FIAPF as an official "noncompetitive festival."

The São Paulo fest now employs nearly twenty commercial screens and has evolved into a business, spinning off its own distribution company to release some of the gems that the event brings in from other countries. The fest partners with a local newspaper to distribute various video titles, from Wenders to Makhmalbaf to Kubrick to Godard.

There are no parties, and little glamour, at the São Paulo International Film Festival, except for the occasional overcrowded interviews with visiting directors such as Jim Jarmusch, Hal Hartley and Mika Kauresmaki. Yet the fest has still witnessed considerable growth, screening around 150 films and, in 1997, drawing almost 200,000 spectators.

—Nelson Hoineff

Molodist International Film Festival

252033, 6, Saksagansky St.
Kiev, Ukraine
Phone/fax: (380-44) 227-4557
Contact: Andrei Khalpakhtchi
Dates: Oct. 18–26
Deadline: Aug. 1

Showcase for student films as well as shorts, documentaries, animation and feature films. Competitive. FIAPF recognized.

Mifed (64th)

Fiera Milano
Largo Domodossola, 1
20145 Milan, Italy
Phone: (39-2) 4801-2912
Fax: (39-2) 4997-7020
Contact: Elena Lloyd
E-mail: mifed@fmd.it
Web site: www.fmd.it/mifed/
Dates: Oct. 19–24
Deadline: Aug. 18

International film and TV market.

ShowEast

244 W. 49th St., Ste. 200
New York, NY 10019
Phone: (212) 246-6460
Fax: (212) 265-6428
Contact: Jimmy Sunshine
Dates: Oct. 21–23

A convention for cinema owners, distributors and equipment/concession manufacturers and dealers.

Uppsala International Short Film Festival (16th)

St. Olofsgatan 33b
751 47 Uppsala, Box 1746, Sweden
Phone: (46-18) 120-025
Fax: (46-18) 121-350
E-mail: uppsala@shortfilmfestival.com
Web site: www.shortfilmfestival.com
Contact: Louise Brown
Dates: Oct. 21–26
Deadline: Aug. 10

International and local shorts, with animation, documentary and children's films. Competitive. FIAPF recognized.

International Hof Filmdays (31st)

Heinz Badewitz
Lothstr. 28
80335 Munich, Germany
Phone: (49-89) 129-7422, 3079-6870
Fax: (49-89) 123-6868

Contact: Heinz Badewitz
Web site: www.media-online.de/HoferFilmtage
Dates: Oct. 22–26
Deadline: Sept. 15

Screening 50 international features and documentaries. Noncompetitive.

Denver International Film Festival (20th)

1430 Larimer Square, #201
Denver, CO 80202
Phone: (303) 595-3456
Fax: (303) 595-0956
Contact: Ron Henderson
E-mail: dfs@denverfilm.org
Web site: www.denverfilm.org/AFF.html
Dates: Oct. 23–30
Deadline: mid-July

New international releases, independents, documentaries, animation, experimental, children's programs. Noncompetitive.

AFI Los Angeles International Film Festival (11th)

2021 N. Western Ave.
Los Angeles, CA 90027
Phone: (213) 856-7707
Fax: (213) 462-4049
Contact: Jon Fitzgerald
E-mail: afifest@afionline.org
Web site: www.afionline.org
Dates: Oct. 23–Nov. 1
Deadline: Aug. 29

Showcase for independent international and domestic filmmakers, as well as tributes and special events. Competitive sections. FIAPF recognized.

Short Attention Span Film and Video Festival and Market

P.O. Box 460316
San Francisco, CA 94146 USA
Phone: (1-415) 576-9335
Contact: Sarah Anderson
E-mail: HYPERLINK mailto:
sasfvf@aol.com sasfvf@aol.com

Dates: Oct. 24–25
Deadline: Aug. 15

An open showcase for short shorts. Competitive.

Valladolid International Film Festival (42nd)

P.O. Box 646
47001 Valladolid, Spain
Phone: (34-83) 305-700/77/88
Fax: (34-83) 309-835
Contact: Fernando Lara
E-mail: festvalladolid@seminci.com
Web site: www.seminci.com/
Dates: Oct. 24–Nov. 1
Deadline: June 30

Shows features, shorts and documentaries, with sidebars on directors, film schools and focus on a country. Competitive.

Founded in 1956 as the "Week of Religious Cinema" at a time when General Franco was making attempts to open up Spain to the world—and particularly to American money—the Valladolid International Film Festival ("Seminci") has a home reputation as the "festival of festivals."

Though it would take second place to San Sebastian on most Spanish festival rankings, Seminci, as the festival is referred to locally, has carved out a prestigious cultural niche of its own. By cleverly finding loopholes in the system during the declining years of the Franco dictatorship—later, between 1973 and 1984 it was known, with supreme

ambiguity, as the "Week of Religious Cinema and Human Values"— Valladolid was able to get official approval to screen pictures that would otherwise have been stopped at customs on ideological grounds: works by Rossellini, Wajda, Truffaut, Fellini and Buñuel himself, after nearly twenty years of isolation, found their first Spanish outlet here.

A film's reception at Valladolid thus became a passport onto the arts circuit right up until Franco's death in 1975, with the Spanish premiere of Kubrick's *A Clockwork Orange* there that year acquiring legendary status as a symbol of the changing times. Ballasted by a reputation for artistic daring and innovation under tough ideological conditions, the festival still casts a keen eye on new cinematic tendencies that come its way, making it perhaps more attractive to critics and buffs than to the general public.

With 1984 came new management, but the recipe remains the same under current director Fernando Lara, with the emphasis firmly on the art house and away from the mainstream: Valladolid seems not to care that the visitors are rarely superstars. Indeed it cannot afford to care, with an annual budget of only just over $1 million, with funding coming from the city and county councils Spanish Culture Ministry and private sponsorship.

Up to twenty features go to make up the official section, and the winner receives—apart from the Golden Spike—$20,000 for its distributor, thereby guaranteeing Spanish distribution. Sidebars are given over to documentaries (the "Time of History" section) and recent world cinema: in 1996 the festival was visited for the first time by a Fipresci international jury. Retrospectives and roundups of neglected moviemakers also feature. Over nine days at the end of October, the festival shows around two hundred films in its nine cinemas, regularly attracting 80,000-plus cinephiles.

Located off the tourist trail two hours northwest of Madrid, Valladolid is an austere, formal town, and the October temperatures can likewise be austere. The festival is still mainly a homely Spanish affair, though anyone who is anyone within the Spanish industry will find time to drop by. Press coverage in Spain is consequently extensive, with the closing ceremony going out live on Spanish TV for the first time in 1996.

As a result of lengthy experience, organization is efficient and friendly, with an increasing number of foreign press in attendance. As Spanish product rises in quantity and quality, it is likely that the Valladolid's star will rise accordingly.
—*Jonathan Holland*

Kinofilm — Manchester International Short Film and Video Festival (3rd)

Kinofilm, 48 Princess St.
Manchester, M1 6HR, U.K.
Phone: (44-161) 288-2494
Fax: (44-161) 237-3423
Contact: John Wojowski
Dates: Oct. 24–Nov. 2
Deadline: Aug. 8

Showcase for innovative international shorts. Animation, U.S. underground, Eastern European, lesbian and gay sidebars. Noncompetitive.

Montpellier Festival of Mediterranean Cinema (19th)

6 rue de la Vieille-Aiguillerie
34000 Montpellier, France
Phone: (33-4) 6766-3636
Fax: (33-4) 6766-3637
Contact: Pierre Pitiot
Dates: Oct. 24–Nov. 2
Deadline: Aug. 31

Annual event focusing on Mediterranean films, with sections for features and shorts and development grants. Competitive.

International Short Film Festival (6th)

Osterbergstr. 9, D-72074
Tübingen, Germany
Phone: (49-7071) 56960
Fax: (49-7071) 569696
Contact: Dieter Betz
E-mail: filmtage.tubingen@t-online.de

Web site: www.cityinfonetz.de/
filmtage/oo.htm/
Dates: Oct. 25–26
Deadline: Sept. 8

Short films.

Abitibi-Temiscamingue International Film Festival (16th)

215, avenue Mercier
Rouyn-Noranda, J9X 5W8, Quebec,
Canada
Phone: (819) 762-6212
Fax: (819) 762-6762
Contact: Jacques Matte
E-mail: fciat@sympatico.ca
Web site: www.telebec.qc.ca/fciat
Dates: Oct. 25–30
Deadline: Sept. 1

Showcase for about 100 features and shorts, with some 20 premieres. Noncompetitive.

Premio Saint-Vincent per il Cinema Italiano (45th)

Via della Lungara 3
00165 Rome, Italy
Phone: (39-6) 6875-331
Fax: (39-6) 6875-338
Contact: Felice Laudadio
Dates: Oct. 25–Nov. 1
Deadline: Oct. 10

Italian cinema showcase. Competitive.

Barcelona International Exhibition of Gay and Lesbian Films (3rd)

Casal Lambda
Ample 5 baixos
08002 Barcelona, Spain
Phone: (34-3) 412-7272
Fax: (34-3) 412-7476
Contact: Xavier Daniel
Dates: Oct. 27–Nov. 7
Deadline: Aug. 30

Forum for homosexual filmmakers to present their work and discuss issues. Competitive.

International Leipzig Festival of Documentary & Animated Films (40th)

Dokfestival Leipzig, Box 940
04009 Leipzig, Germany
Phone: (49-341) 980-3921
Fax: (49-341) 980-6141
Contact: Fred Gehler
Web site: www.mdr.de/dokfestival
Dates: Oct. 28–Nov. 2
Deadline: Aug.7

International documentary and animated films. Noncompetitive.

Geneva Film Festival (10th)

C.P. 5615, 35 rue des bains
CH-1211 Geneva 11, Switzerland
Phone: (41-22) 809-9450
Fax: (41-22) 809-9444
Contact: Gerald Morin
Dates: Oct. 28–Nov. 3
Deadline: Aug. 30

Discovers and promotes new European actors and actresses. Competitive. FIAPF recognized.

Fort Lauderdale International Film Festival (12th)

2625 E. Sunrise Blvd.
Fort Lauderdale, FL 33304
Phone: (954) 563-0500
Fax: (954) 564-1206
Contact: Gregory von Hausch
E-mail: Brofilm@aol.com
Web site: www.ftlavdfilmfest.com
Dates: Oct. 29–Nov. 16
Deadline: Sept. 1

International event showcasing more than 100 features, documentaries and shorts, with galas and educational seminars. Competitive.

Virginia Festival of American Films (10th)

P.O. Box 3697
Charlottesville, VA 22903
Phone: (804) 982-5277
Fax: (804) 924-1447

Contact: Richard Herskowitz
E-mail: filmfest@virginia.edu
Web site: www.virginia.edu/-vafilm
Dates: Oct. 30–Nov. 2
Deadline: July 1

Themed fest (1998 the subject: imprisonment/ freedom), showing films, videos and CD-ROMs of all genres and lengths. Noncompetitive.

Native American Film and Video Festival

Film and Video Center
National Museum of the American Indian
George Gustav Heye Center
One Bowling Green
New York, NY 10004 USA
Phone: (1-212) 825-6894
Fax: (1-212) 825-8180
Contact: Elisabeth Weatherford
Dates: Oct. 30–Nov. 6
Deadline: May 15

Showcases the best new independent, documentary and animated works produced by and about Native Americans and Native Hawaiians.

San Luis Obispo International Film Festival (5th)

P.O. Box 1449
San Luis Obispo, CA 93406
Phone: (805) 546-3456
Fax: (805) 781-6799
Contact: Mary A. Harris
Dates: Oct. 30–Nov. 9
Deadline: Aug. 1

Shows classics and restored films, shorts, documentaries, animation and international features. Competitive for documentaries.

St. Louis Film Festival (6th)

560 Trinity Ave.
St. Louis, MO 63119
Phone: (314) 726-6779
Fax: (314) 726-5076
Contact: Barbara Smythe-Jones
E-mail: slff.mo@aol.com

Dates: Oct. 30–Nov. 11
Deadline: Aug. 15

Presenting European cinema. Competitive.

Speelfilmfestival

Patijntjesstraat 150
Ghent, Belgium B-9000
Phone: (32-0) 9 245 10 71
Fax: (32-0) 9 245 10 71
Contact: Wolfgang Freier
E-mail: pin00974@ping.be
Web site: www.ping.be/film/dedrake.html
Dates: Oct. 31–Nov. 2
Deadline: Sept. 15

Dakino International Film Festival

Calea Victoriei 16-20, Sect. 1
Bucuresti, Romaniq
Phone & Fax: (+40-1) 211-95-44, 211-69-48, 211-07-82
Dates: October
Deadline: July 30

Short films: fiction, documentary, animation

Feminale

Hansaring 86 D-50670 Cologne, Germany
Phone: (49-221) 130 0225
Fax: (49-221) 130 028/417 568
Contact: Katja Mildenberger
Dates: Oct.
Deadline: June 1

Yamagata International Documentary Film Festival

Tokyo Office, Kitagawa Building, 4th Floor
6-24 Kagurazaka, Shinjuku-ku
Tokyo 162, Japan
Phone: (+81) 33266-9704
Fax: (+81) 33266-9700
Contact: Yano Kazuyuki
E-mail: yidff@bekkoame.or.jp
Dates: Oct.
Deadline: March

NOVEMBER

Peachtree International Film Festival

Metropolitan Film Society
2100 Pleasant Hill Rd. #A-5221
Duluth, Georgia 30136 USA
Phone: (1-770) 729-8487
Fax: (1-770) 263-0652
Contact: Michelle Corren
E-Mail: metro@illcnet.com/metro
Dates: Nov 1–8
Deadline: Sept. 1

WorldFest Charleston (5th)

P.O. Box 838
Charleston, SC 29402
Phone:(713) 965-9955
Fax: (713) 965-9960
Contact: J. Hunter Todd
E-mail: worldfest@aol.com
Web site: www.sims.com/worldfest
Dates: Nov. 1–9
Deadline: Aug.24

Focusing on American independent and foreign features, with a special French panorama. Competitive.

Tokyo International Film Festival (10th)

4F, Landic Ginza Bldg. II
1-6-5 Ginza, Chuo-ku
Tokyo 104, Japan
Phone: (813) 3563-6305
Fax: (813) 3563-6310
Contact: Yasuyoshi Tokuma
Web site: www.tokyo-filmfest.or.jp/
Dates: Nov. 1–10
Deadline: Aug. 12

Showcase for the best young Asian cinema. Competitive. FIAPF recognized.

Japan's top event on the international film circuit, the Tokyo International Film Festival was created in 1985 as a biannual affair. Now an annual event, the festival has grown steadily in terms of prestige, attendance and films screened.

In 1997, the festival captured the world spotlight when James Cameron's *Titanic* made its world premiere amongst the 317 film entries from fifty countries. While the film festival is often used to promote mainstream movies that will play in Japan during the coming year, past winners of the event's international Grand Prix award have gone on to win Academy Awards in the best-foreign-language-picture category.

The start date has been pushed back from September to November in order to get more films that would be in theaters for the end-of-the-year holiday season. The result was extremely successful, as the event drew not only *Titanic* but also the German film *Beyond Silence*, from director Caroline Link, and *Perfect Circle* from the Sarajevo-born director Ademir Kenovic. Both *Silence* and *Circle* took home top honors.

Since its inception, the Tokyo festival has offered awards for young directors. Each year, the festival attracts more attention from an increasing number of filmmakers around the world, and it has now established itself as a gateway to

success for up-and-coming direc-
tors. Some past winners include
Yim Ho, Jacob Cheung and Peter
Gothar.

The International Grand Prix
was first given in 1987 along with
special jury prizes for best director,
actor, actress, screenplay and artistic contribution. Past winners for
best film include John Sayles' *City
of Hope* in 1991, Tian Zhuang-
zhuang's *The Blue Kite* in 1993 and
Jan Sverak's *Kolya* in 1996. Awards
are given in the international competition as well as in the young cinema category. The 10th edition of
the festival saw the introduction of
an Asian film award. Generally, 12
or 13 films compete in each category.

The budget for last year's festival was 600 million yen ($5 mil-
lion), half of which was provided by
national and local governments,
with the rest being picked up by
sponsors. Usually a few major stars
and directors attend the event.
Among the notables at the 1997 Tokyo festival were Cameron, Leo-
nardo DiCaprio, Harrison Ford and
Wolfgang Petersen, the latter pair
on hand for the festival's opening
film, *Air Force One*.

—*Jon Herskovitz*

Southern African International Film and Television Market (2nd)

P.O. Box 3832
Johannesburg, 2000, South Africa
Phone: (27-11) 714-3229
Fax: (27-11) 714-3275
Contact: Dezi Roeich
Dates: Nov. 3–7
Deadline: Oct. 9

*Platform for global filmmakers, pro-
ducers, distributors and programmers
to meet with the South African entertainment industry. Noncompetitive.*

Film Art Fest

Presernova 10
10000 Ljubljana, Slovenia
Phone: (386-61) 176 7150
Fax: (386-61) 22 42 79
Contact: Jelka Stergel
Dates: Nov. 3–16
Deadline: Sept. 15

*The aim is to illustrate progress and
continuity of film as an art form. Participation is by invitation only.*

Film Arts Festival (13th)

346 Ninth St., 2nd floor
San Francisco, CA 94103
Phone: (415) 552-8760
Fax: (415) 552-0882
Contact: Mark Taylor
E-mail: filmarts@best.com
Web site: www.filmarts.org
Dates: Nov. 5–9
Deadline: July 11

*Shows northern California indepen-
dent film and video. Noncompetitive.*

Heartland Film Festival (6th)

613 N.East St.
Indianapolis, IN 46202
Phone: (317) 464-9405
Fax: (317) 635-4201
Contact: Jeffrey L. Sparks
E-mail: hff@pop.iquest.net
Web site: www.heartlandfilmfest.org

Dates: Nov. 5–9
Deadline: July 1

The festival serves to recognize and honor filmmakers whose work explores the human journey by artistically expressing hope and respect for the positive values of life. Competitive.

Israel Film Festival in Los Angeles (14th)

IsraFest Foundation
6404 Wilshire Blvd., #1240
Los Angeles, CA 90048
Phone: (213) 966-4166
Fax: (213) 658-6346
Contact: Meir Fenigstein
E-mail: israfest@earthlink.net
Web site: www.israelfilmfestival.com
Dates: Nov. 5–20
Deadline: Sept. 22

Presenting the best new Israeli films. Noncompetitive.

Cinewomen Festival (17th)

Cinema City
St. Andrews Street
Norwich, NR2 4AD, U.K.
Phone: (44-1603) 456-239
Fax: (44-1603) 767-838
Contact: Jayne Morgan
E-mail: J.H.Morgan@uea.ac.uk
Web site: www.parker-barry.co.uk/cinewomen
Dates: Nov. 6–9
Deadline: June 30

Presenting films by women filmmakers only, with a special focus this year on international independents. Competitive.

Nordic Film Days Luebeck (39th)

Nordische Filmtage Luebeck
D-23539 Luebeck, Germany
Phone: (49-451) 122-4105
Fax: (49-451) 122-4106
Contact: Andrea Kunsemueller
Dates: Nov. 6–9
Deadline: Aug. 8

Showcase for Scandinavian, Baltic and North German cinema including unusual films and retrospectives. Competitive.

Northampton Film Festival (3rd)

351 Pleasant St., #137
Northampton, MA 01060
Phone: (413) 586-3471
Fax: (413) 584-4432
Contact: Howard Polonsky
E-mail: filmfest@nohofilm.org
Web site: www.nohofilm.org
Dates: Nov. 6–9
Deadline: June 30

Independent U.S. films and videos, discussions and workshops, with a Women in Film sidebar. Competitive.

Foyle Film Weekend

2nd Flr., Northern Counties Bldg.
8 Custom House St.
GB-Derry, Northern Ireland UK
Phone: (44-1504) 267 432
Fax: (44-1504) 371 738
E-mail: shona@iscm.ulst.ac.uk
Contact: Shona McCarthy
Dates: Nov. 6–10
Deadline: Oct. (TBC)

Competitive.

Margaret Mead Film and Video Festival (21st)

American Museum of Natural History
79th Street at Central Park West
New York, NY 10024
Phone: (212) 769-5305
Fax: (212) 769 5329
Contact: Elaine S. Charnov
E-mail: meadfest@amnh.org
Web site: www.amnh.org/mead
Dates: Nov. 6–12
Deadline: May 3

U.S.'s largest ethnographic/documentary-film festival, screening features and shorts. Noncompetitive.

London Film Festival (41st)

South Bank, Waterloo
London, SE1 8XT, U.K.
Phone: (44-171) 815-1323/4
Fax: (44-171) 633-0786
Contact: Adrian Wootton
E-mail: jane.ivey.@bfi.org.uk
Dates: Nov. 6–23
Deadline: Aug. 15

International cinema, all gauges and lengths, plus video and documentary. Noncompetitive. FIAPF recognized.

If any one event can be said to have invented the concept of a year-end "festival of festivals," it's London. Conceived during a dinner party hosted by Dilys Powell, respected critic of the *London Sunday Times*, it sprang to life in 1957, under the auspices of the British Film Institute, as a boutique showcase of the best of world cinema—among the 15 titles were films by Wajda, Kazan, Kurosawa, Visconti, Satyajit Ray and Fellini. In 1997, it unspooled some 180 features and clocked up more than one hundred thousand admissions—one of the largest and most popular noncompetitive fests in the world.

Under its various directors— Derek Prouse, Richard Roud, Ken Wlaschin, Derek Malcolm, Sheila Whitaker and (in 1997) Adrian Wootton—the LFF has evolved from an arty, buff event for BFI members into an all-embracing gar-

gantuan fest pitched at a wide spectrum of Londoners rather than just a cultural elite. Until the early '70s, it was still physically possible to see every one of its forty-odd films during the two-and-a-half-week span, but under Wlaschin it started to embrace a wider diversity of cinema that turned it into a giant cookie jar for all tastes.

When Wlaschin returned Stateside, his liberal selection policy was expanded on by Malcolm, chief critic of the left-leaning, egghead daily the *Guardian*, who during his three-year guest directorship (1984– 86) popularized the fest by adding downtown hardtop venues, programming popular Hollywood fare alongside the usual arty stuff, instigating national panoramas, and encouraging both British cinema and developing areas like East Asia. Whitaker, who then took over for a ten-year spell, built further on Malcolm's foundations, growing the event into a massive catch-all festival for the capital.

From Malcolm's tenure on, as commercial sponsorship entered the frame, it was clear that the LFF behemoth was rapidly outgrowing its BFI patronage. There was even (sacrilegious) talk behind closed doors of making the event competitive. Tensions boiled to a head in early 1997 when Whitaker, pink-slipped by the BFI, almost succeeded in starting up a rival competitive event of her own and sandbagging the LFF. The debate she started still resonates, unresolved as of early 1998, along with a parallel debate over whether to link a real market (such as the pre-Mifed screenings) to the event.

Though the LFF remains a cinematic banquet for Londoners, in today's combative, crowded fest calendar, it's become more a catch-up stopover for scouters and buyers than a place to discover major new works. (Even with the recent British renaissance, Edinburgh, three months earlier in August, stole its thunder in 1997.) The fact remains, however, that there's still a hole to be filled by an A-grade competitive Euro-fest in the yawning gap between San Sebastian in late September, and Rotterdam and Berlin in late January-February.

London is far from alone in being a massive, locally popular event that has seen its international prestige gradually weakened by feisty upstarts and budget-driven demands. The headline-making days of Godard walloping his producer on stage at the LFF are gone—

indeed, gone from the fest scene as a whole. But with inventive leadership and less constrictive management, London is still well positioned to have the cosmopolitan festival it deserves.

—*Derek Elley*

Banff Festival of Mountain Films (22nd)

P.O. Box 1020, Ste. 38
Banff, Alberta, ToL oCo, Canada
Phone: (403) 762-6125
Fax: (403) 762-6277
Contact: Bernadette McDonald
E-mail: CMC@BanffCentre.AB.CA
Web site: www.banffcentre.ab.ca/CMC/
Dates: Nov. 7–9
Deadline: Sept. 12

Screening the best international films and videos on mountain subjects. Competitive.

Latino Film Festival of Marin

3100 Kerner Blvd. Ste. G
San Rafael, CA 94901 USA
Phone: (1-415) 459-3530
Fax: (1-415) 456-0560
E-mail: sperel@linex.com
Contact: S. Stalman
Dates: Nov. 7–9
Deadline: July 7

Amiens International Film Festival (17th)

MCA, Place Jontiel
80000 Amiens, France
Phone: (33-3) 2271-3570
Fax: (33-3) 2292-5304
Contact: Jean-Pierre Garcia
Dates: Nov. 7–16
Deadline: Sept. 8

171 ∎

the festivals

Includes tributes and regional panoramas. Competitive for features and shorts.

Northwest Film and Video Festival (24th)

Northwest Film Center
1219 S.W. Park Ave.
Portland, OR 97205
Phone: (503) 221-1156
Fax: (503) 226-4842
Contact: Bill Foster
Web site: www.nwfilm.org/nwfv24
Dates: Nov. 7–16
Deadline: Sept. 22

Showcase of new work produced in Oregon, Washington, British Columbia, Idaho, Montana and Alaska. Competitive.

Stockholm International Film Festival (8th)

P.O. Box 3136
S-103 62 Stockholm, Sweden
Phone: (46-8) 677-5000
Fax: (46-8) 200-590
Contact: Camilla Nasiell
E-mail: info@cinema.se
Web site: www.filmfestivalen.se
Dates: Nov. 7–16
Deadline: Aug. 20

Pointing at new directions in filmmaking, a focus on American independents as well as Swedish films. Competitive. FIAPF-recognized.

Augsburg Children's Film Festival (17th)

Filmburo Augsburg
Schroeckstr. 6
86152 Augsburg, Germany
Phone: (49-821) 153-077
Fax: (49-821) 349-5218
Contact: Annette Eberle
Dates: Nov. 7–17
Deadline: Aug. 12

Showing international children's films plus special programs and a school program. Competitive.

London Program Market

Le Meridien Hotel
Piccadilly
London, W1V 0BH, U.K.
Phone: (44-181) 948-5522
Fax: (44-181) 332-0495
Contact: Tim Etchells
Dates: Nov. 10–12

Exclusive market for buyers and sellers of TV programs.

International Sportfilmfestival (19th)

Via Notarbartolo, 1/G
90141 Palermo, Italy
Phone: (39-91) 611-4968
Fax: (39-91) 625-6256
Contact: Vito Maggio
E-mail: sporfife tin.it
Web site: www.tin.it/sportfilm_festival
Dates: Nov. 10–14
Deadline: July 31

Showcase for features, shorts and videos covering the broad subject of sport. Competitive.

Duisburg Film Week (21st)

Am Konig-Heinrich Platz
47049 Duisburg, Germany
Phone: (49-203) 283-4171, 283-4187
Fax: (49-203) 283-4130
Contact: Werner Ruzicka
Dates: Nov. 10–16
Deadline: Aug. 1

Showcase for documentaries entirely in German. Noncompetitive.

Cinanima (International Animated Film Festival) (21st)

Apartado 743
Espinho Codex 4501, Portugal
Phone: (351-2) 724-611
Fax: (351-2) 726-015
Contact: Antonio Gaio
Web site: www.awn.com/cinanima
Dates: Nov. 11–16
Deadline: Aug. 15

Promoting animated cinema including retrospectives, exhibitions and debates. Competitive.

film+arc.graz (3rd)

Hallerschlossstr. 21
A-8010 Graz, Austria
Phone: (43-316) 356-155
Fax: (43-316) 356-156
Contact: Karin Lebinger
E-mail: artimage@xarch.tu-graz.ac.at
Web site: xarch.tu-graz.ac.at/filmarc/
Dates: Nov. 12–16
Deadline: July 10

Biennial fest showcasing film, video and CD-ROM on all aspects of architecture, urbanity and space. Competitive.

Mediterranean Film Festival (5th)

Osterbergstr. 9
D-72074 Tübingen, Germany
Phone: (49-7071) 56960
Fax: (49-7071) 569696
Contact: Dieter Betz
E-mail: filmtage.tubingen@t-online.de
Web site: www.cityinfonetz.de/
filmtage/oo.htm/
Dates: Nov. 12–16
Deadline: Sept. 30

Recent features and shorts from Mediterranean and bordering countries. Noncompetitive.

Okomedia (14th)

Habsburgerstr. 9a
D-79104 Freiburg, Germany
Phone: (49-761) 52024
Fax: (49-761) 555724
Contact: Heidi Knott
E-mail: oekomedia@gaia.de
Dates: Nov. 12–16
Deadline: Aug. 18

International ecological film and TV festival. Competitive.

Verzaubert (International Gay and Lesbian Filmfest) (7th)

Rosebud Entertainment
Wittelsbacherstr. 26
10707 Berlin, Germany
Phone: (49-30) 861-4532
Fax: (49-30) 861-4539
Contact: Schorsch Mueller, Rainer Stefan
E-mail: rosebud_entertainment@t-online.de
Web site: home.t-online.de/home/
rosebud_entertainment
Dates: Nov. 12–Dec. 3
Deadline: Sept. 1

Traveling showcase (Munich, Stuttgart, Frankfurt, Cologne, Berlin) for lesbian and gay films. Noncompetitive.

Kinofest Luenen (8th)

Huelchrather Str. 6
50670 Cologne, Germany
Phone: (49-221) 729-596
Fax: (49-221) 728-611
Contact: Elfriede Schmitt, Ute Teigler
Dates: Nov. 13–16
Deadline: Aug. 30

Charting new developments in German features and short films. Competitive.

Mar del Plata International Film Festival (13th)

Lima 319 piso 3
1075 Buenos Aires, Argentina
Phone: (54-1) 383-2622
Fax: (54-1) 383-9091
Contact: Julio Maharbiz
Dates: Nov. 13–22
Deadline: Sept. 30

Competitive. FIAPF recognized.

Resurrected in 1996 after a quarter-century absence, the Mar del Plata Film Festival has the potential of becoming Latin America's most important film event—a rank to which there currently is no outstanding claimant. Mar del Plata has a $5-million annual budget, huge by Latino standards. It enjoys the close support of Argentine President Carlos Menem and the country's top media group, as well as the national film institute. And it is one of the few Latino fests that is FIAPF accredited. But what it may still lack is strong organization.

In the old days, the seaside resort of Mar del Plata—a short flight from Buenos Aires—was home to a film festival of international renown. Visitors to the 1970 edition, the last before the Argentine government shut it down, recall grand casinos and nightclubs, huge pot-fueled parties, and Pier Paolo Pasolini, Maria Callas and Lee Strasberg wandering in the streets.

Julio Maharbiz, the head of the National Institute of Cinematography and the Audiovisual Arts (IN-CAA) and a close friend of Menem, made it a personal mission to revive the fest in 1996. Stars and other high-profile guests were invited from Europe and the U.S., and around 150 films were slated. But despite its huge budget and lengthy preparation, the fest was a near-disaster. Several stand-in jurors had to be found at the eleventh hour, after late cancellations. The local guest of honor, ninety-year-old actress Libertad Limarque, was left stranded in her hotel room the night of the opening ceremony. Foreign honoree Gabriel Figueroa, himself nearing ninety, was stood up at the airport. Special invitees including Raquel Welch and Gina Lollobrigida left early, fed up—like much of the public—with the frequent screening delays and projection equipment failures.

The 1997 edition of the fest fared much better. Sophia Loren, Alain Delon and Maria Grazia Cuccinotta numbered among the jurors and visiting Euro celebs. Jack Valenti of the MPAA came down for a well-attended press conference and party, and Buena Vista International, whose Latino theatrical topper Diego Lerner has been pushing BVI involvement in local productions, also held a big bash.

Both the opening and closing ceremonies were televised by one of the event's chief sponsors, broadcaster Artear, part of the huge Clarin media conglomerate and an active investor in features. And fittingly, Sally Potter's Argentina-U.K. co-production *The Tango*

Lesson, picked up the cash-heavy top prize, the Golden Ombu, named for Argentina's national tree.

The fest was widely held to be a success, with a high level of public attendance. But some say that Mar del Plata, now a much bigger town than in 1970, has lost most of its old charm—which may explain the recent rumors that the event may relocate to the Andean city of Mendoza. Further, the event was again criticized for lack of coordination of press facilities and visiting artists. Although Maharbiz may be over-criticized by local film folk, who distrust him as an industry outsider, he certainly deserves credit for recreating the fest and reviving some of the old, star-led razzamatazz.

—Andrew Paxman

Hawaii International Film Festival (17th)

700 Bishop St., #400
Honolulu, HI 96818
Phone: (808) 528-3456
Fax: (808) 528-1410
Contact: Christian Gaines
E-mail: hiffinfo@hiff.org
Web site: www.hiff.org
Dates: Nov. 14–20
Deadline: July 15

Showing films and videos from or about Asia, the Pacific Rim and North America. Competitive.

Festival de Cine de Alcala de Henares (27th)

Plaza del Empecinado, 1
28001 Henares, Madrid, Spain
Phone: (34-1) 881-3934
Fax: (34-1) 881-3906
Contact: Pedro Medina
Dates: Nov. 14–21
Deadline: Sept. 30

Showcase for Spanish shorts and feature films. Competitive.

Festival International Cinema Giovani (15th)

Via Monte di Pieta 1
10121 Torino, Italy
Phone: (39-11) 562-3309
Fax: (39-11) 562-9796
Contact: Alberto Barbera
E-mail: ficg@webcom.com
Web site: www.webcom.com/ficg
Dates: Nov. 14–22
Deadline: Sept. 30

Showcase for new international talent, with shorts, features and Italian independents. Competitive. FIAPF recognized.

Oslo International Film Festival (7th)

Ebbellsgate 1, N-0183
Oslo, Norway
Phone: (47-22) 20-07-66
Fax: (47-22) 20-18-03
Contact: Tommy Lordahl
E-mail: filmfestival@login.eunet.no
Web site: wit.no/filmfestival
Dates: Nov. 14–23
Deadline: Sept. 15

Features, documentaries, shorts, U.S. independents and Made in Norway sections. Noncompetitive.

Welsh International Film Festival (9th)

6G Parc Gwyddoniaeth, Cefn Llan
Aberystwyth, Ceredigion
SY23 3AH, Wales, U.K.

Phone: (44-1970) 617-995
Fax: (44-1970) 617-942
Contact: Grant Vidgen
E-mail: wff995@aber.ac.uk
Web site: www.aber.ac.uk/~wff995/
8ffre97.htm
Dates: Nov. 14–23
Deadline: Sept. 1

*Celebrating Welsh filmmaking in an
international context. Noncompetitive.*

**Encontros International de Cinema
Documental Amascultra (8th)**

Centro Cultural da Malposta
Rua Angola—Olival Basto
2675 Olival Basto, Portugal
Phone: (351-1) 938-8407
Fax: (351-1) 938-9347
Contact: Manuel Costa e Silva
Dates: Nov. 15-23
Deadline: Sept. 30

*Portugal's only film festival entirely
devoted to documentaries. Competitive.*

**Oulu International Children's Film
Festival (16th)**

Torikatu 8
90100 Oulu, Finland
Phone: (358-8) 881-1293
Fax: (358-8) 881-1290
Contact: Pentti Kejonen
E-mail: raimo.kinisjarvi@oufilmcenter
.inet.fi
Dates: Nov. 17-23
Deadline: Oct. 13

*Festival of feature-length children's
films, with retrospectives. Competitive.*

Action and Adventure Film Fest

1104 Kortrijkesteenweg, Ghent
B-9051, Belgium
Phone: (32-9) 221-8946
Fax: (32-9) 221-9074
Contact: Jacques Dubrulle

Dates: Nov. 19-25
Deadline: Sept. 15

*This festival focuses on the craft of
the filmmaker.*

**Birmingham International Film and
TV Festival (13th)**

9 Margaret St.
Birmingham, B3 3BS, U.K.
Phone: (44-121) 212-0777
Fax: (44-121) 212-0666
Contact: Sarah McKenzie
Dates: Nov. 19-30
Deadline: by invitation only

*Gala premieres; Cutting Edge; Music
on the Screen; film and TV with a
new thematic and stylistic vision.
Noncompetitive.*

Festival of French Cinema

Unifrance, 4 Villa Bosquet
F-75007 Paris, France
Phone: (33-1) 47 53 95 80/
47 53 27 48
Fax: (33-1) 47 05 96 55
Contact: Stephan Melchiori
Dates: Nov. 20-23
Deadline: Early Oct.

**Vevey International Comedy Film
Festival (17th)**

La Grenette, CP 421
CH-1800 Vevey, Switzerland
Phone: (41-21) 922-2027
Fax: (41-21) 922-2024
Contact: Yves Moser
Dates: Nov. 20-23
Deadline: Sept. 1

*Showing comedy films (long and
short) including retrospectives, homages and tributes, open-air cinema
and video workshops. Competitive.
FIAPF recognized.*

International Festival of Authorial Film

Jugoslavija Film, Makedonska 22/VI
11000 Beograd, Yugoslavia
Phone: (381-11) 324-8554
Fax: (381-11) 324-8659
Contact: Vojislav Vucinoric
Dates: Nov. 20–27
Deadline: Oct. 15

Competitive.

French Film Fest

French Institute
13 Randolph Crescent
GB-Edinburgh, EH3 8TX, UK
Phone: (44-131) 243-3601/225-5366
Fax: (44-131) 220-2443
Contact: Richard Mowe
Dates: Nov. 20–29
Deadline: Sept. 30

Competitive.

Gijon International Film Festival for Young People (35th)

Paseo de Begona, 24-entlo.
P.O. Box 76
Gijon, Asturias, Spain
Phone: (34-8) 534-3739
Fax: (34-8) 535-4152
Contact: Jose Luis Cienfuegos
E-mail: festcine@airastur.es
Web site: www.airastur.es/
gijonfilmfestival
Dates: Nov. 21-28
Deadline: Sept. 30

Presenting worldwide productions made by and for young people and those experimenting innovative film-making. Competitive. FIAPF recognized.

Osaka European Film Festival (4th)

9-5-404, 2-chome
Doshin, Kita-ku
530 Osaka, Japan
Phone: (81-6) 882-6212
Fax: (81-6) 882-6212

Contact: Patrice Boiteau
Dates: Nov. 21–30
Deadline: July 31

Showcase for the diversity of European cinema including exhibitions. Noncompetitive.

International Thessaloniki Film Festival (38th)

36 Sina St.
10672 Athens, Greece
Phone: (301) 361-0418
Fax: (301) 362-1023
Contact: Michel Demopoulos
E-mail: filmfestival@comulink.gr.
Dates: Nov. 21–30
Deadline: Oct. 4

Promotes international independent film, with retrospectives and special events. Competitive.

The title of the Lon Chaney biopic, *Man of a Thousand Faces*, provides an apt metaphor for the Thessaloniki International Film Festival, held in November in Greece's second-largest city, a gray, charmless, provincial port in the northeastern part of the country. It's an event with a thousand faces: shifts in national priorities, economics and the international film scene have made this four-decade-old event into a chameleonlike creature.

Originally, the festival was purely a domestic affair, a forum for presenting the year's Greek product. Although the event has broadened widely—perhaps too widely, with approximately 140 features in 1997—away from its initial purpose, the national competition has remained the most popular component of the festival with the locals. Luckily, the 1997 crop of 14 features revealed a few gems—a rarity in recent years.

Greek spectators are chauvinistic and ignore non-Greek movies during the event, and the foreign guests at this self-proclaimed international festival (director Michel Demopoulos introduced foreign fare after coming on board in 1992) have virtually no interest in Greek movies. Ironically, now that Greek films are coming once again into their own, the Greek Parliament has just declared the national section of the festival noncompetitive.

If Thessaloniki is to have a raison d'être among the plethora of international festivals, it must find a distinctive identity. A priority should be an emphasis on Greek films for the non-Greek audience. One significant achievement has been the creation of the Balkan Survey. Although the festival administration leaves it as an island without a real home among the three main sections (international competition, national competition, New Horizons), it provides a forum for presenting new works from the region surrounding and affecting Greece—countries like Slovenia, Bulgaria, Macedonia and Turkey.

The international competition is yet another of the first-and-second-feature showcases that have been presented more effectively by festivals like Torino's Cinema Giovani, New York's New Directors/New Films, and in Rotterdam with the Tiger Awards. The entries need not be premieres; many have been around the block more than a few times by the time this festival takes place. Others seem to be slot-fillers. But if the festival genuinely wants to support emerging directors, it should reconsider diluting their impact with the noncompetitive New Horizons (the fest circuit's greatest hits, programmed by Toronto's Dimitri Eipides) and far too many almost slapdash retrospectives (good subjects, like Claude Chabrol and Arturo Ripstein in 1997, but not supported by the public and often criticized for poor print quality). Everything shown in Torino and New Directors/New Films, for example, relates in some fashion to new features.

The city of Thessaloniki had the great fortune to be deemed Cultural Capitol of Europe 1997, which brought an infusion of extra-filmic events and hard cash to this somewhat depressed city, far removed from the sun and charm of the south and the more cosmopolitan ambience of Athens. (Athens itself now has a fledgling film festival, which could prove a threat to Thessaloniki's dominance.) One substantial benefit was the $20-million purchase and renovation of the old, centrally located Olympian complex, which now provides two theaters of 750 and 250 seats respectively—although a number of other cinemas are much farther away.

Greece is an extremely political animal—a fact that may explain the weak quality of the few Greek films that cross over from the national into the international competition—and many of the Athens-based politicos are apprehensive about any power in Thessaloniki, center of Macedonia, which, they fear, has nationalistic tendencies. The Ministry of Culture and Environment provides much of the event's funding and has a lot of say in its functioning.

Perhaps more serious is the fest's internal politics: leadership squabbles, a widely recognized nepotism. "Thessaloniki is NOT a 'meritocracy,' " one festival insider said during the last event. If it could emerge from its distracting in-house political problems, and create and maintain a sharp focus on its most unique elements, Thessaloniki might survive the twenty-first century and the threat of Athens—festival and capital.

—*Howard Feinstein*

Festival de Cine Iberoamericano de Huelva (23rd)

Casa Colon, Plaza del Punto
21003 Huelva, Spain
Phone: (34-59) 210-170/1
Fax: (34-59) 210-173
Contact: Jose Luis Ruiz
Dates: Nov. 22–29
Deadline: Sept. 3

Showcase for Latin American cinema trying to mediate between Europe and Latin America. Competitive.

Munich International Festival of Film Schools (17th)

International Münchner Filmwochen GmbH
Kaiserstr. 39
80801 München, Germany
Phone: (49-89) 381-9040
Fax: (49-89) 381-9042
Contact: Wolfgang Langefeld
Dates: Nov. 22–29
Deadline: Sept. 18

Showcase for student films. Competitive.

Dublin Junior Film Festival

C/O Irish Film Centre
Eustache St.
Dublin 2, Ireland
Phone: (353-1) 671-4096
Fax: (353-1) 677-8755

Contact: Alan Robinson
Dates: Nov. 23– Dec. 5
Deadline: Oct. 6

Noncompetitive international show-case of world cinema for young people.

Bilbao International Festival of Documentary and Short Films (39th)

c/o Colon de Larreategui, N.37-4 drcha.
48009 Bilbao, Spain
Phone: (34-4) 424-8698, 424-5507
Fax: (34-4) 424-5624
Contact: Maria Angeles Olea
Dates: Nov. 24–29
Deadline: Sept. 15

Competitive. FIAPF recognized.

Nature Film Festival Valvert

E. Facto S. A. Rue Masui 45
Brussels, B-1000, Belgium
Phone: (32-2) 203 4363
Fax: (32-2) 203-4294
Contact: Sebastian Lob
Dates: Nov. 24–29
Deadline: July

Competitive.

Festival des 3 Continents (19th)

B.P. 43302
44033 Nantes Cedex 01, France
Phone: (33-2) 4069-7414
Fax: (33-2) 4073-5522
Contacts: Alain and Philippe Jalladeau
Dates: Nov. 25–Dec. 2
Deadline: Sept. 1

Exclusively devoted to feature films from Asia, Africa and Latin and black America. Competitive.

International Documentary Filmfestival Amsterdam (IDFA)(10th)

Kleine-Gartmanplantsoen 10
1017 RR Amsterdam, The Netherlands
Phone: (31-20) 627-3329

Fax: (31-20) 630-5300
Contact: Ally Derks
E-mail: idfa@xs4all.nl
Web site: www.dds.nl/-damocles/idfa
Dates: Nov. 26–Dec. 4
Deadline: Aug. 25

Presenting most recent creative documentaries, both film and video. Competitive.

Canadian International Annual Film/Video Fest

25 Eugenia St.
Barrie, Ontario
L4M1P6 Canada
Phone: (1-705) 737-2729
Fax (1-705) 737-2729
Contact: Ben Andrews
E-mail: andrewsb@bconnex.net
Dates: Nov. 27–29
Deadline: Dec. 15

Focuses on amateur film and video and accepts all entries such as Super 8, 16mm, betacam, video8, etc. Open to all nonprofessional productions. Competitive.

CamerImage (International Film Festival of the Art of Cinematography) (5th)

Rynek Nowomiejski 28
87-100 Torun, Poland
Phone: (48-56) 27595
Fax: (48-56) 6210019
Contact: Marek Zydowicz
Dates: Nov. 29–Dec. 6
Deadline: Oct. 15

International festival celebrating the art of cinematography. Competitive. FIAPF recognized.

CamerImage, the International Festival of the Art of Cinematography, was inaugurated in 1993 in Torun, Poland. The festival was founded by the Tumult Foundation, a privately held local group, whose goal is to bring art and commerce to a city that had culturally stagnated under four decades of Communist rule.

The festival's focus is cinematography, because the directors believe it is an important visual art neglected or underplayed by other festivals. Entrants in the competition are nominated by directors of other film festivals, cinematography associations and critics.

A screening committee selects twenty films for the competition, and judges include cinematographers with occasional film critics and a director or production designer. The winners receive Golden, Silver and Bronze Frog trophies, symbolizing a fairy tale deeply rooted in local lore. There is a lifetime-achievement winner with daily screenings from that individual's body of work. Lifetime achievement awards have been presented to Sven Nykvist, Witold Sobocinski, Vittorio Storaro, Conrad Hall, Haskell Wexler and Vilmos Zsigmond.

Twenty other films from around the world are screened during the festival. Screenings are in a theater on the Nicolaus Copernicus University campus, where 15,000 of the city's 210,000 residents are students. There is also a student competition with twenty finalists (Tadpole trophies) and workshops conducted by an international faculty.

CamerImage added a new feature in 1997 with the presentation of seven telefilms from the U.S., selected by the International Photographers' Guild and Local 600.

Don't go to Torun to see celebrity actors and directors—few of them have traveled to participate—but do go to see an eclectic selection of films from around the world in the company of responsive and appreciative young audiences; to the Eastern European media, three hundred film students and locals, the cinematographers are the stars.

There is some local ambience if you like history. A seven hundred-year-old wall surrounds the remnants of the old city in the middle of town. Other Medieval relics include a church dating from the 1500s and a museum dedicated to preserving the memory of Nicolaus Copernicus, the city's most famous citizen.

The foundation has obviously struggled to make the festival financially viable. The money comes mainly from corporate sponsors, local businesses, Polish print, radio and television media, the city and national governments. It's a no-frills environment without hip parties and posh accommodations. Some films have English-language dubs, others have subtitles, but don't be surprised if someone is simultaneously translating the dialogue while the film is being projected.

Torun is a three- to four-hour drive from the nearest international airport, in Warsaw, and there is also train service. The festival assigns volunteer student guides—translators to meet foreign cinematographers and other VIPs at the airport. They come with a driver, stay by your side, and make all arrangements during your entire stay. The festival is staged during the last days of November and the first week of December, so the weather is often bitingly cold.

The instant camaraderie among the forty to sixty cinematographers who participate as entrants, judges, workshop instructors and guests is an uplifting and unforgettable experience, and the entire week is buoyed by a spirit of idealism and the hospitality of locals.

—*Bob Fisher*

Taipei Golden Horse Film Festival (35th)

Floor 7, No.45, Chilin Road
Taipei, Taiwan, R.O.C.
Phone: (886-2) 567-5861
Fax: (886-2) 531-8966
Contact: Jane Yu
E-mail: tghff@email.gen.net.tw
Web site: www.goldenhorse.org.tw/
Dates: Nov. 29–Dec. 3
Deadline: Sept. 14

International and offshore Chinese cinema. Competitive.

German Screenings (22nd)

Jenfelder Allee 80
22039 Hamburg, Germany
Phone: (49-40) 6688-5350
Fax: (49-40) 6688-5399
Contact: Silke Spahr
Dates: Nov. 30–Dec. 4
Deadline: Aug. 20

TV productions of the German public broadcasters ARD and ZDF, presented by distribution companies.

Puerto Rico International Film Festival

70 Mayaguez St., Ste. B1,
Hato Ray, Puerto Rico 00198
Phone: (787) 268-5777
Fax: (787) 268-5769
Contact: Juan Gerard
Dates: Nov.
Deadline: Sept. 1

International cinema with Spanish panorama and the best Latin American fare. Competitive.

Sarasota French Film Festival (10th)

P.O. Box 908
Sarasota, FL 34243-0908
Phone: (941) 351-9010 or 351-4300
Fax: (941) 351-5796
Contact: Tom Loken
E-mail: fffn2zasm@aol.com

Dates: Nov.
Deadline: Sept. 1

Focus on French cinema and French co-productions (with English subtitles). Noncompetitive.

DECEMBER

Cairo International Film Fest

17 Kasr El Nil St.
Cairo, Egypt
Phone: (20-2) 392 3562/3962
Fax: (20-2) 393 8979
Contact: Saad Eldin Wahba
Dates: Dec. 1–14
Deadline: Sept.10

International features, tributes and retrospectives, with adjoining film market. Competitive.

International Festival of New Latin American Cinema (19th)

Calle 23 #1155
Vedado, Havana, Cuba
Phone: (53-7) 34169, 36072
Fax: (53-7) 333078, 334273
Contact: Ivan Giroud
Dates: Dec. 2–12
Deadline: Sept. 30

Presenting Latin American films and videos, including features and animation, with a market. Competitive.

CineAsia (4th)

244 W. 49th St., #200
New York, NY 10019
Phone: (212) 246-6460
Fax: (212) 265-6428
Contact: Jimmy and Robert Sunshine
Dates: Dec. 3–5

Convention for cinema owners in the Asia-Pacific region.

Noir in Festival

Via Tirso 90
Rome 00198, Italy

Phone: (39-6) 884-8030
Fax: (39-6) 884-0450
Contact: Giorgio Gosetti
Dates: Dec. 3–9
Deadline: Oct. 31

Film noir and fantasy shorts, features and retrospectives. Competitive.

Mip Asia (4th)

Reed Midem Organization
P.O. Box 572
11 rue du Colonel Pierre
75726 Paris Cedex 15, France
Phone: (33-1) 4190-4400
Fax: (33-1) 4190-4409
Contact: André Vaillant
Web site: www.mipasia.com
Dates: Dec. 4–6

International TV program market for the Asian and Pacific region.

Cinemagic International Festival for Young People (7th)

4th Floor, 38 Dublin Road
Belfast, BT2 8HN, U.K.
Phone:(44-1232) 311-900
Fax:(44-1232) 319-709
Contact: Shona McCarthy
Dates: Dec. 4–14
Deadline: Aug. 12

International children's films. Competitive.

PIA Film Festival (20th)

5-19 Sanban-cho
Chiyoda-ku, Tokyo 102, Japan
Phone: (81-3) 3265-1425
Fax: (81-3) 3265-5659
Contact: Keiko Araki
Dates: early Dec.
Deadline: July 15

Supports young directors and independent films, with the aim of finding and nurturing new talent. Competitive.

The PIA Film Festival (PFF) is Japan's largest independent film competition. The event, which has helped contribute to the discovery of new talent in the nation's movie industry, is a celebration of the good, the bad and the beautiful offerings of Japan's aspiring filmmakers.

The PFF festival held in Tokyo consists of three main activities: the PFF Award, which is given in order to discover talented young directors; the PFF Scholarship to help young directors; and the introduction of high-quality movies from overseas to create an environment in which people can better watch films. The scholarship program began in 1986, and the prize started in 1988.

Started in 1977 by the entertainment magazine publisher PIA Co. to support a growing 8mm film movement in Japan at the time, PIA currently fields nearly five hundred entries in competition each year. More than thirty award winners have made their debuts as professional directors, including Ryosuke Hashiguchi, Sogo Ishii and Shion Sono.

Since 1992, the festival has been jointly sponsored by PIA and the Japanese movie house Toho Co. The two companies formed the Young Entertainment Square (YES) Project at that time, which was aimed at producing feature-length works from up-and-coming directors. Some of the directors backed by YES include Takayoshi Watanabe, who made *If You Fall in Love With Me*, and Takaro Ogawara, who directed a *Godzilla* movie for Toho.

For the festival's twentieth anniversary, organizers dusted off the first works of such movie giants as George Lucas, Robert Zemeckis, Wim Wenders and Jane Campion. Festival viewers were treated to George Lucas's fifteen-minute film *THX-1138-4EB*, made in 1966. The futuristic piece set in college office buildings and dorms helped show young filmmakers that there is a *Star Wars*–size blockbuster waiting to be had in even the rawest of projects.

—*Jon Herskovitz*

Festival dei Popoli (38th)

Via dei Castellani 8
50122 Florence, Italy
Phone: (39-55) 294-353
Fax: (39-55) 213-698
Contact: Mario Simondi
Dates: Dec. 6–12
Deadline: Sept. 10

Presents documentaries dealing with social, anthropological, political and historical topics as well as the arts. Competitive.

Rencontres du Cinema Italien (15th)

Bonlieu Scene Nationale
BP 294, 74007 Annecy Cedex,
France
Phone: (33-4) 5033-4400
Fax: (33-4) 5051-8209
Contact: Pierre Todeschini
Dates: Dec. 9–16
Deadline: Nov. 1

Featuring films from Italy including tributes and retrospectives. Competitive.

Israel Film Festival in New York (14th)

Israfest Foundation
6404 Wilshire Blvd., #1240
Los Angeles, CA 90048
Phone: (213) 966-4166
Fax: (213) 658-6346
Contact: Meir Fenigstein
E-mail: israfest@earthlink.net
Web site: www.israelfilmfestival.com
Dates: Dec. 9–23
Deadline: Sept. 22

Presents the best new Israeli films. Noncompetitive.

Alphabetical Index

Geographical Index

Geographical Index

Genre Index

the contributors

Peter Bart is editor in chief of *Variety*.

Sheila Benson is a former films critic for the *Los Angeles Times* and reviews films for Cinemania.

Tom Birchenough is the Moscow correspondent for *Variety*.

Peter Cowie is international publishing director of *Variety*, founder of the International Film Guide and author of several books on cinema including a recent biography of Francis Ford Coppola.

Ken Eisner is a Canadian-based freelance writer and frequent *Variety* contributor.

Derek Elley is senior film critic for *Variety* and editor of the *Variety Movie Guide*.

Bob Fisher is a California-based freelance writer and frequent contributor to *Variety*.

Steven Gaydos is *Variety*'s managing editor of special reports and co-editor of *Movie Talk from the Front Lines* (McFarland) and *Cannes: Fifty Years of Sun, Sex & Celluloid* (Miramax/Hyperion).

Jon Herskovitz is *Variety*'s Tokyo correspondent.

Nelson Hoineff is a Latin America–based freelance writer and frequent contributor to *Variety*.

Jonathan Holland is a freelance writer based in Madrid and frequent contributor to *Variety*.

Leonard Klady is a film critic and box office reporter for *Variety*.

Mary Lee is an Asian-based freelance writer and frequent *Variety* contributor.

Joe Leydon is a film critic for *Variety*.

Darryl MacDonald is co-founder of the Seattle Film Festival.

Todd McCarthy is chief film critic for *Variety* and author of the recent biography *Howard Hawks: The Grey Fox of Hollywood* (Grove Press).

Lisa Nesselson is a Paris-based freelance writer and film critic for *Variety*.

Andrew Paxman is a reporter for *Variety*.

Christopher Pickard is U.S. editor of *Moving Pictures*.

Gerald Pratley is a former correspondent for *Variety* and a veteran of the international festival scene.

David Rooney is a film critic for *Variety*.

Judy Stone is a former film reporter for the *San Francisco Chronicle* and author of the recently published *Eye on the World—Conversations with International Filmmakers*.

David Stratton is the former director of the Sydney Film Festival and a *Variety* film critic.

Holly Willis is West Coast editor of *Filmmaker* magazine.

Deborah Young is a *Variety* film critic and Rome correspondent for *Variety*.